Big Book of American Cryptids

50 States of Monsters and Legends

Jannette Quackenbush

ISBN-13: 978-1-940087-69-6

21 Crows Dusk to Dawn Publishing, 21 Crows, LLC

The illustrations in this book are artistically created by Jannette using eyewitness descriptions. Accounts from eyewitnesses may differ.

Jannette Quackenbush is an author of over 50 books, folklorist, naturalist, and paranormal researcher. She focuses on ghost stories, folklore, and hiking trails in the Appalachian and southern U.S. Known for her engaging storytelling, she has published many works on local legends and haunted places. Her project, "Dark Journeys with Jannette," features guided hikes where participants explore haunted and cryptid sites and learn about the region's folklore, connecting them to the rich cultural history and stories of the area. People always ask me, "Do you believe?" And here is how I feel, "Everybody is a skeptic until they experience something out of the norm. Then, all of a sudden, they realize there is more out there to discover, and they become part of this big community of others whose eyes are open to the unknown. And they want to know more, see more, adventure more. Do I believe? Well, I'd certainly rather be racing out to be with the believers, the adventurous ones who get out and explore the likelihood of some undiscovered species, than sitting with the disbelievers with my hands folded obstinately over my chest and shaking my head back and forth. Millions sit on their couches every night doing nothing. I don't want to do *nothing*. I want to be with the believers, the explorers, the adventurers. You can be among this community too—just get out there and explore—

And just so you know, YES, I have searched for cryptids from Florida, up through the Appalachians and into Michigan. I'm a naturalist by trade. I've hiked thousands of miles of remote and not-so-remote trails in my quest of the natural and cryptid/supernatural and I've been to thousands of sites where cryptids are thought to lurk, found more than a few Bigfoot prints on those trails I hike and quests for the unusual, heard the calls, had some stranger than strange incidents occur. You can too. Just get out there!"

Encountering Creatures in the Wild:

In my extensive research on cryptids and the stories of those who encounter them, I've noticed a common theme: many people react with fear when faced with these creatures. They seem to have been conditioned to believe that their first instinct should be to grab a gun and shoot as if the creature intends to harm them for sport. Unlike typical game hunters who find pleasure in killing, these creatures generally only threaten when protecting their territory, cubs, or hunting small prey for survival.

Attributing complex human emotions like hate to animals is a common practice in fiction, portraying them as villains. However, bears, coyotes, wolves, and cryptids like Bigfoot are generally not there to cause harm. If you attempt to hurt them, they might defend themselves. Yes, they are wild. And yes, they can be dangerous. In most cases, encounters with these creatures are coincidental. I found that those who observed quietly and promptly removed themselves from the situation (without running so they appeared like prey) were unharmed. At the same time, those who reacted with fear and violence sometimes faced consequences and were chased away. I found no documented occurrences of people being maimed or killed by these cryptid creatures.

If you plan to visit any wildlife area, it's essential to check the National Park Service's websites for information on handling wildlife encounters, especially larger critters. The National Park Service advises the following in most cases, although they go into greater detail about different circumstances: "If a bear is stationary, move away slowly and sideways. This technique allows you to keep an eye on the bear without tripping. Moving sideways is also non-threatening to bears. Do NOT run; stop and hold your ground if the bear follows you. Bears can run as fast as a racehorse, both uphill and downhill."

Alabama: White Thang

Notable Characteristics: The White Thang is described as a creature standing between 7 to 10 feet tall, covered in thick white or pale fur, with glowing red eyes. Witnesses report that it possesses humanoid features and resembles a large cat or bear. It is agile and can run on all fours or stand upright. Encounters with the creature are often accompanied by a foul smell and blood-curdling screams. Specific locations where these sightings occur are Walnut Grove and nearby Moody's Chapel, Happy Hollow, Natural Bridge, Wheeler Wildlife Refuge near Decatur, and the Hurricane Mountain area. While it covers a large area, much of it comprises vast pockets of wilderness and wooded regions. This indicates that individual creatures may migrate across these expanses or exist as separate entities with distinct territories.

The legendary White Thang gained attention in the 1930s and 1940s, likely because information from remote areas of society became more accessible. This allowed news of such creatures to spread to larger audiences. In the 1930s, there were reports of a creature resembling the White Thang that exhibited behaviors such as running on all fours and climbing trees to observe people walking below. It haunted the Lynn area along Alabama State Route 5, south of Natural Bridge—a town in Winston County near the expansive Bankhead National Forest—and U.S. 278, northwest of Birmingham. Although most people did not consider it threatening, the creature was known to scream, startling anyone wandering its path.

"Spooky Appalachia," an Appalachian storyteller, collected several stories about the White Thang, including one of the earliest accounts told by a preacher around Hurricane Mountain in Alabama, northeast of Birmingham. In the 1930s, a woodcutter from Rabbit Town hauled his firewood by horse and wagon one winter to Jacksonville. It was late afternoon by the time he found a buyer and delivered the wood. When he finished his work, it was already late, and he realized it wasn't wise to take the shortcut along the busier road over White's Gap. Cars and trucks sped down that route as well, making it a risky choice with his horse and wagon. Instead, he chose the longer and more remote Old Forney Road over Hurricane Mountain—an area with few homes with a stretch of backroad that twisted and turned.

Along his journey, however, he discovered that there might be greater threats than getting hit by a car, as he began to hear something following him: footsteps crunching loudly in the autumn leaves. Each time he halted his horses to listen, the footsteps seemed to stop as soon as he did. It was strange; the woods were eerily silent.

At the top of the mountain, a road intersected called Vineyard Road. As the woodcutter approached the crossroads, he heard something running toward him. As he squinted in the dim light, he saw a white figure resembling a person racing directly for his wagon. To his shock, it jumped into the back of the wagon bed, causing the woodcutter to fall from his seat and into the front of the wagon bed.

The mysterious white figure went to the front and sat on the box seat. Since the horses were accustomed to carrying heavy loads and experienced shifts in weight while wood was loaded and unloaded, they continued to work without noticing any difference. This eerie journey continued until they reached the intersection of Forney Road and White's Gap Road, where the figure jumped off and dashed into the woods. From that day on, the woodcutter never ventured across that mountain again!

In a notable encounter from the 1970s, a family driving along a lonely stretch of backroad reported seeing the White Thang. The creature stood upright on the side of the road, watching them as they passed by. It did not exhibit threatening behavior and vanished into the surrounding forest moments later.

Another account describes an individual hiking in a wooded area who heard what sounded like a baby crying nearby. Upon searching for the source of the sound, they encountered a seven-foot-tall white creature, which let out a chilling scream that startled them before they fled. More recently, in 2002, campers at Guntersville State Park observed what they initially thought was a white tiger eating a deer.

Alabama: Slough Thing

Notable Characteristics: Most reports describe a mysterious creature predominantly white and covered in hair. This being stands about 5 feet tall when walking on two legs but can traverse all fours. Its most distinctive feature is its red glowing eyes, which add to its eerie presence. Witnesses have noted its agility and ability to move quickly, upright, and on all fours.

Courtland, Alabama, is home to a creature resembling the "White Thang" that frequents the slough (sounds like slew), a swampy shallow area along Big Nance Creek. Samantha McNamara, writing for the Moulton Advertiser, reported that "some believe it's the same creature as the Alabama White Thang, while others insist that the Slough Thing is a completely different species." Most descriptions of the creature indicate that it stands about 5 feet tall on two legs but can also move around on all fours. Despite differences in size, both creatures share certain traits: neither has harmed anyone, both emit unsettling noises akin to a crying or mewling baby, and both have white fur with red glowing eyes.

In her article, McNamara recounts an incident shared with her by Linda Peebles, Mayor of Courtland. Peebles spoke of a story her mother told her from her childhood during the Great Depression. At that time, many in the community reported hearing the strange cries of the Slough Thing. One night, when her mother was a little girl living near Nance Creek, she went to the outhouse and encountered a creature. "My mother went to the bathroom in the middle of the night, and on her way back, she said it came right up to her and stood on two legs," Peebles related. "It was about the size of a midsize person and was solid white. My mom said she froze when the thing looked at her for a couple of seconds, then the thing turned around and went back into the slough."

Although Peebles did not mention any deaths directly associated with her mother's encounters, sightings of the Slough Thing often seemed to coincide with grave illnesses or deaths in the local community. Peebles recalled a man from Courtland who was very ill. "He lived in a dogtrot-style house, similar to my mother's," she told McNamara. "He was quite sick, and they moved him out to the breezeway to sleep. It was said that the Slough Thing would come and sleep under his bed at night, leaving before morning. It never harmed anyone."

Alabama: Downey Booger

Notable Characteristics: A large, 7-foot-tall hairy creature with unsettling, glowing eyes and a terrifying shriek. At times, it may mimic human voices. Specific locations where witnesses encountered the creature include Winston County.

John and Joe Downey were cousins who lived near Lynn in Winston County in the late 1800s. During their younger days, they spent much of their time together, often riding the rugged backroads from their small community, which consisted of just a few houses, through the thick pine forest to an old log house owned by Oscar Tittle, who hosted Saturday night dances.

One evening, after attending one of these festivities, the two men were riding back on their horses when a strange creature suddenly jumped in front of their path, causing both horses to rear in panic and bolt. Unfortunately, the horses ran in the opposite direction of their home. After settling the horses, they tried to continue along the same route, but the horses refused to go past the spot where they had seen the creature. They ultimately took a longer route home, arriving late and explaining to their skeptical parents why it had taken them half the night to return.

Nobody initially believed their story, but a few months later, a family returning from church encountered the same beast. The children were so terrified that they refused to sleep in their rooms for months afterward.

In late autumn that year, a moonshiner named Jim Jackson was heading to Galloway in his wagon, pulled by his docile mules, Pet and Hattie. Although the mules were quite lazy and tended to move much slower than Jim would have liked, he was determined to sell his whiskey to the miners. He suddenly felt peculiar during the journey, as if he were being followed. Looking to his right, Jim saw a creature ambling alongside his wagon. Knowing that his two old mules could not outrun the beast, he drew his revolver and fired two shots. The creature let out a high-pitched screech and limped away. Although the community formed a posse to search the woods, the trail of blood they found ended without any sign of the beast.

Every now and then, this elusive creature known as the Downey Booger makes an appearance. Its name is inspired by eyewitnesses John and Joe Downey and the term "booger," which refers to something frightening. Bankhead National Forest is home to the Sipsey Fork of the Black Warrior River, which is designated as Alabama's federally recognized Wild and Scenic River.

This makes it an ideal location for canoeing and exploring its diverse wildlife. The forest is also rumored to be inhabited by the legendary big hairy creature, and occasionally, the two themes—canoeing and creature hunting—collide. Here and roughly in the same region as the Downey incident, one evening, an avid outdoorsman was pulling his canoe out of the water along the bank of the Sipsey River near Double Springs just before dark. As he flipped the canoe onto his shoulders, he heard several loud "whoops" coming about a quarter mile away. He mentioned afterward that he left much quicker than planned that day.

On another occasion, while fishing, the same man let out a few "whoops" himself and noticed rustling in the brush behind him. Out of curiosity, he tossed a piece of tangerine toward where the noise had come from. While he continued to fish, he thought he heard something splash in the water nearby. It turned out to be a rock, followed by a second stone from the same direction. Once again, his outdoor trip was cut short by the creature!

Alabama: Crichton Leprechaun

Notable Characteristics: A small bearded man wearing a coat and hat.

In March 2006, witnesses began reporting sightings of a leprechaun in the Crichton neighborhood of Mobile. On March 14, reporter Brian Johnson from local station WPMI-TV was sent to investigate reports of a leprechaun seen in a tree at the dead-end road on Le Cren Street near Bay Shore Avenue. He encountered residents who claimed to have seen it. The videos shared online quickly attracted millions of views. While some witnesses suggested it was simply a hoax perpetrated by a short-statured person, others still assert its authenticity.

Alabama: Wolf Woman

Notable Characteristics: A "pretty and hairy" creature with the lower body of a wolf and the upper body and head of a woman.

In April of 1971, The Press-Register received over 50 phone calls from concerned residents, both day and night, who claimed to have seen a creature that was part woman and part wolf, particularly around Davis Avenue and the Plateau area on the outskirts of Mobile. Witnesses reported sightings of this unusual being for several weeks in various locations. However, the Wolf Woman eventually disappeared without a trace.

Alabama: Huggin' Molly

Notable Characteristics: A towering, gaunt woman dressed in black, with a black hat and a veil covering her face.

Abbeville is a small town in Henry County, located in the rolling hills of farmland and forest in southeastern Alabama. It is known for its southern charm, picturesque downtown area, and a creepy giant woman dressed in black who roamed the streets at night.

This ghoul-like figure lurked in the darkness of Abbeville, most active between 1895 and 1945, particularly after dusk. She prowled for lonely pedestrians, especially young children, from her hiding places. When she spotted a victim, she would leap out and chase them at incredible speeds and with great stealth. Once she caught up with her victims, she would hug them to death. It was well-known in the community to avoid the cemetery and the local Baptist Church, as these were the usual haunts of Huggin' Molly. In the late 1930s, a young man named Bun Gamble walked home along Trawick Street after a late movie. Just as he was about to reach his house, Huggin' Molly emerged from a dark ditch. Since she was in his path, he quickly turned around and ran back into town instead.

The last known sighting of her in the early years occurred in the 1940s when a teen was walking after dark along State Route 95, where it intersected with Elm Street. Huggin' Molly was well-known for lurking in overgrown lots, mainly areas lacking streetlights or sidewalks like the one he was taking. With no streetlamps illuminating his way, Huggin' Molly appeared and blocked his path, refusing to let him go further. In fear, the teen bolted, running past the cemetery and the old school, only to collide with the side of someone's house in the pitch black, knocking himself unconscious. When the owner revived him, Huggin' Molly had vanished.

In a later sighting, a mother witnessed her son chased by a dark figure. She quickly called him to safety. Additionally, in 2010, during a cemetery tour for an annual heritage festival, several attendees reported seeing a ghostly figure resembling Huggin' Molly.

Other Notable Alabama Cryptids

The Alabama Black Panther: For many years, there have been reports of large black cats resembling panthers in rural areas of Alabama, even though such animals are not documented in official wildlife records. Sightings may be attributed to escaped exotic pets or possibly undiscovered species.

The Sipsey Creature: Known to inhabit Walker County, it resembles a combination of a gorilla and a bear, emitting strange, mournful sounds typically heard from deep within the woods.

Coosa River Monster: Witnesses reported seeing a large serpent with bulging eyes, the head of a horse, and a fiery red tongue in the Coosa River during the early 1800s. This creature had knots on its back and a white belly. The most significant wave of sightings occurred in the summer of 1877. Marens Foster, a resident of Etowah County, initially thought he was observing a person in distress but soon realized it was a sizable serpent-like creature. Foster noted that the beast showed no fear as it moved through the water and eventually disappeared after diving beneath the surface. Following this sighting, additional reports came from various eyewitnesses along the Coosa River.

Chokfi Rabbit: The creature is notable as a trickster figure in various Southeastern Native American tribes. Generally portrayed as a light-hearted character, it does not engage in serious wrongdoing. Still, it often exhibits humorously inappropriate behavior, including gluttony, carelessness, and an inflated ego. In the folklore of some Southeastern tribes, it was Rabbit who stole fire and brought it to the people.

Alaska: Amikuk

Notable Characteristics: In Yup'ik lore, there is a shapeshifter known as Amikuk, which takes on many forms but is usually described as incredibly long and almost human-like in shape. In the ocean, it appears hairless, has four spindly arms with pointy fingers, and possesses leathery, slimy skin. It has been observed with both two legs and four legs.

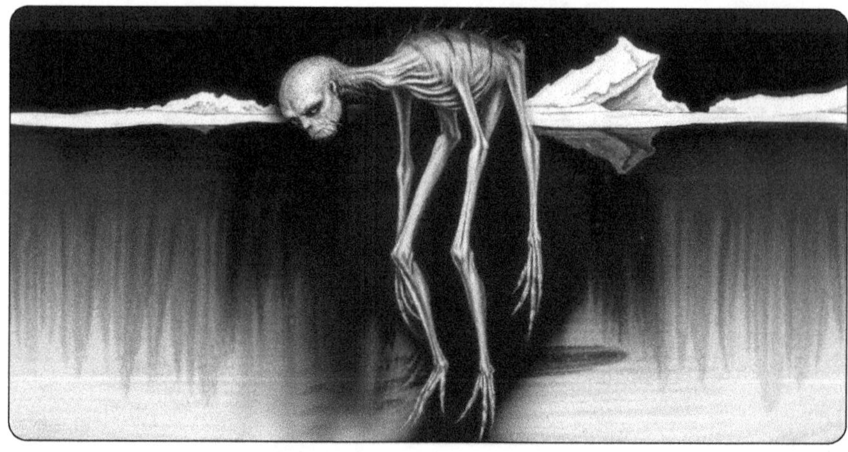

This creature attacks people in boats, patiently waiting for the right moment for a kayak to approach. It then dives off the ice where it rests and swims through the water, surfacing to thrust its arms and legs out of the water to drag its victims underwater and consume them. On land, Amikuk transforms the ground—whether earth or ice—into quicksand, allowing it to move beneath the surface and pull its victims down. While moving, Amikuk creates a thumping noise that can stun its victims. It has also been known to leap into a person, resulting in their death. Interestingly, the Amikuk can only walk in a straight line. If someone encounters it, the best strategy is to sit down in its path with their back to the creature and remain silent. To pass safely, Amikuk will offer gifts that increase in value. Once the gift is accepted, the person can continue and is now quite wealthy.

Alaska: Qallupilluit

Notable Characteristics: An Inuit creature often described as a sea monster or water spirit living underneath the Arctic's icy shorelines and ice floes. It is typically depicted as having very long dark hair, slimy greenish skin, and long fingernails. It wears an amautik, a traditional parka worn by Inuit women; this parka features a hood and a built-in pouch for carrying a baby. The Qallupilluit has two flippers, and one of these can emit a shrill sound that paralyzes its victims. It can alter its appearance using a technique known as pilutitaminik.

The Qallupilluit lures children who wander too close to the water's edge by making an ethereal hum. In some stories, it devours the child; in others, the little one is kept to sustain the creature's youth. Once, there was a grandmother who cared for her grandson. During a long winter, they were close to starving, so the grandmother called upon the Qallupilluit to take the child, believing he would be better off. Later, she was able to hunt again, and a young couple decided to help her retrieve the child. Each time they got close, the Qallupilluit pulled the child deeper into the ocean using seaweed bindings. They finally outsmarted the Qallupilluit, rescuing the child at night when the creature was vulnerable to the darkness.

Alaska: Kushtaka

Notable Characteristics: The Kushtaka, Otter Man, is a shapeshifting creature from the folklore of the Tlingit people, located along the Pacific Northwest Coast of North America. It is described as having a dual form, exhibiting characteristics of both a man and an otter. The Kushtaka is often depicted as having dark intentions, particularly concerning humans, as it is known to use sounds resembling a newborn's cries to create perilous situations for them.

This creature can emit a distinct high-pitched whistle to draw attention, typically following a three-part pattern of low-high-low. Interestingly, while the Kushtaka can lead individuals into danger, it can also exhibit a protective side.

In certain narratives, it saves lost people by distracting them with visions of their family and friends, which may help guide them away from freezing in harsh conditions.

Contrarily, the Kushtaka is also associated with more malevolent actions, as it is believed to lure victims into its grasp, dragging them into the depths or transforming them into creatures of its own kind. This transformation involves stealing the person's soul, effectively preventing them from achieving reincarnation.

During a time of starvation, a man and his wife struggled to catch enough halibut to survive. One day, they discovered two devilfish mysteriously left for them outside. The wife believed that the fish had been sent by their son, who had drowned a year earlier. Overjoyed, the couple used the devilfish as bait and successfully caught halibut.

That night, they heard a whistle outside and invited their son, now an Otter Man, to join them, convinced he had returned to help. Their son appeared in spirit form, taking the father to his boat and assisting the family with fishing and meeting their needs before vanishing again.

The Kushtaka is often linked to many of the mysterious disappearances in Alaska, a state known for its unusually high number of missing persons. While most of these cases can be attributed to the remote, rugged wilderness and harsh weather conditions, some people believe that this Otter Man creature plays a more sinister role in the vanishing of individuals.

Alaska: Adlet

Notable Characteristics: The Adlet is described as a creature that is half man and half dog. Known for being swift and aggressive, its roots stem from a story about a woman who marries a dog and gives birth to ten children. Five of these children are dogs, and the other five are Adlets.

The origins of this story can be traced back to a woman named Niviarsiang, also known as Uinigumissuitung, which means "she who wouldn't take a husband." Niviarsiang lived with her father, Savirqong, and after rejecting all her suitors, she chose to marry a dog named Ijirqang. Together, they had ten children: five were dogs, and the other five were Adlet—creatures with the lower bodies of dogs and the upper bodies of humans.

Ijirqang does not hunt or provide for the family, so Niviarsiang's father must feed their large, noisy household. Angered by this, he places Ijirqang and the children in a boat and takes them to a remote island, instructing Ijirqang to swim back each day to bring meat. When Ijirqang paddles to the shore with his boots hanging around his neck, Savirqong deceives him by filling the boots with rocks instead of meat. As a result, Ijirqang drowns.

In revenge against her father, Niviarsiang sends her pups to gnaw off her father's feet and hands. He, in turn, retaliates by kicking Niviarsiang overboard while she is in his boat. As she clung to the boat, he cut off her fingers; these fingers fell into the ocean and transformed into whales and seals. Niviarsiang, fearing for her children, sends some inland away from Savirqong's wrath, and others she sends across the sea. From these children spring forth numerous peoples.

Other Notable Alaska Cryptids

Bushman: In Alaska, legends speak of the Bushman, also known as the Tornit, a creature resembling a giant, wild humanoid. These large, hairy beings are said to roam the wilderness, occasionally destroying hunters' traps. Renowned for their incredible strength and size, they can move massive rocks and catch whales with their bare hands. It is believed that they carried lanterns to melt ice for drinking water. The Tornit eventually fled the area after one of their own was killed by an Inuit. Since then, numerous stories have emerged about hunters disappearing or being discovered dead and mangled, leading some to believe that Tornit may still inhabit the wilderness.

Keelut: The Keelut is often depicted as a large, hairless black dog, with fur only on the pads of its paws, allowing it to move silently. This creature possesses both physical and supernatural attributes and inhabits the remote and unexplored areas of Denali National Park, adding to its mysterious legend. The Keelut has a reputation as a predator, stalking lone travelers who stray off well-trodden paths. It leads these individuals into confusion, causing them to forget their identity and purpose. This disorientation can ultimately result in death, after which the Keelut consumes their remains.

Kaats: Creatures from Tlingit mythology are described as the offspring of a union between a man and a bear. Some accounts characterize them as deformed beings, such as two-headed or one-legged bears. They are occasionally depicted as monstrous hybrids, combining human and animal traits. A prospector in Thomas Bay, south of Juneau, reported an encounter with one of these creatures, which he described as a mix between a man and a monkey, featuring long, coarse hair and scabby flesh.

Tizheruk: Tizheruk are 7-10 feet long serpent-like ocean creatures with a flipper-like tail lurking in the waters of Alaska. They are rumored to pull people from docks and boats.

Arizona: Mogollon Monster

Notable Characteristics: The creature is described as ape-like, with matted gray hair covering its body, talon-like fingers, and long claws. It is named after the mountainous region of the Mogollon Rim where it has been seen. Its face appears sunburned and brown with deep-set and striking green eyes. Eyewitnesses report that the Mogollon Monster stands between 7 to 10 feet tall, with a muscular build and thick dark or reddish-brown hair. The monster emits an eerie scream and primarily forages at night within dense forest landscapes, leaving a strong odor reminiscent of dead fish.

In 1903, newspapers reported the account of I.W. Stevens from Cedar, Colorado, who encountered a strange "wild man" near the Grand Canyon. The creature was seen carrying a club in one hand. After Stevens fled the area, he discovered the wild man was feasting on a cougar he had killed. In the 1940s, 13-year-old Don Davis, who later became a well-known cryptologist, was startled to awaken during a Boy Scout camping trip to find the beast rummaging through their campsite. Occasionally, hikers in remote areas report sightings of this Bigfoot-like creature.

Arizona: Rake

Notable Characteristics: The Rake is depicted as an eerie and unnaturally tall figure, often described as a gaunt, hairless humanoid that strikes fear in those who encounter it. When fully upright, it stands around six feet tall. Still, it often adopts a more unsettling posture, frequently crouching or moving on all fours, which adds to its unsettling presence. Its face lacks distinctive features, creating an almost blank canvas that amplifies the unease it evokes.

Primarily a nocturnal creature, the Rake emerges during the cover of darkness, prowling through the desolate, scorched landscapes of the southwestern deserts. It typically makes its lair within the shadows of deep caves, where it can remain hidden from the world's prying eyes. It may be aggressive, and when cornered, the mouth opens like a hinged skull at the chin, exposing hundreds of teeth.

The creature is known to lurk in the shadows of bedrooms, inducing vivid nightmares to its victims. At the same time, it watches them almost hungrily before ultimately killing them. One of the most famous stories about the Rake involves a woman who wakes up at night to find the monster crouched at the foot of her bed.

Arizona: Skinwalker

Notable Characteristics: Window Rock serves as the capital of the Navajo Nation. In this region, tales and sightings of Skinwalkers—known as "Yee Naaldlooshii" in Navajo—are prevalent among residents. The Skinwalker is a type of shapeshifting witch often linked to malicious activities and dark magic.

Due to their ominous nature, discussions about Skinwalkers are frequently approached with caution, as the topic is considered taboo. According to Navajo beliefs, an individual must commit a grave act, such as harming a family member, to become a Skinwalker. This act endows the person with the ability to shapeshift and grants them formidable powers associated with fear and malevolence.

One notable account is that of "The Laughing Ram." This story involves a contractor working on an old ranch home near Tuba City. While there, he heard unsettling laughter from nearby sheep pens. Driven by curiosity, he approached the sound. He discovered a group of sheep huddled in fear at one end of the pen while a lone ram stood upright on its hind legs on the other side, crossing its front hooves over its chest. The ram emitted a maniacal laugh, and its gaze seemed disturbingly familiar. When the contractor locked eyes with the ram, he experienced an overwhelming dread. However, almost instantaneously, the ram reverted to all fours and behaved as if nothing unusual had occurred.

Arizona: Lizard Man

Notable Characteristics: The Arizona Lizard Man is a cryptid inhabiting the deserts of Arizona. This creature is characterized by its green, scaly skin and glowing eyes, and witnesses have described it as standing approximately six feet tall with a muscular build. It is often said to lurk near rocky outcrops or within the shadows of desert vegetation. The Arizona Lizard Man possesses sharp claws and a long tail, and produces guttural noises.

One notable account involves a group of hikers near Phoenix exploring a trail just before dusk. They observed a large figure moving quickly on two legs between cacti and boulders during their hike. When illuminated by their flashlight, the creature's eyes glowed, prompting the hikers to investigate further. The figure stood upright as they approached, growled gutturally, and vanished into the surrounding darkness.

Arizona: Thunderbird

Notable Characteristics: The Thunderbird is a prominent figure in Native American mythology, often depicted as a massive bird with wingspans reaching up to 20 feet. According to legend, Thunderbirds can create thunder and lightning while in flight. They are said to be powerful enough to carry off large animals and, in some stories, even small children. In many Native American cultures, the Thunderbird is regarded as a powerful spirit and protector. Its influence is believed to extend to the control of weather, which is crucial in bringing rain and storms vital for sustaining life in arid regions, such as Arizona. This creature symbolizes strength and protection, underscoring its importance in the cultural narratives of various indigenous peoples.

The Whetstone Mountains and the Huachuca Mountains are both located in southeastern Arizona. On April 26, 1890, the Tombstone Epitaph published an article about a strange, winged creature discovered in the region. The bird was too exhausted to fly and was subsequently shot by two ranchers who were pursuing it on horseback.

Upon examination, they found that the creature measured 92 feet in length, with a head approximately 8 feet long and eyes as large as dinner plates. Its jaws were thick and lined with teeth. The wings consisted of a transparent membrane, resembling those of a bat, and were devoid of hair or feathers.

There is a twist to the story. Much later, one of the men came forward, admitting that he had seen the Thunderbird. However, it was not shot down because their horses were too spooked to get close to the bird, and it flew away.

Other Notable Arizona Cryptids

The Bo-Bo: In the St Johns area, a creature inhibits graveyards that digs up corpse bones and steals them. Described as walking on two legs, it is covered in dark fur and is about 6-7 feet tall with lanky arms and legs. Its eyes are deep-set, and its brow pronounced. It reeks of mungy towels and wet fur. It is seen mainly around dusk and has a range of low growls to high-pitched squeals.

The Cactus Cat: This feline is predominantly found in the deserts of Arizona. It is described as having a coat covered in spines that resemble cactus needles. It is particularly noted for its haunting yowls and its elusive behavior.

The Aswang: This cryptid is deeply embedded in Filipino folklore. It is known for its ability to shapeshift into various forms associated with malevolence, such as vampires and ghouls. Recently, there have been reports in Two Guns, Arizona, of an entity resembling the Aswang, depicted as a tall, shadowy figure that roams the desert at night. Witnesses describe hearing unsettling sounds like “tik-tik,” which adds to the confusion about the creature’s proximity to potential victims.

Arkansas: Boggy Creek Monster

Notable Characteristics: The Fouke Monster, often referred to as the Southern Sasquatch or Boggy Creek Beast, is a giant, hairy creature reported to inhabit the swamps of Miller County. It is generally described as standing between 7 to 10 feet tall and weighing nearly 800 pounds. The first documented sightings occurred in 1834 when a large, hairy "wild man" was reported roaming around Arkansas. The creature gained notoriety again in the early 1970s following several sightings and an infamous incident involving the Ford family.

Fouke was a small rural farming community with a population of 394 residents when a colossal creature made its first known appearance at the home of Elizabeth and Bobby Ford on May 2, 1971. This creature, described as being six feet tall and black, reached through a screen window around midnight while Elizabeth was sleeping on a couch. Elizabeth Ford said, "I saw the curtain moving on the front window and saw a hand sticking through the window," she declared. "At first, I thought it was a bear's paw, but it didn't look like that. It had heavy hair all over it and it had claws. I could see its eyes. They looked like coals of fire, real red."

Elizabeth's husband, Bobby, and her brother chased the creature away, firing several shots at it, but no blood was found. Afterward, scratch marks appeared on the porch, and three-toed footprints were discovered nearby. This creature, later dubbed the Fouke Monster or Boggy Creek Monster, returned to the area located along Boggy Creek.

During a subsequent encounter, Bobby was on the porch steps when the creature grabbed and pulled him down. Although he managed to escape, he was so rattled that he forgot to open the front door and ran through it instead. Bobby was so unnerved that he had to be taken to a hospital, nearly senseless. Three witnesses reported seeing the creature along U.S. Highway 71 only a few weeks later. One described it as resembling a "giant monkey" that weighed more than 200 pounds. The driver of a vehicle feared hitting the creature, stating, "It was really moving fast across the highway, faster than a man. Its arms were swinging like a monkey's, and it didn't seem to notice us or look at the car." Until that moment, like most people, the trio had assumed the monster was a hoax. Over the years, there has been a significant increase in reported sightings, fueling public interest and curiosity about the unknown.

Arkansas: Ozark Howler

Notable Characteristics: The Ozarks are known for their sheer cliffs, natural bridges, rock promontories, and caves. The remoteness is the perfect habitat for those wild beasts that are nocturnal and elusive as within the Ozarks, witnesses have seen a large, cat-like creature with horns and glowing eyes. It has an eerie cry akin to a wolf's howl, an elk bugle, and a high-pitched scream. Eyewitness accounts vary from a huge black cougar to a massive black mix of goat and cat creatures with horns protruding from the head and glowing eyes.

There are occasional sightings. In the autumn of 2014, after dusk, a motorist almost collided with a strange bear-sized gray mammal in the moderately populated area of Springdale at Pump Station Road. Wildlife officers were dispatched, but no trace could be found.

Arkansas: Wampus Cat

Notable Characteristics: In Appalachian folklore, the Wampus Cat is often described as a sizeable cougar-like creature mixed with another entity, such as a bear or a human. It is a creature that can run erect or on all fours. It is seen just after dark or before dawn all throughout the Appalachians. It is blamed for missing livestock and pets.

In southern Appalachian folklore, there is a legend of an old woman who lived alone in the mountains. She tended to the sick with forest herbs and was often seen talking to herself in her ragged clothes. The locals, wary of her eccentricities, accused her of witchcraft when livestock began to go missing. They believed she transformed into a housecat to sneak into homes and cast spells on families.

To catch her, townspeople followed her one night and witnessed her transforming into a cat and entering a house. When they confronted her in the barn during her spell to revert to human form, she became trapped as a half-woman, half-cat creature. She fled into the darkness and is said to still steal livestock and occasionally snatch a child.

In Arkansas, it is sometimes called the Whistling Wampus. It is associated with various tales of livestock killings and mysterious sightings. Much of its popularity centers around the early 1900s when, in March of 1914, the Greencastle Herald reported that a Wampus Cat had been caught by hunters, wounded, and brought in for exhibition in the Arkadelphia area. It was first described as black, more vicious than a lion, with four long claws and a nine-foot-long tail used like a kangaroo's tail as an extra leg to propel themselves and thump to scare its enemies. The front feet are like those of a bear with the burrowing feet of a badger. The rear legs were cloven like a deer, and the gait shuffled like a hog or bear. As the newspaper went into print, it also noted that since the discovery, the creature had escaped into the wild.

Madison County is primarily a rural and unspoiled region of the Ozarks. In 2008, a man living in the county spotted a mountain lion sitting on the bank of a pond. Around the same time, others reported similar sightings, but the Arkansas Game and Fish Commission did not have enough evidence to verify them.

In Hot Springs, several individuals have reported hearing strange noises and seeing large feline shapes moving through the woods. Some have attributed the peculiar sights and sounds to the Wampus Cat, which enhances the lore surrounding its existence.

Arkansas: Gowrow

Notable Characteristics: The creature is distinguished by its odd appearance, characterized by legs with webbed feet tipped with sharp-edged claws. Its skin is armored with scales, while prominent sharp horns extend from its neck to its tail. The tail is elongated and culminates in a bone-like sickle, which can be wielded as a formidable weapon.

In the sparsely populated farming community of Blanco during January 1897, several notable citizens brought a mysterious monster to the attention of businessman William Miller. This monster had been slaying and eating horses, hogs, and pets in the village, coming down from the mountains at night and breaking into barns and sheds. While hunting for rabbits, a child found puzzling tracks in the snow.

A posse was formed to investigate. The footprints led along the shoreline of a creek and reappeared downstream. After following a well-worn path between some shrubby cedar trees, they discovered a frequently used cave. As the men explored the dark cavern with torches, they found bones and corpses of all sorts of animals and even a few human skulls.

The men felt emboldened by their numbers and set a trap. They concealed themselves behind boulders, waiting for the creature to return. Soon enough, they heard a loud splash on the far bank and braced themselves for battle. Then, too quickly for their comfort, a sickly green monster appeared before them. Its head resembled a man's, but it had two large tusks protruding over its lower lip. The creature's legs ended in webbed feet, each equipped with horrifyingly sharp-edged claws. Its skin was covered in scales, featuring a long series of sharp horns that extended from the neck to the tail. The tail was long and ended with a bone-like sickle, which could be whipped around and used as a weapon. Their courage failed far too quickly; the men drew their guns and shot the creature dead without a fight, except for one man who lost his leg by the tail whipping as the beast was in the throes of death. The men then lashed out with macabre, childlike delight, taking their anger out on the creature and butchering its body until little was left but pieces of slimy flesh and bits of bone.

The story sparked both panic and skepticism. A second Gowrow was said to be captured by tricking it into eating so many dried apples that its belly swelled, preventing it from escaping its burrow. The live creature was displayed in an exhibit, allowing the curious to glimpse the beast for a fee. However, just as the audience grew, a man would stagger out from behind the curtain where the Gowrow was hidden. His clothing was tattered, as if he had been attacked. Despite the excitement, no one ever saw the creature at this sideshow.

Other Notable Arkansas Cryptids

Wild Man: In July 1902, near Hot Springs, a discovery was made by local farmers Abe Cullum and John White in a densely wooded ravine. They found footprints measuring 14 inches in length and 5.5 inches in width. This find was part of a broader search effort initiated when White's son reported seeing a creature resembling a wild man. It stood about seven feet tall and was covered in hair. The creature was spotted while the boy was searching for a missing cow.

The Minashunka: The Minashunka, Knife Dog, is a cave-dwelling creature weighing 20 pounds with four pointed, sharp teeth and a vampire-like thirst for blood. It is over 2 feet long and walks on all fours with overly long front legs. It feeds on its prey, drinking the blood with saliva containing anticoagulants so its bites are nearly painless; this allows larger prey like grazing cows to remain unaware during an attack, still feeding and unafraid. The Minashunka generally hunt in complete darkness. It relies on sound, smell, and a specialized heat sensor on its nose to locate these warm-blooded animals. Like the noises a bat makes that are typically not heard by humans, witnesses have reported hearing tick-tick-clicking sounds made by the creature as it uses echolocation to locate food. Encountering a Minashunka is considered a harbinger of death.

White River Monster/Newport Sea Monster: In the summer of 1937, a plantation owner and his workers witnessed a mysterious creature in the White River, six miles from Newport, Arkansas. Some described it as a legless, slick elephant the size of a boxcar. Others believed it to be a hippopotamus with a catfish-like head and a long, serpentine body. It was 10 to 30 feet long with skin like an elephant, a spiny dorsal ridge, and an antler protruding from its forehead.

Charles Brown, a deep-sea diver for the Army Corps of Engineers from Memphis, set out to investigate the Bateman Eddy, which was 60 feet deep and a mile long. He brought along a harpoon to entertain the eager crowd that had gathered to catch a glimpse of the creature. The monster was never captured but has been occasionally sighted over the years. In the 1970s, sightings significantly increased, prompting the Arkansas legislature to pass a resolution creating the White River Monster Refuge. This refuge is situated in a section of the White River between Old Grand Glaize and Rosie, and the laws prohibit harming the monster.

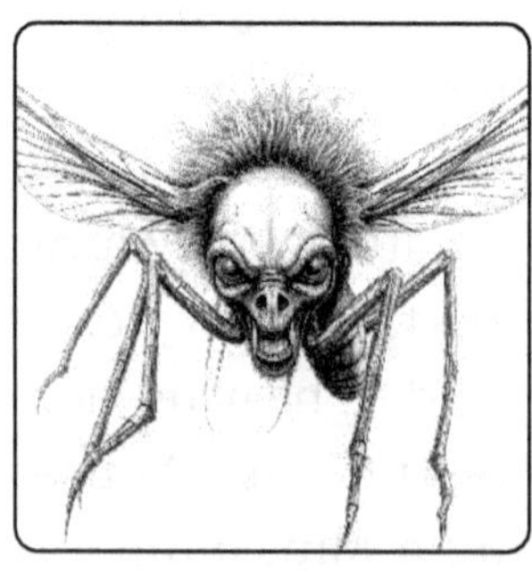

Skeeteroo: This giant insect, known to devour livestock like horses and cows, is tied to lumberjack folklore. One story recounts a lumberjack who got lost in the forest and returned to find his horse missing, devoured by two Arkansas Snipes, who also ate the saddle, spitting out the horseshoes. Once, a mosquito-like creature consumed a cow and lured in other cattle with the cowbell to feast upon them, too.

California: Bluff Creek Bigfoot

Notable Characteristics: The creature is approximately 7 to 8 feet tall and has a robust and muscular build. Its body is covered in shaggy dark brown or black fur with a coarse texture. Additionally, it has a pronounced brow ridge and a flat nose resembling an ape.

Bluff Creek is a tributary of the Klamath River in Northern California, right in the heart of Six Rivers National Forest. The creek runs through dense forested terrain characterized by a diverse range of coniferous and hardwood trees. The area is known for its rugged landscape and remoteness, including canyons and various elevations contributing to its unique ecosystem. Bluff Creek is historically significant as it is famously associated with Bigfoot or Sasquatch.

A notable encounter was in August 1958, when Jerry Crew, a logging tractor operator, came across the beast while working in the remote wilderness of Six Rivers National Forest. Crew discovered giant footprints, measuring 16 inches long, that resembled a human's tracks. This discovery occurred near Bluff Creek, located in Humboldt County.

Not long after, one of the most famous encounters took place in the 1960s at Six Rivers National Forest in California, the same location as Jerry Crew's experience. Roger Patterson, who hailed from Yakima, Washington, was deeply passionate about nature and cryptids, particularly Bigfoot. His fascination began in December 1959 when he came across an issue of Ivan T. Sanderson's True magazine, which sparked his quest to research sightings and locations of the creature in the Bluff Creek area of Northern California.

To support his expeditions, he founded the Northwest Research Foundation. During his journeys, he met Robert "Bob" Gimlin, who shared his interest in studying Bigfoot and became close friends and collaborators.

On October 20, 1967, Patterson and Gimlin rode horseback along Bluff Creek. Around 1:15 p.m., they came across an overturned tree with a massive root system, and as they took a turn in the creek, they encountered a logjam. Just beyond it, they spotted a figure—approximately 7 feet tall—crouching beside the creek. Patterson quickly grabbed his camera from his saddlebag and began filming.

This footage would become Patterson's most significant contribution to the field of cryptozoology, known as the Patterson-Gimlin film (PGF), shot near Bluff Creek. The short film captures a large, unidentified, hairy bipedal figure walking through the forest. It is often cited as one of the most compelling and controversial pieces of evidence for the existence of Bigfoot. Numerous reports and research collected by organizations such as the Bigfoot Field Researchers Organization (BFRO) indicate that the majority of Bigfoot sightings occur in the Pacific Northwest of the United States. Within this region, Washington State consistently reports the highest concentration of sightings, followed closely by Oregon and California.

California: Lone Pine Mountain Devil

Notable Characteristics: The creature is notable for its large, furry appearance and multiple wings, resembling a bat. It is equipped with razor-sharp talons and several layers of venomous fangs, which enhance its predatory capabilities. Its name is linked to its habitat near Lone Pine, California. It has a ferocious reputation when it comes to hunting prey.

The Lone Pine Mountain Devil is a creature linked to the Sierra Nevada region of California. It is described as a large, winged, bat-like carnivore that preys on various animals and even humans. The legend of this creature emerged in the mid-19th century. It circulated among early settlers, particularly those who came during the Gold Rush, known as the Forty-niners.

The tales were fueled by the discovery of coyote and bobcat carcasses along the wagon trails in the rugged desert and mountainous areas as settlers moved into California. During this time, horrific stories circulated about entire groups—settlers, families, and gold prospectors—vanishing without a trace and being found gruesomely mutilated.

In 1878, a wagon train of migrating homesteaders had a horrifying encounter with unknown creatures. Among the group was Father Justus Martinez, who traveled with several Spanish settlers—men, women, and children—totaling 37 individuals. They were traversing the Sierra Nevada Mountains when they mysteriously vanished.

Two months after their disappearance, a group of copper miners stumbled upon the grisly scene: the rotting corpses of the settlers had been found scattered across the area. Their faces were unrecognizable, having been eaten away, and their torsos appeared to have been stripped clean to the bone. What remained was nothing but bone and rotted, dried flesh. Amidst this horror, Father Justus Martinez was found alive but in a weakened and near-death state. He had no supplies and was only wearing his garments.

After being rescued, Father Martinez traveled to a mission about 110 miles north of San Diego. There, he wrote about his harrowing experience in an old journal he had kept during his travels. His narrative detailed how the settlers had set up camp for a celebration in honor of Saint Roderick. Chaos erupted as they celebrated late into the night, using burning trees for light and warmth.

From his tent on the outskirts of the camp, Father Martinez watched in horror as "winged demons" emerged from the trees. These creatures attacked without mercy, slaughtering men, women, and children alike in what he characterized as a horrific bloodbath.

His journal entries expressed his terror as he witnessed these beings attacking his fellow travelers. The final entry in Father Martinez's journal powerfully conveyed his despair: "My God. My God. They are all gone. The winged demons have risen! What sin have they committed against each other and thy sacred earth? May the forgiving Lord not abandon their souls, which were taken from them into the depths of hell! And through the earthly fires of man, a sole tree remained on the mountain's peak. And the Devils that spared me returned to the refuge of the Lone Pine of the Mountain."

Recent reports indicate that there have been no confirmed sightings of the Lone Pine Mountain Devil. However, some individuals have shared their experiences online, claiming to have encountered creatures exhibiting similar characteristics to those reported by the ill-fated party.

California: Dark Watchers

Notable Characteristics: Dark Watchers (Los Vigilantes Oscuros) are a group of tall, mysterious entities, 7 to 15 feet in height, associated with the Santa Lucia Mountains. They are described as featureless, dark silhouettes frequently adorned with wide-brimmed hats and carrying walking sticks. When approached, they vanish. The shadow-like beings are primarily seen at twilight and dawn, where they silently observe travelers from the ridges and peaks of the mountains. They are not aggressive but instead passive observers, disappearing without a trace.

The Santa Lucia Mountains, a breathtaking and rugged coastal range in central California, rise dramatically from the edge of the Pacific Ocean. Their steep cliffs, often shrouded in mist, create a stunning contrast against the deep blue waters below. This majestic landscape is woven into the fabric of the Los Padres National Forest, and within its borders lie a variety of pristine wilderness areas, each teeming with diverse wildlife and vibrant plant life. The mountains invite adventurers to explore their rugged trails and experience the enchanting beauty of nature at its finest. But, there are also rumors of mysterious beings lingering there, their watchful presence casting an intriguing veil over the land.

The legend of the Dark Watchers has its roots in the oral traditions of several Native American tribes, particularly the Chumash people who inhabited the coastal areas of California. Although these entities hold significance in local folklore, there is no definitive evidence linking them to specific Chumash myths. The term "Los Vigilantes Oscuros" was coined by early Spanish settlers in the 1700s. They documented encounters with these enigmatic figures during their explorations of the mountainous terrain. The featureless silhouettes wearing hats would appear at twilight as if from nowhere, observing those passing by before vanishing.

For centuries, numerous witness accounts have emerged, with individuals reporting encounters with these mysterious dark entities. In the mid-1960s, a local from the Monterey Peninsula recounted an interesting experience during a hiking trip. The group spotted a dark figure standing on a rock, which disappeared when one of the hikers called out to it.

California: Fresno Night Crawlers

Notable Characteristics: The Fresno Nightcrawler is a thin, humanoid form with long legs and arms lacking. The height of these creatures is approximately five feet, with most of their stature attributed to their elongated legs. The upper body is notably tiny, rounded, or cone-shaped and difficult to discern in the footage captured during sightings.

The first noteworthy sighting of the Nightcrawler occurred in 2007 in Fresno, California. A man named Jose reviewed footage from his front yard security camera after hearing his dogs barking in alarm. He observed what appeared to be a strange creature with long, spindly white legs moving across his yard. Although this initial footage was lost, it sparked interest in the creature. Subsequent sightings included videos taken in Yosemite National Park. A retired couple, attempting to catch the perpetrator of break-ins at their private property, aimed a security camera at their driveway to monitor passersby. Two Nightcrawlers were captured in the footage: one was smaller than the other and exhibited webbing between its knees and torso.

California: Evil Gnomes

Notable Characteristics: The creature described resembles a gnome, standing under three feet in height. It features jagged teeth, a wide grin, and small, beady eyes. Its attire consists of maroon pants paired with a yellow shirt, contributing to its distinctive appearance.

Porterville is in the foothills of the Sierra Nevada Mountains in Tulare County. It is known for its small-town charm but also for the eerie tales of evil gnomes. In one home along the Tule River, two families experienced terrifying encounters with a gnome-like creature.

Tammy moved into a two-story home in rural Porterville with her three children in 2009 and soon noticed strange disturbances. She often felt like she was being watched, particularly in the direction of a dilapidated barn on the property. One day, after returning from the store, she heard something coming from the barn. "One evening, my son and I had just come back from grocery shopping," Tammy recalled.

"We parked and got out of the car, and as I was opening the back to get the groceries, I noticed a movement out of the corner of my right eye." She heard a very unsettling, evil-sounding chuckle as she turned to investigate. "I looked in that direction, and standing about fifty yards away from us was what I can only describe as a gnome." Terrified, she ran inside, slammed the door, and watched in horror as the tip of its hat crept beneath a window as if trying to get inside. The family described the creature as a tiny, grotesque being that appeared at night, causing various disturbances, including strange noises.

The second family, the Thomases, moved to the same property in 2010 and began to experience similar phenomena. Charlie Thomas recounted an incident where she and her husband were awakened at 3 a.m. by a hideous sound outside their window. Upon investigation, they saw what they described as a gnome-like figure standing near their pond. This creature was less than three feet tall, had jagged teeth and beady eyes, wore maroon pants and a yellow shirt, and held one of their garden gnomes. The situation escalated when the creature grabbed a koi fish from the pond and swallowed it right before their eyes. "It was 3 a.m., and we were woken by a sound I can only describe as a raspy gurgling noise," Charlie Thomas said. "It was without a doubt the most hideous sound I have ever heard. It freaked us out." They called 9-1-1, but the creepy visitor had already vanished when law enforcement arrived, so they didn't mention what they had seen. The officers assumed it was an intruder; Charlie explained, "When they were satisfied that it was gone, they told us they had only found some small shoeprints, like a kid's. We knew it was no kid."

Jason Offutt covered the story in his blog, "True Tales of the Paranormal." He revealed that the gnome returned each night.

It was obsessed with one of the family's yard ornaments, a garden gnome, and enjoyed feasting on the fish in their pond. The Thomases thought the creature would go away if they removed the fish and garden gnome. They were mistaken.

"One night, after we had removed the greenery and gnomes and fish from the yard, the creature showed up at the usual time, 3 a.m.," Charlie said. "When it came and found that the yard ornaments and fish were gone, it went crazy. It screamed and yelled in a way we couldn't understand, but we knew it was furious and wanted us to know it." In a panic, Charlie frantically ran around the house, shutting windows and doggie doors, fearful that the creature would come inside.

The last thing they saw was the tip of its hat as it moved beneath the living room window outside. They quickly decided to move out to escape the terror.

Both families noted a striking resemblance in their experiences, even though they lived on the property at different time periods. The eerie similarities in their stories, filled with fear, suggested that the neighborhood itself held a deeper, haunting significance, weaving a dark thread connecting their lives across time.

Other Notable California Cryptids

Joshua Tree Skinwalkers: Joshua Tree National Park is in Southern California, at the boundary between the Mojave and Colorado Deserts. Hikers in this area have reported sightings of the strange Skinwalkers—shapeshifting witches believed to be able to cast spells and imitate their loved ones. These tales draw from legendary stories of the Mojave Desert that have persisted for centuries. It is highly discouraged to whistle at night as Skinwalkers respond to the call, causing harm to those who encounter it.

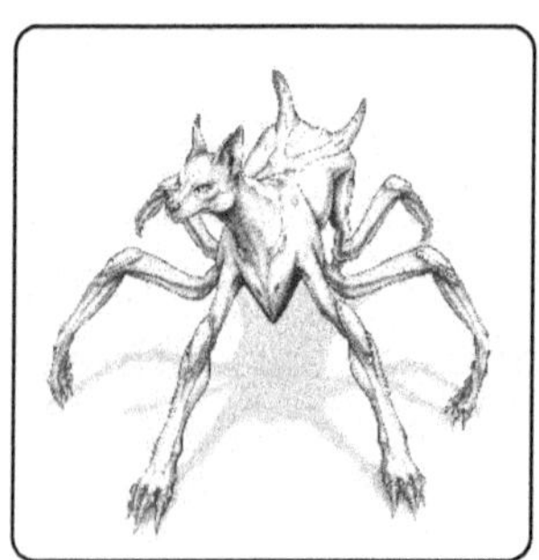

The Whintosser: A bristle-haired creature from lumberjacks' lore, linked with the coastal ranges of California during the late 19th and early 20th centuries. This cryptid inhabits social groups, such as families or packs. Distinctive features of the Whintosser include a triangular body shape, a neck, and a short tail, with the head and tail's ability to swivel and spin at an impressive rate of up to 100 revolutions per minute. Despite its relatively small size, the Whintosser is known for its aggressive demeanor and a notable sense of ego. One of the most intriguing aspects of the Whintosser is its unique locomotion. It possesses three sets of legs that provide stability during earthquakes, a common occurrence in the region. These legs are strategically positioned around its body, allowing the creature to walk in various orientations, whether upside down, sideways, or right-side up.

Colorado: Devil Ram

Notable Characteristics: This slender, bipedal cryptid features the skull of a goat adorned with three horns (the female's horns curve downwards, while the male's horns curve upwards). It stands slightly over 7 feet tall when upright on its hind legs. The Devil Ram has extended arms, which makes it stealthy chasing prey, with double-jointed fingers to aid in catching and grasping its prey and long, sharp claws.

Its origins can be traced back to the early 19th-century farming settlements in Colorado, where starving travelers sought food and shelter from the homesteaders but were turned away. Those who were rejected became desperate as they starved and lost their will to live, eventually transforming into what is now known as the Devil Ram.

It is often compared to Wendigo. Both creatures are depicted as malevolent, predatory creatures that embody themes of hunger and destruction, frequently associated with cannibalism or livestock consumption. Additionally, they share supernatural strength and intelligence characteristics, allowing them to effectively plan attacks on their victims. They are clever, can pry open wooden doors of barns or farmhouses, and ambush adults and children.

This unusual ram has occasionally been spotted in northwest Colorado nowadays. Although it has not harmed anyone, it gives off a threatening impression.

On August 15, 2019, the Johnson family was camping near Steamboat Springs when they spotted a large, ram-like creature standing on two legs. The creature had dark brown fur and three sets of horns. When the family made noise, it retreated from their campsite.

Around October 3, 2020, a farmer in Routt County reported that several sheep were missing from his pasture. He mentioned seeing a tall figure with a goat skull for a head lurking near his barn late at night, which left him with an overwhelming sense of dread.

On May 22, 2021, a group of hikers in the Flat Tops Wilderness Area reported an encounter with a being approximately 7 feet tall, featuring elongated arms and sharp claws. The creature moved stealthily through the trees before disappearing into the underbrush, matching the descriptions of a Devil Ram.

On February 14, 2022, a local news outlet reported an incident where residents of a small town near Craig heard odd noises, saw a shadowy creature resembling a ram walking around, and experienced disturbances with their livestock at night.

Colorado: Tommyknocker

Notable Characteristics: Tommyknockers are rooted in Cornish folklore and are linked to mining in Colorado. The creatures are about two feet tall and resemble gnomes. They are known to be attired in miners' clothing, including the miners' hats.

Tommyknockers possess both benevolent and malevolent characteristics. They are helpful spirits that guide miners toward rich ore deposits or warn them of impending dangers such as cave-ins. Their noises can be heard within caves and mines, as well as knocking or tapping, which could be a warning or an indicator of good fortune. Yet, they are also pranksters, stealing miner's tools and returning them much later, only if they feel like it.

Miners often leave offerings such as food (notably saffron cake, a rich, buttery-tasting pound cake) to appease and protect these spirits while working underground. The belief was that neglecting to honor the Tommyknockers could lead to bad luck, rock falls, or accidents. The presence of Tommyknockers is sometimes linked to dead miners who continued to watch over their living counterparts.

In the early years, there was a miner who was careless with his tools, often putting them down in one spot and forgetting where he had left them. One day, he misplaced his pickaxe and could not find it or work without it. He searched everywhere, but with only the dim light from the carbide lamp on his mining cap, he couldn't see it. Frustrated, he called for help, winding his way through the mine tunnels.

After searching for quite some time, he finally sat down on a stone and sighed. He caught the faint sound of knocking from a wall as he did. Curious, he stood up and followed the noise until it seemed to concentrate just above a pile of rubble. When the miner looked down, he discovered his pickaxe partially buried beneath the stones. That evening, when he went to eat his meal, he decided to leave a bit of his food as a thank-you to the Tommyknocker for helping him find his tool.

Colorado: Slide-Rock Bolter

Notable Characteristics: The creature has a large, whale-like body featuring a large head and small eyes. Its tail resembles a dolphin's, with a fluke that aids movement. It possesses specialized grabbing hooks at the end of its tail, which it utilizes to secure itself to mountain ridges or crests. It releases its hooks when the creature spots food, typically unsuspecting tourists. It rapidly slides toward its prey, leaving a trail of avalanches and fallen trees in its wake. The creature harnesses the power of gravity to glide down, aided by a lubricant that drips from its saliva. Once it reaches the bottom, the momentum propels it back up the other side to another mountaintop, where it hooks its tail and waits for the next unsuspecting hiker.

Rico is a small town in southwestern Colorado, nestled within the San Juan Mountains. It was founded in 1879 after miners discovered silver ore. The rapid growth that followed attracted many prospectors eager to exploit the area's natural resources. By 1892, with the railroad's arrival, Rico's population exploded to 5,000. This boomtown drew many tourists seeking adventure in the surrounding wilderness.

Rico was home to a large lumber mill, where timbermen shared tales and wild stories about life in the wild, scaring one another and travelers alike. One of those stories was about the Slide-Rock Bolter, a gruesome creature that preyed on tourists.

In 1910, the legend of the Slide-Rock Bolter emerged when William Cox, a state forester, wrote: "Fearsome Critters of the Lumberwoods, with a Few Desert and Mountain Beasts." The book had tales he collected from logging camps. Among them was the story of the Slide-Rock Bolter. Cox described the beast this way: "In the mountains of Colorado, where the woods become infested with tourists during the summer, much uneasiness has arisen from the presence of the Slide-Rock Bolter. This frightful creature resides exclusively in the steepest mountain regions, where the slopes are greater than 45 degrees. It has an immense head with small eyes and a mouth resembling that of a sculpin, extending back beyond its ears. Its tail is a divided flipper with enormous grab hooks, which it uses to anchor itself to the crest of a mountain or ridge, often remaining motionless for days while watching the gulch for tourists or other unsuspecting creatures. When the Bolter spots a tourist, it lifts its tail, loosening its grip on the mountain. With its small eyes fixed on the unfortunate victim and thin, slippery grease drooling from the corners of its mouth, the Bolter comes down like a toboggan, scooping up its prey as it descends. Its momentum carries it up the next slope, where it once again secures its tail over the ridge and waits. Whole groups of tourists have been reported missing after being swallowed in a single scoop by venturing too far into the hills. The Bolter is not only a threat to tourists but also to the forest itself. Many clearings through spruce-covered slopes have been laid waste, with trees uprooted or mowed down as though by a scythe due to the Bolter crashing down from the peaks above."

Other Notable Colorado Cryptids

Vampire: Todor Glava, originally from Transylvania, was 43 years old and employed at the Simpson Mine when he died suddenly on December 4, 1918, following a relapse of influenza. He was buried at the Lafayette Cemetery in Boulder County. Some believe he was a vampire, and local lore suggests that the townspeople feared an outbreak of vampirism. To investigate, they exhumed his grave and claimed to have found that he had blood near his mouth, and his hair and nails were still growing. Some sneaked into the cemetery and placed a stake through his heart so he could not escape. A rosebush sprouted over the grave from that stake, and the nearby rose bushes grew from his fingernails. In July 2010, an unusual incident occurred near Fruita, Colorado. A woman crashed her SUV into a canal late at night after reportedly seeing a vampire while driving down a dirt road. According to the Colorado State Patrol, the woman claimed that the sighting caused her to panic, leading her to put her SUV in reverse and back into the canal. The police investigation found no evidence of drugs or alcohol influencing her driving at the time of the accident.

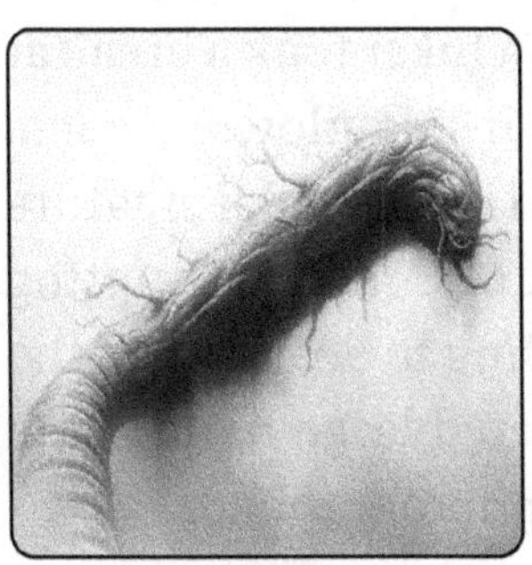

Augerino: The Augerino is a worm-like creature found in the drier regions. It burrows into the ground, creating holes in dams and irrigation ditches that allow water to drain out. The Augerino lines them with silica to prevent their burrows from collapsing.

San Juan Sasquatch: The San Juan Sasquatch is an ape-like creature noted by deep-set eyes, a pronounced brow ridge, and dark fur. Its long arms facilitate agile movement through forested areas. In 1975, two hunters encountered a large, upright figure while hiking in the mountains. They reported hearing loud vocalizations echoing through the forest. The beast emitted a strong fetid odor like wet dog fur.

The Sleeping Warrior: Near Cortez, a mountain resembles a reclining Native American warrior with his headdress facing north. His arms are folded across his chest. According to Ute folklore, the warrior fell asleep years ago, allowing Spaniards, Plains Indians, and miners to enter Colorado. It is said that he will one day awaken and drive everyone from the state.

Bigfoot: According to the Bigfoot Field Researchers Organization (BFRO), Colorado has recorded more than 130 reported sightings since 1926. In 2019, while on the trail, a hiker took a break at an old log cabin in Mayflower Gulch. During the stop, a large bipedal creature was spotted at 11,000 feet, attempting to climb a 20-foot snow wall but struggling to do so. After the encounter, the hiker and others discovered large handprints and footprints in the snow which were photographed.

Connecticut: Winsted Wild Man

Notable Characteristics: Witness accounts of the Winsted Wild Man present a range of descriptions, noting variations in height from six to eight feet. Despite these differences, the sightings have consistent themes, including the creature's substantial size and dark, hairy exterior.

Winsted is a suburban town in Connecticut known for its scenic landscapes. Nearby is Highland Lake, a 445-acre area popular for boating and fishing, surrounded by rolling hills and wooded areas. The lake's shoreline is heavily developed with houses, leaving only a small, forested area. With a significant portion of the population living along the shoreline, it is common for people and wildlife, including large animals like bears, to come into contact with each other.

This includes occasional sightings of a creature similar to Bigfoot, known locally as the Winsted Wild Man.

One of the earliest sightings occurred in the autumn of 1895 when Riley Smith, a farmer and businessman, encountered what was described as a wild man in the woods while searching for a lost hog. He was accompanied by his typically bold bulldog, which suddenly ran back to him in fear. Riley spotted a creature about 40 feet away in a clearing. Described as approximately 5 feet 10 inches tall, weighing 180 pounds, and covered in hair, the wild man was picking blackberries when he noticed Smith. After a horrifying scream, the creature quickly vanished into the woods.

Over the years, there have been occasional sightings of a mysterious creature. In 1952, enormous footprints—pigeon-toed and shaped somewhat between a human's and a bear's feet, but three times the size—were discovered at Highland Lake in Winsted Woods by Argyle Throckmorton, a local resident. In 1972, two local teenagers, David Chapman and Wayne Hall, reported seeing a man-like creature on Winchester Road, near Crystal Lake Reservoir and a barn. They observed it from inside Hall's home for nearly 45 minutes. "From what we could see, it was about 8 feet tall and covered with hair. We could only see its arms, legs, and head; we couldn't see its face," Hall revealed. He was sure it was not a black bear and described the creature as being black in color and stooping as it walked on two legs. The two boys first became aware of its presence when they heard strange noises resembling loud frog croaks and the yowls of a cat.

One of the last reported sightings of the Winsted Wild Man occurred in September 1974. Two couples parked at Rugg Brook Reservoir and saw a "six-foot, 300-pound creature covered in dark-colored hair" illuminated by the moonlight. They quickly fled the area after witnessing the creature.

Connecticut: Glawackus

Notable Characteristics: The creature is described as a large, tawny, or black cat-like animal, resembling a blend of a bear, panther, and lion. It measures about 4 feet long and stands between 2 to 2.5 feet tall, featuring a bushy tail. The creature has glowing eyes and emits a piercing scream. Some witnesses have compared it to a large cat or dog. In contrast, others suggest it has characteristics similar to a bear's.

The term "Glawackus" is derived from the town of Glastonbury, Connecticut, where it was first reported in January 1939 during the winter months. The name combines "Glastonbury" with the word "wacky." This fascinating creature is approximately four feet long, which is comparable to the size of a large dog, and features a cat-like head. It stands about two and a half feet tall and has a physique that resembles a mix between a bear, a panther, and a lion.

Typically, the Glawackus is described as having either black or tawny fur, along with a long, bushy tail. One of its most distinctive characteristics is its fierce vocalizations, which include screeches and cackles like those of a hyena. In January 1939, a hunting party was organized after Wells Strickland, a resident of Bush Hill in Manchester, observed a mysterious creature that made a deep, unusual sound resembling "wuh," which piqued his curiosity. Strickland, a deacon at the Buckingham Congregational Church who owned a quarry and lumber business, was inspecting damage to his timber tract between Hebron Avenue and Neipsic Road when he spotted a large feline about 400 feet away. The creature appeared to be roughly three feet long and two feet tall, featuring a long, buff-colored coat like a mountain lion. After witnessing the animal scratch its ear, Strickland referred to a book and concluded that it was a cougar that had escaped from a game farm during the storm. However, the hunting party could not find evidence of such a creature in the woods, leaving Strickland's conclusion unchallenged.

The last confirmed sighting of the Glawackus occurred in the mid-1950s. During this time, reports indicated that the creature was attacking animals, eluding capture or identification. The sightings extended from Glastonbury to areas north and west, reaching as far as Granby, Connecticut. However, after this resurgence in sightings, the Glawackus disappeared altogether. It does not stop the legend from growing. During the 1900s, this creature was merely known for stealing small farm animals and pets. Over time, the legend of the Glawackus has gotten more fantastic and unsettling. Its reputation has grown, with added qualities such as the belief that it is blind but possesses heightened senses of smell and hearing. An alarming aspect of its mythos is that looking into its eyes can erase a person's memories.

Connecticut: Faded Black Dog

Notable Characteristics: A large, silent, "faded" black dog about two feet long, friendly, with huge, sad eyes.

The Hanging Hills of Meriden, Connecticut, are a range of trap rock ridges that overlook the Quinnipiac River Valley. These hills were formed by volcanic activity 200 million years ago, when two lava flows covered the valley, cooling and hardening into trap rock. The area is renowned for its dramatic cliff faces and distinct linear ridge formations. It offers excellent hiking opportunities during certain times of the year. However, in the dead of winter, when snow covers the ground and icy winds howl, the landscape transforms into a more sinister and lonely setting for those who view it from below. It is within these Hanging Hills that, for centuries, a mysterious faded black dog has been spotted on the desolate peaks, becoming a part of local legend in the region.

Stories passed along since the 18th century relate that encountering the black dog leads to different fates: seeing it once is considered joyful, seeing it twice brings sorrow, and seeing it three times results in death. Still, it gained broader recognition in 1898 when William Pynchon used it to write a fictional account published in the April–June issue of the Connecticut Quarterly. According to this narrative, a New York geologist, identified only by his initials, F.S., met a peculiar black dog while conducting research in the Hanging Hills. He described the dog as black but faded and ghostlike, about two feet long, friendly, with huge, sad eyes. It oddly left no footprints as it traveled silently beside F.S.'s wagon.

F.S.'s first encounter with the black dog occurred during a solo trip into the hills. The dog vanished without any trace or sound as he prepared to leave. Three years later, F.S. returned to continue his research, accompanied by his friend Herbert Marshall. This United States Geological Survey member had seen the dog twice on previous trips. After sharing stories about their encounters with this spectral pup, both men saw it again during their camping trip. Tragically, shortly after their sighting, Herbert Marshall fell to his death when a rock he was standing on broke loose. Six years later, F.S. returned once more to where Marshall had died. On November 2nd, he disappeared, prompting the formation of a search party. They found his corpse at the foot of the southern cliff of the peak, where he had fallen from the top, landing forty feet below, near the spot where Herbert Marshall had met his demise.

Occasionally, the Black Dog appears, as happened in the early 2000s when a photographer took pictures of the area and captured a short-haired black dog in some of his shots. Interestingly, those who encounter the Black Dog during their visit typically report that it will be their last visit if they see it again.

Connecticut: Taugwonk Bigfoot

Notable Characteristics: Giant and hairy Bigfoot-type creature 6 to 7 feet tall.

In April of 1926, a giant, hairy creature terrorized two teenagers who had recently inherited their deceased father, Horace D. Miner's sprawling farm estate near the Taugwonk neighborhood in Stonington, Connecticut. He had passed away three weeks earlier. The large, hairy creature, the size of a man with huge paws and a cumbersome walk, was spotted sliding off a big rock, frightening horses near a bridge, and lurking in a nearby swamp. It scared off the hired hand, Frank Miller, who had worked on the farm for quite some time; he found work elsewhere, stating he had seen enough of "things popping up on rocks and hopping about the place."

It was assumed that Muriel, 19, and Mildred Miner, 16, who were orphans, were being scared into selling the valuable farm for cheap. Still, the local wildlife officer investigated who might be responsible. Around April 1, a newspaper reported that state policeman Clifford Gorgas from the Groton barracks had been directed to a high mountainous area nearby, Haystack Rock. He discovered that Muriel had placed an ape mask on a dummy wrapped in a sheet with a large "April Fool" sign hanging on it. Gorgas stated that Muriel confessed to the hoax. However, after the story was published, she angrily and adamantly denied the claims.

This mediocre investigation by the local police and game warden sparked outrage among the residents, who claimed to have seen the Bigfoot creature. Several locals had seen the beast, including Harry Main, who had traveled to Anguilla to hunt turkey. While he was there, several children came running toward him, excitedly pointing at an outcropping known as Haystack Rock. A small group of onlookers gathered, and they watched the creature hop around the rock. When they moved closer, it let out a piercing shriek. It fled into the thickets and woods, eventually disappearing into the swampland. Harry described the creature as being wrapped in a white shroud. Later, when a man from a neighboring farm arrived at the scene, he found his 14-pound white cat lying there unharmed and took it home.

The community rallied around the girls, defending them and criticizing the state police for their alleged neglect and laziness in the investigation and failing to find out who or what was tormenting the family. Determined to protect their property, the girls armed themselves with guns, and eventually, the Bigfoot creature moved on.

Recent reports from small towns near Taugwonk have highlighted unusual vocalizations possibly linked to Bigfoot.

In October 2023, a witness described hearing distinct "whoops" and cries that did not match the sounds typically produced by local wildlife, such as coyotes or bobcats. These vocalizations were particularly notable for their intensity, causing nearby dogs to bark excessively. The Bigfoot Field Research Organization (BFRO) has classified this incident as a credible sighting. However, it falls under the "Class B" category due to the absence of direct evidence.

Other Notable Connecticut Cryptids

Downs Road Bigfoot: Downs Road in Hamden was a route connecting Hamden to Bethany. In recent years, the isolated road has been closed at both ends. It has become a haven for a 5-foot Bigfoot creature often creeping along the road from the woods.

Black Fox of Salmon River: Long ago, white hunters heard a captivating legend from their Native American guides about a mysterious black fox living along the Tatamacuntaway (Salmon) River. This fox possessed a beautiful, magical coat that anyone who saw it was driven to capture it. However, no hunter ever succeeded; arrows would pass through the fox without causing it any harm, leading to endless and frustrating chases that only deepened their obsession. Some brave hunters returned exhausted after days of pursuit, eager to share their tales, while others mysteriously vanished, believed by the Indians to have been taken by the fox's enchanting spirit.

Melonheads: Melonheads are small humanoids with bulbous heads that occasionally emerge from their hidden lairs in Stratford, Shelton, and Trumbull to scare teens in the backwoods of Fairfield County.

The Higganum Mucket: The Higganum mucket is a mysterious, fish-like creature believed to inhabit only Candlewood Hill Brook, which flows through the heart of Higganum, Connecticut. This elusive creature is known for its aggressive eating habits, indicating that it may be a predatory species within its fantastic narrative.

Connecticut River Serpent: The Connecticut River serpent is thought to inhabit the waters of the Connecticut River. Various historical accounts, including reports from the New York Times in 1886, detail sightings of this serpent. Witnesses have described it as having a large black head, prominent eyes, and a copper-colored back, along with hissing sounds that it reportedly made.

Long Island Sound Kraken: The Long Island Sound is home to various marine life, including crabs, snails, and jellyfish. However, it also harbors a Kraken-like sea monster occasionally reported in newspapers from 1879 to 1909. One notable incident in 1895 involved a crew that had a terrifying encounter with a 60-foot-wide octopus whose arms measured 100 feet long. They accidentally collided with the creature, but it was eventually driven away by a group of porpoises.

Delaware: Prime Hook Swamp Creature

Notable Characteristics: This particular animal typically stands between 2.5 to 3 feet tall, characterized by its long legs and tan body. It also has a long tail and a facial structure reminiscent of a pug, giving it a distinctive appearance.

The Prime Hook Swamp Creature is a cryptid that was reported to inhabit the Prime Hook National Wildlife Refuge in Delaware. The first significant encounter with this creature occurred in July 2007 when a witness named Helen J. spotted it while driving along Broadkill Road, which runs adjacent to the swamp. Helen described the beast as standing approximately 2.5 to 3 feet tall, with long legs, a tan body, and a long tail. Its facial features were said to resemble those of a pug. Since then, there have been additional sightings of the creature, including a report from a local shop owner who claimed to have seen it while biking.

Delaware: Selbyville Swamp Creature

Notable Characteristics: The Selbyville Swamp Creature is portrayed as a large, hairy entity between 6 and 7 feet tall.

Burnt Swamp, or the Great Cypress Swamp, is a freshwater forested wetland near Selbyville. It received its name after a moonshiner's still exploded, causing a fire that swept through the area in 1930. The marshland is rumored to be inhabited by a Bigfoot-like creature, the Selbyville Swamp Creature.

In the 1920s, two raccoon hunters ventured into the swamp at night. Unexpectedly, their dogs froze, tucking their tails and pulling their ears back as they began to whimper.

The hunters didn't have time to react before a horrifying scream echoed across the marshy waters, drawing closer to them. Fearing for their safety, they quickly fled, hearing the sounds of snapping branches and swirling water behind them.

This incident was likely not the first run-in with the creature, nor would it be the last. In the 1960s, a series of sightings were reported in the area. During the peak of this phenomenon, a hoax was orchestrated by Ralph Grapperhaus, an editor for Delmarva News, and his friend Fred Stevens. They created costumes and staged sightings to promote the legend of the creature. Despite the newspaper's deception, reports of the beast have continued, and sightings persist. Some residents claim to have seen the creature lurking in the woods, while others have reported hearing strange noises and cries from the swamp.

Delaware: Bigfoot

Notable Characteristics: The creature is known for its dark brown or black fur, standing at an approximate height of 7 to 8 feet. It is also noted for its loud scream.

Sussex County, Delaware, is characterized by a mix of towns, forests, and farmland. A woman traveling with her family on August 16 along Route 1 spotted a dark brown, hairy creature in a cornfield near Milton in this county. She observed it for about ten seconds and noted its Bigfoot-like features. She reported the sighting to the Bigfoot Field Researchers Organization.

In autumn 2012, a man unpacking groceries heard screams and wood knocks nearby, while in 2004, a driver spotted a nearly 8-foot-tall figure covered in thick black hair by a utility pole on Asbury Road.

Other Notable Delaware Cryptids

The Fence Rail Dog: This creature originates from folklore in Delaware, specifically along a stretch of Highway 12, known as Midstate Road, that runs through the towns of Frederica and Felton. It resembles a dog, standing 4 feet tall and measuring 10 feet long from the tip of its nose to the end of its bushy tail. The creature has glowing red eyes and possesses remarkable speed, able to outpace vehicles on the road. Some stories suggest it is the phantom of an outlaw who took his own life or the spirit of a boy who was killed by the man who enslaved him, both roaming the area in search of peace.

Deer Man: A creature that is part man and part deer, with the ability to transform, is said to lurk in Delaware. One notable sighting occurred in Hockessin in 1993. An 8-year-old witness related an encounter while staying with his grandparents. The child described seeing a creature that initially looked like a deer but then transformed into a humanoid figure when it stood on its hind legs.

Mhuwe: A creature from the Lenape Native American tribe in Delaware known as a man-eating ice giant involving themes of starvation, cannibalism, and sin. Individuals who have tasted human flesh or have gone mad from the cold and starvation can transform into a Mhuwe.

Florida: Skunk Ape

Notable Characteristics: The Florida Skunk Ape is a large, hairy, bipedal creature characterized by its height of 5 to 7 feet, covered in mottled reddish-brown hair, and known for emitting a foul odor similar to a skunk.

The Skunk Ape is a well-known cryptid in Florida, often compared to Bigfoot. This creature is primarily reported in the swamps and forests of Southern Florida, particularly within the Everglades. Eyewitness accounts describe the Skunk Ape as a massive, ape-like being that stands approximately 8 feet tall and weighs around 450 pounds. It is infamous for its foul, rancid odor, contributing to its distinctive reputation.

Not long ago, a man was driving slowly along State Road 50 between Lake and Sumter counties when he noticed an enormous hairy animal emerge from the forest beside the road. At the same time, his wife slept peacefully beside him.

Remarkably, she slept through the incident when the creature hit the side of the car with a clenched fist. The impact was strong enough that a body shop had to fix a dent in the car. However, the driver was more focused on the creature, as he sped up to 80 miles an hour, and the hairy thing ran alongside him for quite some time.

Scott Marlowe, a Bigfoot enthusiast, anthropologist, and a well-known figure in the cryptid community, experienced a shocking moment in October 1975 while unloading groceries at his apartment in Lakeland. He had a strange feeling of being watched, and when he looked up, he found himself staring eye to eye with a hairy, 7-foot-tall "man-ape" standing under a light across the parking lot. The creature vanished shortly after their encounter.

In August 2004, about a week after Hurricane Charley, Jennifer Ward drove along a remote stretch of road after visiting a friend's house with her kids in the car. She glanced into a ditch and saw something rising from a squatting position. It stood between 6 and 8 feet tall and covered in long, thick hair. It was close enough for her to see that the creature's lips were textured like a dog's paw.

The Skunk Ape has fascinated people in the southeastern United States for the past two centuries. This elusive creature thrives in dense, swampy areas, allowing it to remain hidden. Stories of its sightings have been passed down through generations, adding to the rich folklore surrounding this mysterious being.

Florida: Hog Kong

Notable Characteristics: The Florida Hog is a large, stocky animal with a long snout, tusks, and wiry black, brown, or brindled fur. It can weigh over 150 pounds and measure between 5 and 6 feet in length.

The Florida hog, commonly called the wild hog or feral pig (Sus scrofa), is a non-native species that has inhabited Florida since at least 1539. It is believed that these animals were introduced to the region by the Spanish explorer Hernando DeSoto. Florida hogs can grow to impressive sizes, often exceeding 150 pounds and measuring 5 to 6 feet long. They are highly adaptable and thrive in various habitats, including oak-cabbage palm hammocks, freshwater marshes, and pine flatwoods. One example of the monster side of this pig is the Florida Hog Kong. One of the largest hogs on record, Florida Hog Kong, weighed over 1,000 pounds and was killed in 2004 by a Florida man named Larry Earley. This event sparked speculation and belief among enthusiasts that larger specimens may still lurk in the wild.

Florida: Croczilla

Notable Characteristics: The giant crocodile of Florida, also known as "Croczilla," is a massive American crocodile spotted in the Everglades National Park. Its enormous size is around 14 feet long, although some say it certainly can be more extensive. It has a greyish-green color with a narrow, tapered snout, and its fourth tooth on its lower jaw is exposed when its mouth is closed.

Florida is well-known for its alligators but is also home to a small population of American crocodiles found at the northern edge of their range in South Florida. These crocodiles inhabit brackish or saltwater ponds, coves, and mangrove swamps. There is a cryptid associated with these creatures that is compared to the Mahamba of Congo, a giant crocodile said to measure 50 to 60 feet in length. The St. Johns River flows north along Florida's east coast and is renowned for its large population of alligators. In 1907, workers constructing a bridge over the river spotted a massive crocodile swimming beneath them nearly as long as the bridge itself. Panicking, they hurriedly left the site but returned the next day to find scraps of clothing where the creature had been.

Florida: Muck Monster

Notable Characteristics: The creature was described as shadowy and approximately 10 feet long, with footage capturing a glimpse of its tail fin.

The Florida Muck Monster is a cryptid reported to inhabit Lake Worth Lagoon in Palm Beach County. This lagoon extends about 21 miles and has undergone significant ecological transformations over the past 130 years, primarily due to dredging activities to create inlets. At first, the lagoon functioned like a freshwater lake, getting its water from natural sources that seeped in from the nearby Everglades. This hints that there might be many types of marine life yet to be discovered in the lagoon.

The Muck Monster first gained public attention in August 2009, when Greg Reynolds and Dan Serrano from Lagoon Keepers encountered what they thought was a floating log. Yet, the object consistently submerged when their boat came within ten feet of it. A marine biologist reviewed video footage from the incident, concluding that the creature exhibited behavior typical of an animal moving through the water without disturbing the surface. This behavior is unusual for common marine species, such as dolphins or manatees, which typically cause surface disturbances while swimming.

Other Notable Florida Cryptids

The Gulf Breeze UFO: This incident refers to a series of UFO sightings in Gulf Breeze, Florida, in November 1987. The central figure in this event was local contractor Ed Walters, who apparently photographed a UFO and communicated with extraterrestrial beings. Walters reported numerous encounters, including being immobilized by a beam of blue light and witnessing a UFO landing, from which he claimed extraterrestrial beings emerged.

Florida Chupacabra: This is a creature reported in the state since the 1990s, described as a blood-sucking monster resembling a dog or coyote with mange, which is a condition that causes hair loss and gives the animal a bony appearance. Many sightings of chupacabra have been misidentified animals suffering from this condition. Reports of the creature often coincide with incidents of livestock deaths occurring outdoors. The chupacabra can be differentiated from a mangy dog by its spines on the back and scaly skin.

One notable sighting took place in Sweetwater in 1996, where livestock owners claimed their animals were found drained of blood and showing puncture wounds on their necks. In July 2024, residents of a Florida community reported seeing a strange creature characterized by scaly skin and sharp spines along its back, adding to the ongoing intrigue surrounding the chupacabra phenomenon.

Monster Snakes: Florida is home to several monster snake species, one of the most notable being the Borinkus, commonly called "Johnnie." This massive serpent-like creature is reported to inhabit the St. Johns River. Accounts of its existence date back to 1849 when Captain Adams described an encounter with an estimated 90-foot-long creature. Witnesses typically characterize the Borinkus as having a dirty brown coloration and a neck that tapers from its head, giving it a snake-like appearance complemented by distinctive, frightening fins.

Buster Farrel was a Seminole Indian who, in 1892, went on a crocodile hunt. He followed wide, flattened pathways in the sawgrass, hoping to find an enormous crocodile. That day, Farrel noticed an unusually broad path. He anticipated encountering a crocodile more massive than the 15-foot one he had previously shot. However, instead of finding his prey, he faced a monstrous snake with the triangular head shape of a rattlesnake and a body as thick as a wooden barrel. It emitted a hissing sound that was so loud it could be compared to the noise of an underinflated tire being filled at a gas station air pump. Farrel was not one to run in fear, but on that day, he froze and was unashamed to admit he fled the scene as quickly as possible.

Georgia: Coweta County Belt Road Booger

Notable Characteristics: The Belt Road Booger stands about 5 feet tall, with a face resembling a dog or monkey, large eyes, and a broad, bushy tail.

The origin of the name "Belt Road Booger" dates to August 1979 and has captivated the imagination of residents in Coweta County, Georgia, particularly around the city of Newnan. This creature is often described as ape-like, standing approximately five feet tall. Witnesses report features that include a dog-like face or monkey-like appearance, large eyes that glow like diamonds when illuminated, and a broad, bushy tail resembling that of a beaver. The creature got its name from Belt Road, where numerous individuals encountered this mysterious being.

In one notable incident in 1979, Nancy Jackson, a resident of the Meadowview subdivision near Arnco—about a mile and a half from Newnan—pulled into her driveway at around 7 a.m. after returning home from a night of work. She described the creature standing on her patio as four to five feet tall.

It had a bushy beaver-like tail and an odd dog-like face. Jackson said it was "the ugliest looking thing I've ever seen." The creature was eating plants directly from her clay pots on the porch. Additional reports indicate that this being has been heard bellowing in the area and has allegedly attacked local pets.

Georgia: Coweta County Happy Valley Horror

Notable Characteristics: A large, bipedal, ape-like creature with glowing red eyes, long, sharp claws, and a foul odor.

About seven miles away from the home of the Belt Road Booger, as the crow flies, a creature known as the Happy Valley Horror appeared 26 years later. One of the earliest reports was documented in a letter to the local newspaper, The Times Herald, where a witness described seeing a hairy beast wandering around Happy Valley Circle, a wooded area.

In August 2005, 18-year-old Jeff Robards was traveling along Cedar Creek Road toward the intersection with Happy Valley Road around 2:30 a.m. when a large, hairy creature walked down the center of the road toward his vehicle. He recognized that it was not a bear, as the beast had a flat face, but he did not stick around to investigate further. Three nights later, his mother, Donna, was driving the same road when she suddenly had to stop as two creatures walked past her car before disappearing into the woods.

Georgia: Altamaha-ha

Notable Characteristics: An alligator-like creature that is 30 to 70 feet long, featuring a green or gray snake-like body, front flippers, and no hind legs.

The Altamaha River is a significant waterway that stretches 137 miles, originating from the confluence of the Oconee and Ocmulgee Rivers and flowing into the Atlantic Ocean. The riverbanks are richly lined with various trees, including cypress, Ogeechee lime, and tupelo. Historically, the Muscogee tribe and later settlers encountered a legend called the Altamaha-ha near the river's mouth. This creature is said to resemble an alligator, measuring between 30 to 70 feet in length. It has a serpentine body shape, characterized by a gray or green coloration, front flippers, and a lack of hind limbs.

In 1981, several fishermen reported seeing a giant, snake-like creature in the Altamaha River, estimated to be 15 and 20 feet long and "as big around as a man's body." Larry Gwin, a former newspaper reporter who lived along the riverbank north of Darien, shared his own experience with reporters.

He and his fishing partner, Steve Wilson, encountered the creature while fishing near an oxbow called Smith Lake that December. “We don’t really know what it was,” Gwin said. “It was too slender to be a manatee and undulated up and down.” He recounted how Steve saw it first and yelled, “What in the world was that?” Gwin looked and observed two brownish humps about five feet apart, along with a large swirl of water.

The giant, snake-like creature rocked their boat in a frightening way; they felt the swell it created. “It was like the wake from a racing boat,” Gwin declared. “What really scared us was that it dipped the boat, and at that time of year, the water was cold.” After their encounter, the creature submerged and did not resurface.

Another witness, 74-year-old Harvey Blackman from Brunswick, described a similar sighting in the Altamaha several years earlier. He and two friends were standing on a floating dock at Two-Way Fish Camp when he saw something grayish with a slick-looking body. “I have always wanted to know just what it was,” Blackman said. He wasn’t frightened by his close encounter with the unidentified creature. “I wasn't afraid; I was just looking,” he added. “I've been looking ever since, hoping to see it again, but I never have.”

Frank Culpepper, the founder and former owner of Two Way Fish Camp, did not see the snake-like creature surface, but he observed the wake it created that pushed boats against the dock. “I saw the wake as the thing went down the other dock, angling toward the hill,” he noted. However, it vanished as quickly as it appeared.

Georgia: Werewolf

Notable Characteristics: Disheveled, wild hair and thick eyebrows. Teeth are sharp and pointy, like a carnivore's. Suffers from chronic insomnia with nighttime wandering and notable livestock attacks.

Talbot County, Georgia, has long been known for its legend of a werewolf. This story has been passed down through local lore for over a century. The Burt family, wealthy and well-liked in the community, played a central role in this tale. Among the siblings—Alpheus, Sarah, Mildred, and Emily (Emmie) Isabella Burt—Emmie stood out.

After their father passed away, Emmie, like many affluent young women of her time, was sent to Europe for her education. However, upon her return, she began exhibiting symptoms that some interpreted as signs of lycanthropy—a rare condition in which a person believes they can transform into a wolf. Emmie showed signs including sleepwalking, a detached demeanor, and many sleepless nights. Frequently, she would leave the house to wander the countryside alone in the dark, which only fueled gossip in the community and at home. Her hair looked shaggier, and her eyebrows were thicker and more prominent, making her eyes appear smaller and darker. Perhaps the most striking feature was her teeth; her canines had grown sharper and pointier, resembling those of a carnivore.

Following her return, there was a noticeable increase in the number of livestock killed by a mysterious predator that only hunted at night. Unable to identify this creature, the townspeople began to wonder if it was something more sinister lurking in their community. Werewolf stories became quite popular in the 1800s, with many gothic short stories, novels, and sensationalized newspaper articles featuring the werewolf theme. This led them to consider that a werewolf might be in their midst. Armed with guns, a posse was formed to patrol the community during the dark hours.

Finally, someone spotted the predator and shot at it; however, the beast managed to escape. Not long after, Emmie's mother discovered that the young woman had been wounded by a bullet, which further fueled the belief that she had been transformed into a werewolf. Shortly after, Emmie was sent away—this time across the Atlantic, presumably for treatment for lycanthropy from a noted physician. Upon her return, the livestock killings ceased. Emily lived out her life respected within her community until she died in 1911 at 70.

Georgia: Nodoroc Wog

Notable Characteristics: According to historical accounts, particularly those documented by G. J. N. Wilson in his book 'The Early History of Jackson County, Georgia,' the Wog is described as the size of a small horse, with a bear-like head and large, visible white teeth, as its lips never fully close. It has long, jet-black hair and an unusual body structure resembling a horse but with disproportionately short legs. Notably, its front legs are longer than its hind legs, contributing to its peculiar gait. Additionally, the Wog has a forked red tongue and glowing eyes.

Nodoroc is a notable mud volcano located in Winder, Georgia. It is believed to have formed from the decaying organic matter beneath the surface, resulting in the eruption of mud, gases, slurries, and water. The last recorded eruption of Nodoroc occurred around the year 1800.

This site features a vast muddy expanse and holds historical significance for the Creek Indians, who used the area to execute their enemies. They regarded Nodoroc as being protected by supernatural entities. There was a temple and altar at the site in the past, although these were later stolen.

Despite its cultural importance, the Creek Indians sold the pond and surrounding land to the English for a mere 14 pounds of beads. This decision may have stemmed from their belief that the site was inhabited by evil spirits and served as a gateway to hell. The Creek passed along that a creature known as the Wog guarded the gate to hell. The creature was depicted as a jet-black hybrid of bear and dog, possessing a white tip on its tail, a long red forked tongue, and the size of a horse. According to their beliefs, the Wog would leave them alone if they did not provoke it.

Georgia: Pig Man

Notable Characteristics: Descriptions of Pigman vary, but he is commonly portrayed as an old man with a pig's head or wearing a mask resembling a pig. His appearance is unsettling, evoking fear among those who claim to have encountered him.

According to various accounts, a Pig Man exists in Hawkinsville, Georgia. He was a murderous recluse who staked pig heads near the bridge as warnings to trespassers. When teenagers disregard these ominous signs and visit the bridge, Pigman avenges them by killing them and displaying their heads likewise. Another version of the tale suggests that he is the ghost of a circus hog trainer who met a tragic end, possibly at the hands of his own pigs. Pigman lurks in dark, isolated areas such as abandoned bridges or secluded roads, particularly around Hawkinsville.

Other Notable Georgia Cryptids

The Plat-eye: The Plat-eye is a malevolent spirit most commonly depicted as a black dog with a single flat eye in the center of its forehead. This entity can also take on the form of a person it once was, as well as other animals such as a cat or cow or even a headless human.

The Plat-eye manifests when an individual dies without a proper burial or their remains are interred carelessly, resulting in an unsettled spirit seeking vengeance. Those who encounter the Plat-eye may experience extreme terror, potentially leading to insanity or death. The only effective way to pacify this spirit is to properly locate and bury the remains of the person associated with it.

Camp Rainey Mountain Beaver Shark: Camp Rainey Mountain is a scout camp located in the foothills of the Appalachian Mountains, and it has an eerie legend associated with it. In July 1980, a troop from this camp reportedly captured a creature known as the Beaver Shark and skinned it. The skin is still displayed more than 40 years later. Descriptions of the Beaver Shark vary, but it is generally described as having a beaver's head and a shark's body. This legend likely originated as a cautionary tale told by camp counselors to discourage children from swimming in unsafe areas.

Hawaii: Lizard Spirit-
Mo'o of Mākua Valley

Notable Characteristics: Mo'o are shapeshifting lizard spirits often portrayed as fierce, monstrous creatures. These entities are revered as ancestral spirits providing guidance and protection. Mo'o inhabit freshwater like creeks and ponds and possess significant powers over these natural elements.

In Hawaiian legend, Mo'o are mainly female beings known for their dual nature; they can serve as caring guardians of water sources or terrifying predators. Many stories describe their interactions with humans, often emphasizing their shapeshifting abilities. Mo'o may appear as a woman, luring men into dangerous situations that sometimes lead to death.

Kalena Stream is a waterway in Maui County flowing from Ko'iahi to Mākua. It is associated with a particular Mo'o—Mo'o of Mākua Valley—who lived in a valley on the west coast of O'ahu known as Mākua whose parents changed her into a Mo'o so she would not marry the Shark-man Kupua. Mo'o was once a pretty girl who, during rains, would descend from the Kalena Stream to meet Kamohoali'i, the Shark-man of Kāneana Cave. She would sit on a rock and call out to him, and he would swim through the caves to her. They would then transform into humans and unite. When the water is green, the Mo'o is in the stream; when the water is clear, she is not.

Hawaii: White Lady-Pele

Notable Characteristics: The White Lady, a depiction of the goddess Pele, is often portrayed as a woman with long white hair who roams the Hawaiian Islands. She is sometimes seen hitchhiking or appearing at the foot of volcanoes. The White Lady is known to test the kindness of strangers. She embodies benevolence and the potential for catastrophe for those who do not show her respect.

The White Lady of Hawaii is a spirit linked to Pele, the Hawaiian goddess of fire. This entity is typically described as wearing white clothing and having long, flowing white hair. She appears in various forms, youthful or elderly, particularly on full moon nights as she roams the island. Witnesses report seeing her hitchhiking along roads or accompanied by a small white dog.

Sightings of the White Lady have frequently occurred on Highway 30. One notable account involves a man traveling to Wailuku who picked up a woman hitchhiking. He noticed an unusual glow surrounding her, initially attributing it to the moonlight. When he inquired about her destination, she did not respond, and he later realized that she appeared nearly transparent when observed in the rearview mirror. When he looked back to ask her again, she had mysteriously vanished.

Hawaii: Night Marchers-Huaka'i po

Notable Characteristics: The Night Marchers, or Huaka'i po, are significant figures in Hawaiian folklore, embodying the spirits of ancient warriors who are believed to march through specific areas at night. This spectral procession is often accompanied by haunting sounds of drums and chants, with sightings of these entities frequently occurring during particular phases of the moon. When faced with an encounter, it is said that visitors should show respect by either removing their clothing or lying flat on the ground to avoid incurring the wrath of the warriors.

The Koloa Tree Tunnel—a long stretch of trees imported from Australia—is known for its eerie occurrences that may be due to these entities. This area was originally part of a wealthy man's estate, where he planted trees, later donating the excess to the Koloa community to line Maluhia Highway.

Reports of strange lights and mechanical failures have emerged from this location. Two young men driving a new truck experienced sudden sputtering and stalling of their vehicle. Despite attempts to restart the truck, it remained inoperable until a mysterious light appeared on the road, resembling an approaching vehicle, although no car was found. After a brief period, the lights disappeared, and the truck resumed functioning. Many who have encountered similar phenomena surmise that a supernatural force, possibly the Night Marchers, influenced their journey.

Hawaii: Little People-Menehune

Notable Characteristics: The Menehune are one of the most well-known cryptic entities in Hawaii. This race is characterized by small, dwarf-like individuals ranging from 2 to 3 feet tall. They inhabit the dense forests and secluded valleys of the Hawaiian Islands. They are notably recognized for their remarkable craftsmanship.

The Menehune are responsible for constructing significant structures across the islands, including temples, fishponds, roads, and houses, completed in the dark and in one night. Their diet is believed to consist primarily of fish and bananas. The Menehune are also noted for their elusive nature, often working at night. They are also known for their playful and mischievous behavior, frequently engaging in tricks that can surprise unsuspecting individuals.

Mo'okini Heiau is one of the Hawaiian Islands' oldest and most sacred temples. It is in the Kohala Historical Sites State Monument on the Island of Hawai'i. Originally built as a luakini heiau, a type of temple used for rituals involving human sacrifice, it is believed to have been constructed between the 13th and 14th centuries. The temple also served as a primary place of worship for Native Hawaiians.

According to Hawaiian legend, the Menehune, known for their extraordinary skills in construction and craftsmanship, built this structure, among many others on the Hawaiian Islands, overnight. Under cover of darkness, the Menehune transported stones from 12 miles away in Pololū Valley, passing them hand to hand.

On Friday, May 24, 1929, a teacher at Waimea Elementary and Junior High School in Kauai observed students running wildly around the schoolyard during morning recess. The children of all ages were out of breath as they chased a creature they described as a "little fellow about a foot high with pointed shoes who was eating peanuts." This *fellow* had been spotted on the school grounds and at the nearby Waimea Foreign Church, now known as the United Church of Christ.

When the teachers arrived at the scene, the students had surrounded the minister's house. Some even crawled beneath it in an attempt to capture the little creature. "Watch out for that crack!" some children shouted, while others called, "Don't let him get away!" and "Keep the house surrounded!"

When a teacher scolded the children for leaving the school grounds and asked what they were trying to find beneath the house, one wide-eyed and expectant student replied, "The Menehune! He went right past us, a little fellow about a foot or so high, with a long beard; he wore pointed shoes and was eating peanuts." The students pointed out tiny footprints on the ground as evidence.

Eventually, the students were rounded up after the commotion. However, during lunch, accompanied by more students and a few elderly Hawaiians who had heard about the incident, they began their search again. The tiny menehune had eluded capture and managed to escape.

After school, Principal Dallas McLaren questioned each student individually about the incident. All of them told the same story. As afternoon turned into evening, adult community members joined the search. Still, the little fellow remained elusive and was not found.

There is one thing for sure: do not anger a Menehune. Three young people ventured out on a moonlit night to an isolated beach on the south shore of Kauai. The air was eerily silent, and something felt *off*. They built a small fire and soon noticed that the rocks and tree roots appeared strange. "I noticed that the rocks, roots, and trees around us looked like gnarled, grotesque faces," one girl recalled. "I pointed it out to my two companions, who agreed. I wasn't scared because I thought they were merely hallucinations."

However, as they walked through the tall grasses, shadows of small people began to emerge in the darkness. "We were right next to a heiau—a pre-contact place of worship for Hawaiians, like an altar," the girl reported. "I was very miffed that he would bring us to such a creepy and spiritually charged place." Realizing their mistake in coming so close, she worried that they had offended some ancient entity. To make amends, two teens offered a pear at the altar as a gift. The girl, feeling uneasy, could not bring herself to approach.

The boy walked to the grass, placed the pear down, and vanished. Moments later, he came sprinting back, chased by tiny figures around him. Terrified, the three teens fled the scene and vowed never to return to the area again.

Other Notable Hawaiian Cryptids

The Green Lady of Wahiawa: This entity is an important figure in Hawaiian folklore. She is known for her deep connection to the island's lush rainforests. She is often depicted as a woman transformed into a nature spirit, with green skin adorned with leaves, moss, grass, and seaweed in her hair. According to legend, she tragically lost her children in the woods and now roams the forest in search of them in the afterlife. In her anguish, she may grab any child she encounters, regardless of whether they are hers or not.

Kamapua'a, the Hog-child: This entity was born to Hina and Kahikiula on the northern coast of O'ahu. He was abandoned by his mother's eldest son, discovered wrapped in a kapa garment, and raised by his grandmother. Fueled by rejection from his stepfather, Olopana, Kamapua'a became angry and rebellious. Still, he became a handsome and skilled man. Kamapua'a could transform into different forms, including that of a hog or a kukui tree. Once, Kamapua'a transformed into a pig to escape his enemies after stealing chickens from Olopana. Cornered at a waterfall, he shifted into hog form, helping his followers climb to safety. Once atop, Kamapua'a released the water, sweeping away Olopana's men. Kamapua'a's relations with Pele, goddess of fire, were marked by conflict and passion. They often shifted between being enemies and lovers. Kamapua'a used his ability to summon rain to extinguish Pele's flames when she attacked with lava.

Idaho: Slimy Slim

Notable Characteristics: Witness accounts describe Sharlie as 30 feet long and two feet wide, having a dinosaur-like head, humps along its body, and a texture reminiscent of a shell.

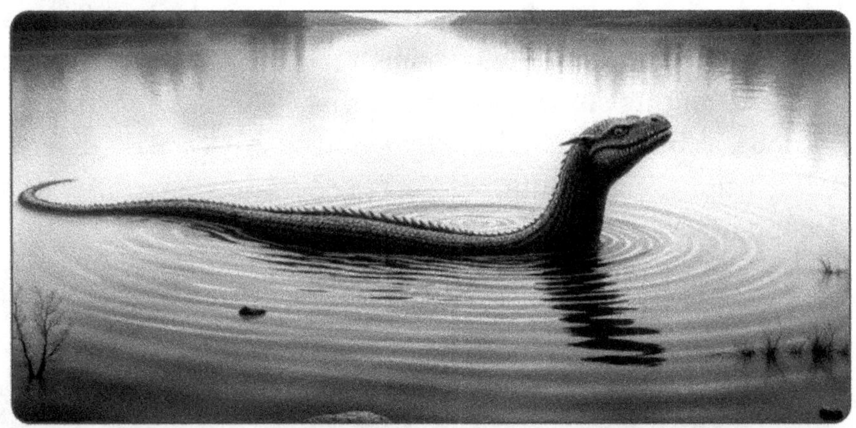

Payette Lake is a prominent 5,330-acre body of water in McCall, Idaho, that was formed through glacial activity. The lake has significant depths, with some reaching up to 392 feet. Historically, local Native American tribes shared stories of a powerful spirit believed to inhabit Payette Lake, expressing caution about a potentially malevolent entity thought to reside beneath its surface.

In the 1920s, sightings of an odd creature in the lake were first documented when railroad workers reported observing a large, log-like figure estimated to be between 30 and 35 feet long moving swiftly through the water. Occasionally, sightings still occur. In 1976, 21-year-old Nick McGough of Boise said he and four others observed a puzzling ripple in the smooth lake surface. Shortly after, a creature 30 feet long and two feet wide surfaced about 350 yards offshore. It turned and vanished. Initially named Slimy Slim, the beast was renamed Sharlie in the mid-1900s.

Idaho: Bear Lake Monster

Notable Characteristics: The Bear Lake Monster is an intriguing creature, typically described as a large entity measuring at least 40 feet long. Witness accounts often depict it as having short, powerful legs and a body resembling an alligator or crocodile. Its coloration is commonly described as grayish-green. Additionally, some reports suggest it features spikes along its spine and a head that bears resemblance to various animals, including cows and walruses. The diverse descriptions contribute to the mystery surrounding this legendary creature.

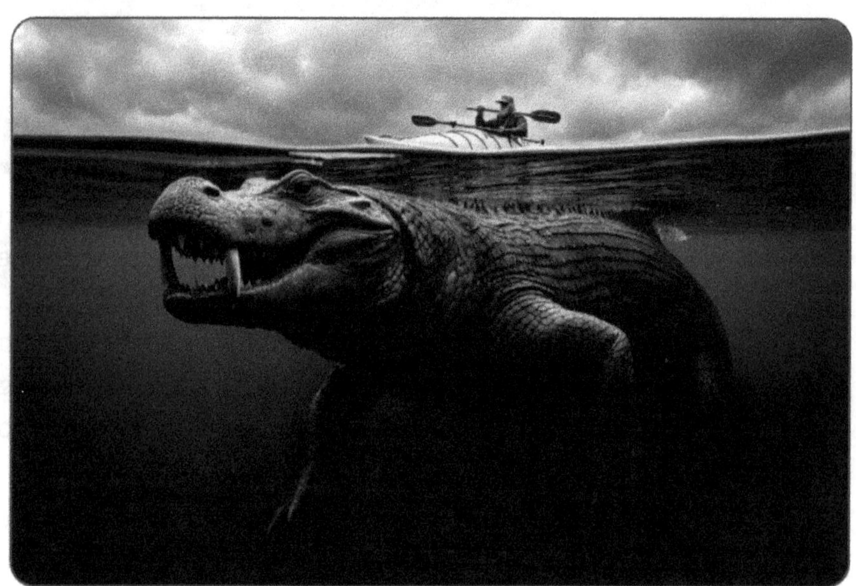

Bear Lake is 20 miles long and eight miles wide, with a maximum depth of 208 feet. It straddles the border between Utah and Idaho. It is home to a mysterious creature that resembles a combination of a crocodile and a walrus. This creature has sturdy legs, a snake-like tail, a horse-like head, extended nostrils, and a forked tongue. Sightings of this creature date back to the 1860s.

The monster gained fame after being credited with eating a horse in the early 1900s. Soon after, it was discovered that the young man who reported the incident lost the horse in a poker game, and the monster became the scapegoat for his father's missing steed. The sensationalized newspaper stories surrounding this creature originated in the 19th century, mainly due to articles written by Joseph Rich, a Mormon settler in the region. These articles, published in the Deseret News, detailed local Native American traditions about a serpent-like creature inhabiting Bear Lake. Although Rich claimed to report second-hand accounts of sightings, he later recanted these stories. Despite his admission that the tales were fabricated, others continued to assert that they had seen the creature clearly, and the legend persists.

According to an Idaho Statesman newspaper interview with local historian Patrick Wilde, a colossal skeleton was found in the 1920s, "Then in 1928, when Bear Lake was at its lowest point in drought years," Wilde told reporters. "The health director for the State of Utah identified part of the skeletal structure of a large aquatic animal, so who knows whether the monster is real or not."

Sightings of the creature pop up from time to time. In 1937, a four-year-old boy claimed to have seen the monster; in 1946, a Boy Scout leader reported a sighting. More recently, in 2002, local businessman Brian Hirschi saw "these two humps in the water" while anchoring his boat. He described it as having two humps and dark, slimy green skin, along with deep beet-red eyes. The humps vanished under the water's surface then something huge lifted his boat. It roared and disappeared.

Idaho: Nimerigar

Notable Characteristics: According to the stories of the Shoshone people, there is a race of small creatures, particularly associated with the Rocky Mountains, including regions in Idaho. These beings, known as "Nimerigar," which translates to "people eaters," reflect their cannibalistic tendencies. Nimerigars are 2 to 3 feet tall, aggressive, and vicious. They possess sharp canine teeth and fight using poisoned arrows.

Legend has it that Nimerigars would kill members of their own tribe who were too ill or unable to contribute to society by striking them on the head with large rocks. This act was seen as a means of survival and to engage in cannibalism.

They often targeted the Shoshone and Paiute tribes, playing tricks on them or stealing their children.

In 1932, gold prospectors discovered a 14-inch-tall mummy near Casper, Wyoming, which led some to speculate on the reality behind these legends. Subsequent examinations revealed that the mummy was that of an anencephalic infant; however, the presence of teeth resembling those described in Nimerigar folklore led some to question this conclusion. The mummy mysteriously disappeared from public view.

Today, there have been reports from hikers and locals who claim to have experienced strange sounds or sights while exploring the remote areas of Idaho's mountains. Some individuals report hearing rustling noises or noticing quick movements out of the corner of their eyes.

Other Notable Idaho Cryptids

Malad Gorilla: A massive creature, standing 7 to 10 feet tall and covered in dark fur, named after the town where numerous sightings occurred. It has broad shoulders, long arms, and a robust build. Eyewitnesses frequently mention facial features such as a flat nose and deep-set eyes, enhancing its resemblance to primates. The legend of the Malad Gorilla dates back several decades. In 1902, the Montpelier Examiner reported a sighting near Chesterfield, where skaters on the Portneuf River—a tributary of the Snake River—saw an 8-foot-tall creature covered in hair. A posse was formed, and 16-inch-long tracks were discovered in the snow. Another notable sighting occurred in the 1970s when campers heard unusual vocalizations and reported seeing a prominent figure moving through the trees at dusk. In the following years, more reports emerged of large footprints found near streams or wooded areas, further fueling interest in the existence of the Malad Gorilla.

Wapaloosie: The creature is comparable in size to the short-legged, long-bodied dachshund and exhibits characteristics like a woodpecker, including specialized feet adapted for climbing trees. Its diet consists exclusively of mushrooms that grow on these trees. Notably, the fur of this creature possesses a remarkable quality; it continues to exhibit movement even after being transformed into clothing.

Illinois: Big Muddy River Monster (The Thing)

Notable Characteristics: Standing 7 to 8 feet tall, with white or silver hair, and weighing about 400 pounds, this creature leaves footprints measuring 10 to 12 inches long and is typically covered in mud.

Two police reports, one from June 25 and a second from June 26, are remembered in Murphysboro, Illinois, as a time when many locals faced the unexplained. That summer of 1973, residents reported seeing a tall, white creature covered in mud near the Big Muddy River, prompting them to call the police for an investigation.

The initial report came in around midnight on June 25 from a couple parked near a boat dock on the southwestern edge of Riverside Park. Nineteen-year-old Randy Needham and Judy Johnson heard loud screams coming from the woods. Then, they witnessed a 7-foot-tall creature with light-colored hair, matted with mud, walking on two legs toward their car. Terrified, they sped off into the night and reported their experience to local law enforcement.

Police searched the area using flashlights and discovered footprints measuring 10 to 12 inches long, 3 to 4 inches deep, and 3 inches wide. Officers also heard a scream emanating from the woods. However, despite their thorough search, no additional signs of the creature were found.

At the time, the police chief of Murphysboro, Ron Manwaring, was the officer on duty when a second call came in the following evening from the Westwood Hills subdivision. Two teenagers relaxing on a porch spotted a tall, white-haired creature moving through a field near a wooded lot, and a five-year-old neighbor witnessed it as well. Officers, including Manwaring, once again searched the area. They followed a local footpath until they encountered a foul odor and a slimy film coating the tree branches.

The canine unit was brought in, led by Jerry Nellis, who was in charge of the trained dog, Reb. He told reporters from the Southern Illinoisan newspaper, "I saw this substance and smelled the odor myself. The dog tracked the scent to a barn," he explained. "But once we got to the barn, the dog refused to go inside." At that time, Nellis speculated that it might be a bear; however, they did not get a good look at the tracks. Just a couple years later, in July of 1975, two men reported seeing the Big Muddy Monster north of Murphysboro. However, if they looked into the past, they might have noted that this was not the first time the creature had appeared in the region.

In October of 1942, The Daily Independent from Murphysboro reported on what they called "The Thing," a massive, hairy, silver ape-like creature weighing over 400 pounds and standing 8 feet tall. It was seen by a bartender and a police officer. Then, it was sighted at the Big Muddy Bridge just outside Murphysboro. On the night of the sighting, Chief Floyd Jones was working when a frightened motorist rushed into the police station to report that a giant hairy creature had run in front of his car at the bridge. The creature known as the Silver Monster had been sighted on multiple occasions and had garnered a range of reactions from the community. While some dismissed it as mere fanciful tales, others suggested it might have escaped from a traveling circus. However, a few individuals understood the true nature of the creature. It is still out there.

Illinois: Enfield Horror

Notable Characteristics: The Enfield Horror first gained public attention in 1973. It is described as having a short body, two arms, and grey skin with a slimy texture. The creature has three legs and distinctly deep red eyes. It is named after the town of Enfield, where it was sighted.

On April 25, 1973, Henry McDaniel, a veteran, heard a strange scratching sound at his back door between 9:30 and 10 p.m. When he peered outside, he thought he saw what appeared to be a bear. However, after grabbing his flashlight and gun, the man stepped outside into the blustery wind. He noticed a creature in his rose bushes.

McDaniel described the strange being that looked almost human: "When I first saw it, I thought it was an animal. I went back inside the house to get a gun and a flashlight," he recalled. "It was right about three feet from me. I wasn't scared. Then I saw those pink eyes shining at me like reflectors on a car. It had pink eyes, a large head, and a dirty gray color. It was about four or five feet tall, standing right in front of the door on three legs, just like a human being."

Yet, in a moment of sheer panic, he lifted his gun and took a shot. He knew he had hit the creature as it made a wildcat-like hiss and then leaped 75 feet in three jumps before escaping along a railway embankment, vanishing from sight. The footprints left behind measured three to five inches across, with six toes and little hoof marks.

The creature returned later, drawing McDaniel's attention when his dogs started barking. He got up, looked outside, and saw the same three-legged creature staring back at him from the railroad tracks about 75 feet away. He stated he was not scared this time either; he just wished to keep it as a pet and charge admission. Undoubtedly, the creature would probably disagree with this notion, given that the man shot at it.

Some have proposed that it was either an escaped ape or a kangaroo. Others have suggested a connection between the Enfield Horror and local UFO sightings, implying a possible link to extraterrestrial activity during the same period.

Illinois: Wolfman of Chestnut Mountain

Notable Characteristics: The Wolfman is a five-foot-tall hybrid resembling a wolf and a human. It has dark fur and yellow eyes that reflect light at night. Its hands are human-like, similar to a raccoon's, and witnesses depict it as cunning and feral and moving fast when running on all fours rapidly.

Sightings of the Wolfman have typically been reported along backroads near Galena, with accounts dating back several decades. Notable reports began emerging in the early 1980s. One memorable sighting took place in 2010 when a psychologist, who was on vacation with her fiancé, was driving on a remote stretch near Chestnut Mountain. They encountered a wolf-like creature that ran on two legs, staring at them for a long moment in the moonlight before disappearing. The creature stood over five feet tall and had dark, shaggy fur.

Illinois: Monster of Salt Creek

Notable Characteristics: This cryptid is described as a tall creature with a hairy body, resembling Bigfoot. It is noted for its glowing yellow eyes and a strong, unpleasant odor reminiscent of decaying refuse.

The Farmer City Monster, also known as the Monster of Salt Creek, is a cryptid that gained notoriety in the early 1970s. The first sighting occurred in July 1970 when a group of teenagers was camping at a local lover's lane near Salt Creek. They began to feel as if they were being watched, and almost simultaneously, a terrible smell filled the air. One of the boys turned on their car's headlights and spotted a tall, hairy, human-like figure with glowing yellow eyes lurking in the nearby woods. Terrified, they left immediately.

Local law enforcement was called to investigate, and one of the officers, Robert Hayslip, reported witnessing the creature walk directly in front of his patrol car during one of his shifts. After receiving reports from concerned citizens about strange occurrences around Salt Creek, conservation officers investigated the area. They discovered large, human-like footprints along the muddy banks of Salt Creek. Throughout the summer, more locals began to report encounters with the creature, with sightings reported from Heyworth to Waynesville.

One particularly striking report came from construction workers who spotted the creature while commuting early in the morning. These numerous sightings—from teenagers to police officers and locals—provided substantial evidence of the creature's existence. However, just as it gained popularity, the Farmer City Monster vanished.

Illinois: Chicago Mothman

Notable Characteristics: The flying "Mothman-like" humanoid creature measures six to ten feet in height, with a wingspan of around ten feet. Witnesses report a variety of eye colors, including red, green, yellow, and orange. Despite the differences in individual accounts, common characteristics include fur, leather-like skin, bat-like wings, and an absence of a neck.

Since 2011, there have been hundreds of sightings of a large, winged humanoid creature with leather-like skin and bat-like wings in the Chicago area. Many people have linked these sightings to the Mothman, a flying humanoid reported in the 1960s in West Virginia around the abandoned West Virginia Ordnance Works, known as the TNT Area. As a result, this creature has been dubbed the Chicago Mothman.

A notable phenomenon emerged around 2011, peaking in 2017, with sporadic reports continuing to surface in subsequent years. Most sightings are reported near bodies of water, particularly around Lake Michigan. One significant account occurred in 2019 at O'Hare International Airport, where a USPS employee described encountering a tall figure with glowing red eyes and large wings that appeared to charge toward her.

In 2020, airport security was startled by the sight of a massive black-winged being taking flight. Additionally, in May 2017 at Adler Planetarium, two bystanders observed giant bats performing aerial maneuvers. These incidents highlight an ongoing interest in unexplained aerial phenomena in the region.

Other Notable Illinois Cryptids

The Piasa Bird: A legendary creature from Alton, Illinois, often described as dragon-like, featuring wings and distinct mismatched characteristics. "Piasa" originates from the Algonquian language, translating to "a bird that devours men." The first known documentation of the Piasa Bird was by Father Jacques Marquette in 1673, when he discovered a painting of the creature on the bluffs along the Mississippi River. According to local legend, the Illini Native American tribe experienced ongoing torment from the Piasa. To address this threat, their chief, Ouatoga, undertook a period of fasting and received guidance from the Great Spirit. Through this vision, he developed a strategic plan to defeat the bird using poisoned arrows. This plan ultimately succeeded, leading to the Piasa's demise as it crashed into the river, where it is said to remain. Or so they thought because in 1977, near Lincoln, a 10-year-old boy was attacked by a giant bird and carried 30 feet before being dropped.

The Cole Hollow Road Monster: The Creature is a hybrid resembling an 8 to 9-foot-tall ape combined with a caveman. It has white hair and emits a foul smell—tracks with three toes. The initial sightings of the creature began in May 1972 as a teen prank. Interestingly, police received a report from an anonymous caller who described an 8-foot-tall hairy beast that picked up the back of her vehicle and held on for quite some time. Occasionally, folks still see it today.

Indiana: The Crawfordsville Phenomenon

Notable Characteristics: A headless, pure white entity resembling the snake-liked movements of a flag flapping in the wind with several sets of propelling fins floating in the air. The object was about 16 to 20 feet long and 8 feet wide.

On an early Saturday morning in September 1891, in Athens, Indiana, Methodist minister G.W. Switzer stepped outside for a drink from the parsonage's well pump between midnight and 1 a.m. Suddenly, Switzer felt a strange awe and looked into the night sky beyond the streetlight's glare. He saw an odd, headless object resembling a drapery floating in the air. The object was about 16 feet long and 8 feet wide, moving in a snake-like motion above him. Alarmed, he called out to his wife, who observed the peculiar creature as it hovered over the Methodist Church, dipped down, and ascended again. Eventually, they grew tired of watching it and returned inside, leaving the object still hovering in the sky.

In Crawfordsville, two ice men, Marshall McIntyre, and Will Gray, were preparing for deliveries at their employer's barn at about two o'clock on Saturday, September 5, 1891. As they hitched up the teams, both men were overcome by an intense dread. McIntyre stepped into the alley and looked up at the night sky. To his astonishment, he saw what he could only describe as an apparition—20 feet long and 8 feet wide—rushing toward him from the west, propelled by several pairs of fins. Strangely, it seemed to lack a head, yet it emitted a wheezing, mournful sound from an invisible mouth. As it hovered above their employer's home, McIntyre suggested waking the family to warn them but ultimately decided against it. The creature circled for a while as they sought refuge in the barn. After moving east, it returned as the men fled in their wagon. When they returned later that day, the mysterious creature was gone.

As reporters flocked to the community and fear surged across the U.S., a practical and less alarming explanation needed to be found quickly. John Hornbeck and Abe Hernley observed the entity swooping through the town. They believed they had just that explanation: a massive flock of hundreds of Killdeers, a shorebird known for its shrill cry, which had become confused by the city's bright lights. Others speculated that it could be balloon parachutes, a craze among certain devious young boys at the time, possibly with a cat attached that would eventually be released. Still, many believed the entity was ultimately unexplainable. Those out during the early morning hours reported hearing birds chirping in distress as if they sensed something unsettling in the air that was swooping at them occasionally. Regardless, the event left an aura of doom hanging over the area, and the creature never returned.

Indiana: Pukwudgies

Notable Characteristics: The Pukwudgie is a creature with its roots in Indiana, particularly within the legends of Indigenous peoples such as the Lenape (Delaware) and Wampanoag tribes. These tiny beings are typically described as goblin-like figures, measuring about 2 to 3 feet tall. They are characterized by large noses, long ears, and porcupine-like quills along their backs, contributing to a troll-like appearance.

Pukwudgies are known for their mischievous tendencies, often playing tricks on humans. They possess a range of magical abilities, including shapeshifting and invisibility. Historically, Pukwudgies had amicable interactions with humans. Still, they have become more hostile over time due to grudges resulting from human behavior. Their elusive nature makes them hard to spot in the wild, as they can transform into animals as a means of concealment.

Paul Startzman, a passionate hiker, author, and amateur archaeologist in Indiana, had a notable encounter with the elusive Pukwudgie in 1927 when he was just 10 years old.

He described the creature as resembling a half-sized man with dull blonde hair and protruding ears. Other sightings have also been reported; for instance, a child playing alone in a park was approached by a group of Pukwudgies, who exhibited curiosity about her activities.

Mounds State Park in Anderson is recognized as a significant location for Pukwudgie sightings, with its dense forests offering an ideal habitat for these creatures to remain hidden while engaging in their playful behavior.

Indiana: Ohio River Thing

Notable Characteristics: A large aquatic creature characterized by its fur-like covering and claws.

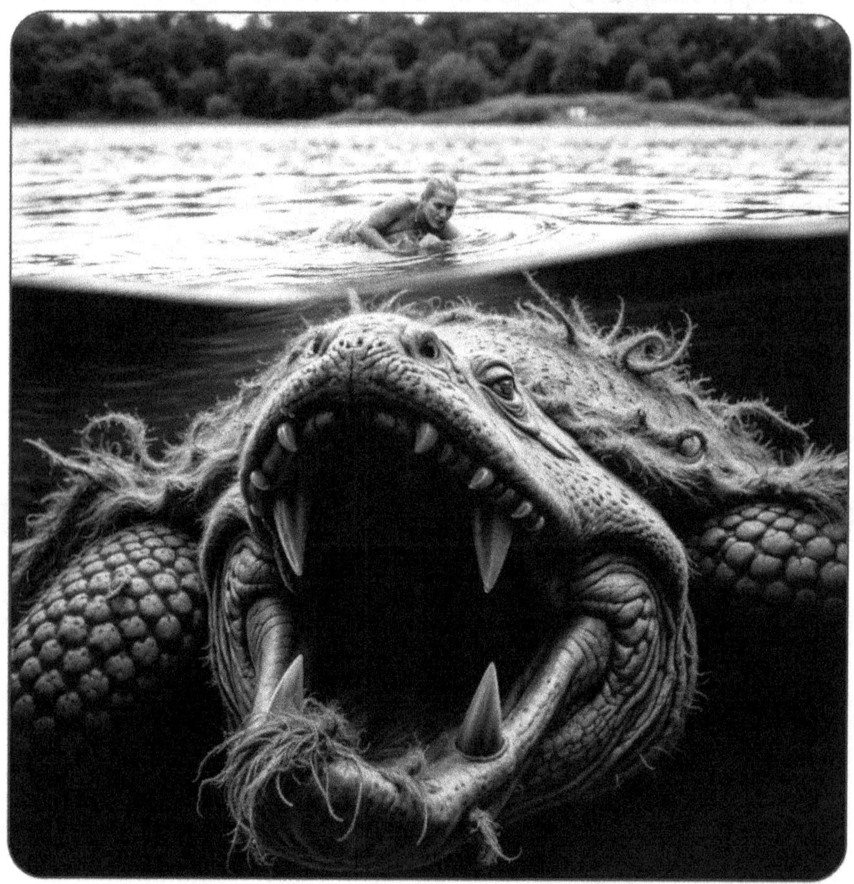

In August of 1955, a 35-year-old mother from Evansville, Naomi Johnson, her three children, and a friend named Missus Lamble went swimming in the murky Ohio River near Dogtown. While the children played on the shore, Missus Lamble floated on an inflated inner tube, and Naomi paddled about fifteen feet from the bank. A few minutes later, Naomi felt a creature with furry paws grab one of her legs just below the knee and attempt to drag her underwater.

She struggled to return to the shore as Missus Lamble paddled closer. Naomi eventually managed to free herself and frantically swam to safety, exclaiming, "It was a frightening experience, and I want to warn everyone not to swim in the Ohio River. I'm certainly glad it did not grab my little boy; he might not have been able to get away." She had several scratches and bruises on her leg as evidence of the encounter.

Some old-time fishermen dismissed the incident as merely a turtle covered in moss. However, strange things have been discovered in the murky waters of the Ohio River. For instance, a bull shark was caught by fishermen in 1937, about 700 miles from the ocean in Alton. In 2010, after floodwaters receded, a juvenile shark was found on a boat ramp in Olmsted, Illinois. Even more frightening is the possibility that Naomi encountered a legendary creature, the Ogua, rooted in Native American folklore. Descriptions of the Ogua depict it as a massive aquatic beast resembling a large turtle or alligator, with rough skin that ranges in color from dark green to reddish-brown. The creature is said to reach lengths of 15 to 20 feet and weigh between 400 and 500 pounds or more. The name "Ogua" is thought to derive from Native American languages, possibly translating to terms like "river demon" or "water devil."

There are legends that curious individuals in Cincinnati once dragged the carcass of an old cow to the Ohio River. They clamped one of the enormous grip hooks used to hang pigs in the slaughterhouse to butcher them onto a chain and connected it to the corpse. They dropped it off a dock, left it in the water all night, and returned to drag it out in the morning. A huge bite mark on the dead cow took up most of its belly. Perhaps Naomi Johnson's words should not be taken so light-heartedly, especially when the only alternative advice comes from those who have never ventured into uncertain waters.

These individuals sit comfortably on the banks in the sunshine, occasionally baiting a hook with a plastic worm and casting it into the water. They have yet to explore the depths of darkness that lie within. But she has.

Indiana: Mill Race Monster

Notable Characteristics: The creature observed was approximately six feet tall and possessed an upright posture. Its body was characterized by a coating of hair and slime and exhibited a green coloration.

Mill Race Park is an 85-acre public park located in Columbus, Indiana. It is known for its scenic beauty along the White River, featuring wooded areas and open fields. Previously, the property was home to the Commerce Roller Mill, which served local farmers.

In November 1974, a mysterious creature was reported to be lurking in Mill Race Park. Witnesses described it as a large, hairy, green monster standing upright on two legs. The first sighting occurred on Friday, the 1st, at approximately 3:30 p.m. at the paved boat ramp by the East Fork of the White River, near the west end of Fifth Street. This sighting was made by a couple of women.

Later that night, around 11:45 p.m., two girls observed the same creature emerge from the East Fork of the White River, covered in green slime. This time, the beast jumped onto their car and scratched the paint while attempting to break through the windshield.

One witness recounted her experience: "I just happened to look to the right and saw the weirdest thing. The big, black, blurry-looking figure came toward the car. Its face was pale, with long fingernails resembling claws and fangs. I sat there stunned, thinking it was a joke." The creature pounded on the car, and she noted, "It didn't look like a mask or a person playing a prank. The face was greenish, really yucky looking." She was so frightened that she struggled to put the car in reverse and speed away.

On November 4, at 4 p.m., two men near the mill race spotted the creature hiding in the trees near the covered bridge. They returned to the park that night with binoculars for a better look, but the creature chased them away.

City Park Director Robert Gillikin temporarily closed the park because too many curious visitors showed up each evening. The growing crowds were becoming unsafe, so he felt it was best to take this action. Eventually, the mysterious creature sparking so much interest disappeared. While some people believe the sightings were a hoax—pointing to an alleged confession from a teenager who later admitted to wearing a ghillie suit—others remain unconvinced and ponder the phenomenon's true nature.

Indiana: Crosley Monster

Notable Characteristics: A mysterious creature is reported to inhabit the Crosley Fish and Wildlife Area in Jennings County, Indiana. Some believe it resembles Bigfoot, standing upright and reaching 7 to 8 feet. The creature is covered in matted hair and has glowing red or yellow-orange eyes.

In 2006, four teenage boys—Corey Mullikin, Terry Snyder, Clint Maschino, and Robbie Evans—gained much attention after a camping trip to Harsin Pond in Crosley one late July evening. They were excited for a night of fishing and camping. Still, around 11:00 p.m., they began to hear unusual sounds.

"We heard some strange noises and tree branches snapping behind us," Snyder told Bryce Mayer, a North Vernon Plain Dealer newspaper reporter.

"I didn't know what it was at first and thought it might be a deer," Mullikin piped in. The noise came from right at the tree line, but the animal remained concealed behind the trees. Not long after, they saw a seven-foot-tall silhouette standing on two legs with yellow-orange eyes reflecting from their lantern.

"I saw his shadow from our lantern, and it was huge," Snyder continued. "You could see from the shadow he had a bunch of hair, too. He looked filthy."

When the boys spotted it, they sprinted down the nearest road. The creature began to pursue them through a cornfield adjacent to Grayford Road, knocking down cornstalks in its wake. While they ran, German shepherds from a neighboring house started barking. Fortunately, the boys managed to escape.

Corey Mullikin encountered the creature again while squirrel hunting on a different day, this time in the evening a little farther from Harsin Pond. He heard a scream, turned around, and saw the creature so close that it frightened him to his very core. "He was big and covered in black fur," Mullikin said. "I started running. He was running on all fours, but he was still huge and ran in like a circle around me as I ran through the woods," Mullikin said. The teenager sprinted nearly three miles backward during his escape. And once again, he was able to evade the beast.

An Indiana natural resources officer was initially skeptical about these reports; however, the Crosley Fish and Wildlife Area manager claimed he had received numerous accounts over his 34 years in the area, averaging at least a dozen each year.

Despite numerous sightings and reports over the decades, definitive physical evidence of the Crosley Monster remains mysterious. This has led to various theories regarding its nature, ranging from an undiscovered primate species to supernatural explanations. Local witnesses have also reported glimpses of dark figures and unusual sounds attributed to this elusive creature.

Other Notable Indiana Cryptids

Beast of Busco: On his farm in Churubusco in 1898, Oscar Fulk observed a giant snapping turtle in a seven-acre lake. Later, Gale Harris owned the property and reported seeing the massive creature. In the late 1940s, Harris confirmed his previous sighting of the giant turtle. However, it wasn't until July 1948 that the creature gained widespread attention when two local fishermen, Ora Blue and Charley Wilson, reported seeing a massive turtle estimated to weigh around 500 pounds while fishing in the same lake. Following Blue and Wilson's sightings, word spread quickly through the community, and newspapers picked up the story, attracting curious visitors to Churubusco. This increased interest led to attempts to capture the creature, including efforts to drain the lake and send divers into its depths, ultimately failing. The turtle was named "Oscar" in honor of Oscar Fulk and was never captured.

Ghoul Snake: In the late 1880s, The Lafayette Courier reported sightings of a creature known as the Ghoul Snake, which was described as a monstrous snake observed in a cemetery near Oxford, Indiana. This unusual serpent was noted for its disturbing behavior of burrowing into mausoleums and graves, where it would reportedly break open coffins and tombs to consume corpses.

Cistern Creeper: In June 1960, Dan Craig publicly revealed that a monster had been living in his cistern for at least a year, located four miles south of Lynn, Indiana, on the Randolph County line. Craig described it as "an eerie beast with a dome-shaped head, two bulbous eyes, and eight flailing tentacles as long as a man's arm." The creature was fascinatingly likened to a plate-sized mushroom, complete with long legs and feet. Intrigued, the man decided to explore by pumping out the abandoned 12-foot well, clearing it of debris until it was dry. Excitedly, he lowered a fish to the octopus-like creature, which eagerly sprang into action, tearing the fish into pieces with impressive speed. Craig theorized that it was brought from the tropics when asked how it ended up there. "When it grew to a dangerous size," Craig stated, "they looked for a place to dispose of it and chose my well." Afterward, he covered the well to protect his family.

Bremen Troll: Those who drive to a small bridge in Bremen not far from Little Egypt (Ewald) Cemetery, turn off their car, and exit the vehicle may come face to face with a troll 7 to 8 feet tall with an aggressive demeanor. Groups visiting the site have reported hearing strange noises, such as a baby crying. Some describe seeing a prominent figure on or near the bridge during late-night visits. One night, after tossing a coin at a tombstone in a nearby cemetery, a group heard an eerie cry and was chased by a dark entity.

Iowa: Dogman

Notable Characteristics: The Iowa Dogman is often described by witnesses as significantly larger than an average dog, typically standing between 6 to 7 feet on its hind legs and weighing up to 400 pounds. Its muscular physique resembles a large wolf or dog yet exhibits more human-like features. The animal's fur tends to be dark or grayish with long limbs ending in clawed paws or hands. Some accounts highlight glowing eyes. Observers have reported that the creature appears to track them from a distance, mirroring their movements without revealing itself until it decides to do so.

In Cedar Falls, there have been several encounters with the Dogman. One notable account took place in March 1981 when a young man reported a frightening experience while attempting to access his parents' home. He was looking for a hidden key in the garage but couldn't find it. To get inside, he started to pry open a window screen.

When unsuccessful, he returned to the garage to search for the key again. At that moment, deep, guttural growls began emanating from the driveway. The young man decided to confront whatever it was. Still, it remained hidden in the darkness at the edge of the woods bordering the property. He felt an overwhelming fear and instinctively recognized that the entity making those growls was not an ordinary dog; it was much larger and more aggressive. Suddenly, it let out a roar reminiscent of a lion's, prompting the man to run back to his car and speed away.

In 2014, a deputy sheriff was patrolling around 11:30 p.m. along a bike path near Cedar Lake, where a possible drowning had been reported. He noticed a couple of red lights in the distance but dismissed them as taillights. Suddenly, he heard sniffing and snorting sounds. When he turned to investigate, he came face to face with an 8-foot-tall creature that he estimated weighed over 400 pounds. He quickly shone his flashlight on the creature, revealing its long, pointed ears and elongated muzzle before it bolted into the dark woods. The deputy managed to keep his composure but quickly returned to his vehicle!

Iowa: Van Meter Visitor

Notable Characteristics: The Van Meter Visitor is a cryptid that haunted the town of Van Meter over several nights from September 29 to October 3, 1903. Descriptions of the creature depict it as a half-human, half-animal being with dragon-like features, most notably large bat-like wings and a horn on its forehead that emitted a blinding light. Its movements resembled a hopping crow. A strong, unpleasant odor accompanied the creature.

Sightings were made by several prominent townspeople, including U.G. Griffith, a local implement dealer. Griffith and others reported seeing the creature flying above the town's buildings. Griffith fired shots at the beast; however, it seemed unaffected by the gunfire.

Other witnesses included a doctor and a bank cashier, Peter Dunn, who took plaster casts of its three-toed tracks. The pursuit of the Van Meter Visitor ultimately led witnesses to an old mine shaft. While investigating the mine, they heard sounds from within and discovered a smaller version of the creature. Despite their efforts to scare it away using noise and gunfire, the beast and its companions retreated deeper into the mine.

Iowa: Lockridge Monster

Notable Characteristics: The creature is about 5 feet tall, walking upright like humans, and has a footprint of 10 inches, which is notably smaller than the typical footprints attributed to Bigfoot. Its body is covered in thick hair, resembling that of a bear, while its facial features are more akin to those of an ape. This specific measurement has prompted some researchers to consider that it may represent a distinct type of creature, differentiating it from the more widely recognized Bigfoot.

In the autumn of 1975, a predator was on the loose in southeastern Iowa's Jefferson County. One sighting occurred on October 3 when Herbert Peiffer, a local turkey farmer, observed a large, hairy creature illuminated by the lights of his tractor while tending to his turkeys.

Initially, he hesitated to tell anyone out of fear of ridicule. However, shortly after, a hunter named Lowell Adkins discovered 10-inch tracks near the remains of four partially eaten turkeys. He speculated that the tracks might belong to a bear, but bears were a rarity in that area. Witnesses described the creature as standing around 5 feet tall, walking upright like a human, with a hairy, bear-like body and an ape-like face. Due to its proximity to the town, it was dubbed "The Lockridge Monster" by the Milwaukee Sentinel on October 28, 1975.

Gloria Olson, another eyewitness whose family owned a nearby farm, would not have believed such a creature existed until she saw it herself in July 1975, likely marking the first sighting in the area. She and her husband, Wendell, spotted a bushy-haired creature walking on two legs with a monkey-like face while creeping around the dilapidated buildings of a deserted farm. "It was just before dark, and I was driving past an old, deserted farmyard when I saw it," Gloria recalled. "To me, it looked like it had a monkey's face and was covered in hair. I didn't linger too long," she added.

Iowa: Dragons

Notable Characteristics: The creatures have features similar to traditional dragons, featuring elongated, snake-like bodies and bat-like wings with brown skin tones. Unique head shapes distinguish them, with prominent, protruding eyes, a forked tongue, and a scaly exterior.

Reports of dragons in Iowa have been documented for over a century, with notable sightings occurring in Burlington. The first significant encounter dates back to August 11, 1887, when The Bedford Times-Independent reported that farmer Lee Corder had seen a flying serpent. He described it as having protruding eyes, a forked tongue, and scales that glistened in the sunlight. The creature reportedly landed in his cornfield before taking off again.

In October 1890, multiple witnesses in Independence, Iowa, claimed to have seen a monster with wings and a monstrous head adorned with horns. This creature was described as green and covered in scales. In 2005, a witness named Megan recounted an experience while driving through Burlington at night. She saw a dragon-like creature that was approximately 10 feet long, with bat-like wings and a head resembling that of a seahorse.

Other Notable Iowa Cryptids

The Okoboji Lake Monster: Okoboji is a group of lakes in Iowa. Within is a large dark brown creature with a head as big as a basketball that some say is a fish, and others say it is the serpent. It causes small wakes and has even almost tipped over boats.

Big Cats: Historically, cougars once roamed the state but were eradicated by the early 20th century. However, numerous sightings have been reported across the state in recent decades. One significant spotting occurred in 2008 when a Davenport, Iowa, resident observed a sizeable cat-like animal crossing a road. The animal had a long tail and was much too large to be a housecat, weighing around 200 pounds.

Monster Turtle of Big Blue: A gigantic turtle has been spotted in a pond called Big Blue in Mason City. Although it resembles a regular snapping turtle, it is comparable in size to the hood of a Volkswagen Beetle. Divers often use the pond, and many assert they have seen the monster turtle.

Kansas: Sinkhole Sam

Notable Characteristics: Sinkhole Sam is often characterized as a sizable creature resembling a worm or serpent. It typically measures between 15 and 30 feet in length and has a thickness comparable to that of a car tire.

The Inman sinkhole site resembles a marshland and is characterized by a series of depressions in the ground that are often filled with water, creating the appearance of ponds. Surrounding these depressions is wetland marshland populated with various grasses and cattails, contributing to the area's unique ecosystem. Among the inhabitants of this environment is Sinkhole Sam, also known as the Foopengerkle—a worm-like creature that resides in a part of Inman Lake referred to as "The Sinkhole." This lake is the largest inland lake in the state.

Before the 1920s, the region was characterized by small freshwater lakes and wetlands. However, farmers and land developers drained many of these lakes in the early 20th century, resulting in a few low-lying areas known as sinkholes. The remaining wetlands in Inman are referred to as the Farland Lake Marshes, which include Little Sinkhole No. 1, Little Sinkhole No. 2, and the largest one, known as "The Big Sinkhole."

Witnesses at The Big Sinkhole have reported sightings of Sinkhole Sam. The creature is typically described as a large worm-like or serpent-like creature that measures between 15 and 30 feet long and is as thick as a car tire. In 1952, two Mennonite boys, Albert Neufeld and George Regehr, were fishing on a small bridge over the Big Sinkhole when they reported seeing a massive serpentine form breaking the water's surface. They described it as 15 feet long, with a flat head and a tail.

Some people believe Sinkhole Sam is a prehistoric creature that once resided in a flooded underground cavern. It is thought that this creature made its way to the lake after the surrounding area was drained. In the 1920s, an oil company drilled in the region, an activity believed to have brought the creature into the open.

Kansas: Dogman

Notable Characteristics: Witness descriptions often depict the Dogman as a large creature, standing 6 to 7 feet tall, resembling a wolf. It has a muscular build and stands on two legs. Its head looks similar to a dog's, featuring pointed ears and a short muzzle, though some reports mention a flatter face and glowing eyes when lights are shined on them.

The Dogman is a cryptid characterized by its combination of human and canine features, reported across the United States, including Kansas. Furthermore, sightings often highlight unusual behaviors for known wildlife, such as running on two legs, standing upright, and showing an almost human-like recognition of those who witness it.

The North American Dogman Project and the Dogman Encounters collect a variety of sightings from individuals who often encounter the creature by chance. Both serve as valuable resources and communities for anyone who encounters the creature and seeks answers. For instance, one woman from Osage County was traveling on a winding road during the summer of 2016 when, at the first turn, deer suddenly leaped across the road. The driver slowed down, waiting to see if more deer were coming. Just then, a gray figure emerged from the woods. It had a dog-like head, short muzzle, cropped pointed ears, and a sleek coat. The creature sprinted on all fours in a manner reminiscent of a human running. In a swift motion, it sprang onto the road and cleared to the other side in a single bound. Its gaunt body resembled a human's as it loped over the embankment.

In Jackson County in 2015, a young man living on the outskirts of the city was tending to his chickens. While carrying a bucket of corn to the coop, he looked up into nearby tall grass and thought he saw a deer standing not far away. However, upon closer inspection, he discovered it was a dead deer rotting there. As he started back to his house, he heard a deep, snarling growl similar to that of a wolf and saw what appeared to be a wolf with cropped ears and long front legs. It had hands with long claws, and when it stood upright, its body made a creepy popping sound. The creature let out a horrifying howl, causing the young man to race back to his house in fear.

Kansas: Bigfoot

Notable Characteristics: The creature is six to eight feet tall, standing upright, covered in hair, and capable of easily jumping over high fences.

In November 1977, the Wichita (Kansas) Eagle reported a short note about 15-year-old John Mark Breeze jogging near his rural residence after dusk. On a full moon night, around 10:30 p.m., he heard bushes rustling and the strange squawk of a bird. When he turned to investigate, he saw a creature that appeared six to eight feet tall and covered in hair. The beast effortlessly jumped over a barbed wire fence and disappeared into a field. "It looked like it didn't have a neck," Breeze told his incident to a reporter. "Its arms hung down to about its knees.

Well, it wasn't real shaggy hair, kind of like a dog's hair." Later, Deputy Dwight Posey discovered a track one and a half feet long and seven inches wide alongside the road. Breeze admitted that he was frightened by the encounter.

He was not the only one in Kansas to have a startling encounter with Bigfoot. In mid-October 1978, over 120 miles away in Lawrence, hunters, landowners, two Douglas County sheriff deputies, two officers from the Kansas Highway Patrol, and a Kansas Fish and Game officer were tramping through the brush in search of Bigfoot. This followed sightings by squirrel hunters Fred Hadl and Jim Swager, who reported seeing an eight-foot-tall creature with dark hair standing upright on its hind legs. "I'll be damned if I was seeing things," Hadl remarked. "Two of us saw it." Their report was taken seriously after a driver on the Kansas Turnpike near Bonner Springs, just inside Leavenworth County, also reported seeing a strange, Bigfoot-like creature running in front of their car.

Other Notable Kansas Cryptids

Headless Men: The Wichita tribe historically inhabited areas now known as parts of Kansas, Oklahoma, and northern Texas. In Native American folklore, especially among tribes like the Wichita, there are legends of headless men. These figures are often portrayed as dangerous monsters or bogeymen that embody fear. Encountering a headless man is considered a very ominous sign. In some accounts, these headless figures may have their heads hidden or obscured, while in other descriptions, they are entirely without heads.

The Deer Woman: She is a figure in various Native American traditions, often characterized as a shapeshifting entity capable of appearing as a beautiful woman or a deer. Deer Woman is commonly regarded as a guardian of women and children, taking on the role of a protector who punishes those who have caused harm to them. In many descriptions, the Deer Woman is depicted with hooves instead of human feet. She possesses eyes that bear a resemblance to those of a deer. Certain narratives emphasize her ability to attract men with her beauty, only for her to reveal her true nature and exact vengeance upon them once they have been lured in. This duality highlights her role as a benevolent protector and a fearsome avenger.

Kentucky: Pope Lick Monster

Notable Characteristics: The creature described is a humanoid figure that typically stands between 7 and 8 feet tall, exhibiting distinct goat-like characteristics such as horns and hooves. This mysterious being is believed to reside in the vicinity of Popelick Creek.

The Pope Lick Trestle, constructed in the late 1800s, stands ninety feet above the Pope Lick, a tributary in the Fisherville neighborhood of Louisville, Kentucky. Measuring 742 feet in length, it continues to serve trains operated by Norfolk Southern. A chain-link fence surrounding the trestle bears a warning sign stating, "Keep Off. Danger. Private Property."

This area is also associated with the legend of the Goat-Man, which describes a grotesque creature that is part goat and part man. According to folklore, the Goat-Man lures unsuspecting individuals to their deaths with a siren-like call. There are various interpretations of the creature's origin; some stories suggest it stems from a farmer who, in a desperate drought, made a pact with the devil. In contrast, others depict it as the offspring of an abusive farmer or a mistreated circus child. Regardless of its origins, the legend maintains that the Goat-Man resides *beneath* the trestle, waiting for potential victims.

Tragically, several individuals have attempted to cross the trestle and have suffered fatal accidents, including a notable incident involving a 15-year-old girl in 2019. Despite the allure of the Goat-Man legend, there is no evidence that the creature actively lured these individuals. Typically, it is said to remain hidden in the shadows, preying on the unwary. For those drawn to the excitement surrounding the Goat-Man, it is essential to recognize that the real danger lies in the active train traffic above, as the legend itself does not necessitate crossing the tracks.

Kentucky: Spottsville Monster

Notable Characteristics: The creature is imposing, standing between seven to eight feet tall. It has a hairy exterior, a reddish tint to its fur, and distinct red eyes. One observer noted its elderly appearance.

Not far from the banks of the Green River in Eastern Henderson County, the Red and Rose Nunnelly family moved to a remote farmhouse on Mound Ridge Road to raise farm animals and grow tobacco. For nearly a year, a giant hairy creature with red eyes, known as the Spottsville Monster, seemed obsessed with terrorizing them.

They had received warnings from a previous tenant, who had once shot at the hairy monster right through the back door. Red Nunnelly brushed the story aside; he was not easily frightened and had a 12-gauge shotgun in case of trouble. Everything was fine until some chickens began disappearing, and their 9 and 10-year-old boys noticed dead dogs in the nearby fields. The dogs had been mutilated. Their internal organs were removed along with eyeballs and tongue. It was gruesome but not as strange as the lack of blood near the corpses and the fact they lay there decaying without a single vulture, fox, or dog dragging them away.

In January 1976, during the harsh winter, the Nunnellys discovered that their farm animals, including 200 chickens, several pigs, and a horse they had carefully tended to, had been mutilated. Soon after, strange sounds emanated from the deep forest and its swampy areas at night. Their older son, Harold, decided to move his trailer onto the property.

One day, a nearby neighbor stopped by to warn the Nunnellys about a peculiar, hairy creature he had seen running away on its hind legs. This encounter sparked an immediate bond between Red Nunnelly and the neighbor.

Not long after, Rose Nunnelly witnessed the creature for herself. While calling the family in for supper from the fields, she spotted a monstrous shadow, standing 8 feet tall, lurking near a shed. Terrified, she screamed and rushed inside to call the police. However, the beast had vanished without a trace by the time they arrived.

Rose would see the creature again while Red was chased from the field. Ten-year-old Dean was working by a shed when he heard an explosion near the woodlot, followed by an eerie silence. When he peered behind him, he saw the creature with patchy reddish hair standing in a small gully.

The newspapers referred to the creature as "The Spottsville Monster" but mistakenly described it as green and placed it in the wrong location. The monster became a sensational story in newspapers, and the family faced ridicule. Monster hunters flocked to the community but headed in the wrong direction.

However, the neighbor who had befriended Red began tracking the creature. One day, while seeking shelter from the rain, he came face to face with the monster inside an abandoned house. It was almost within reach when he saw it lurking in the shadows—a short muzzle, fangs, and strange red eyes staring at him. He was so startled that he could only gaze at the creature, frozen in place. Then he heard a voice inside his head reassuring him not to be afraid, claiming it would not harm him. After that, the creature turned and vanished into a nearby field. Eventually, the Nunnelly family moved away; they had enough of the monster. And somewhere along the Green River, it still lurks.

Kentucky: Kelly Green Men

Notable Characteristics: Short alien figures, measuring between 2 to 4 feet in height, are distinguished by oversized heads and glowing yellow eyes. They also have large, pointed ears, claw-like hands, and spindly legs. Observers have noted that their bodies seem to shimmer in the moonlight, enhancing their otherworldly appearance.

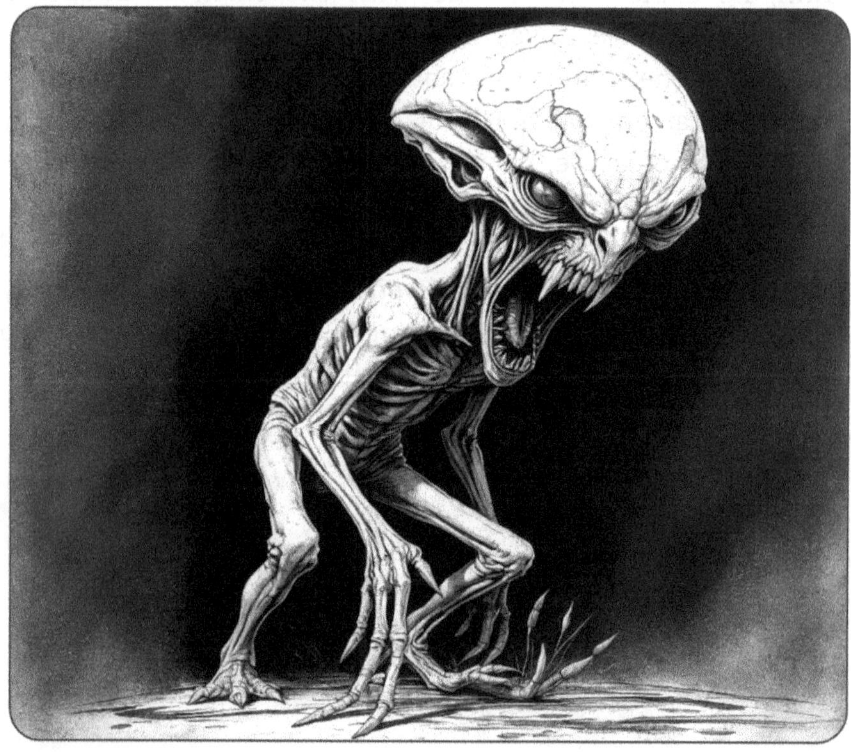

On the night of August 21-22, 1955, a peculiar incident unfolded at an isolated farmhouse on Old Madisonville Road near Kelly in Christian County, Kentucky. It was a night of terror that profoundly affected one family and prompted an extensive investigation involving four city police officers, five state troopers, three deputy sheriffs, and four military police officers from the nearby United States Army Fort Campbell.

Eight adults and three children were gathered at the farm:

Glennie Lankford - The matriarch of the family and owner of the farmhouse.

Elmer "Lucky" Sutton – Glennie Lankford's adult son.

John Charley "J.C." Sutton - Another adult son of Glennie Lankford.

Vera Sutton - Elmer "Lucky" Sutton's wife.

Alene Sutton - John Charley "J.C." Sutton's wife.

O.P. Baker – Alene Sutton's brother, who was also visiting.

Billy Ray Taylor - A family friend and carnival worker visiting from Pennsylvania with his wife.

June Taylor - Billy Ray Taylor's wife.

Lonnie Lankford - Glennie Lankford's younger child.

Charlton Lankford - Glennie Lankford's younger child.

Mary Lankford - Glennie Lankford's youngest child.

Around dusk, Billy Ray Taylor was standing outside when he saw what appeared to be a flying silver disc land in a nearby field. His story was initially met with skepticism by the family. However, around 8 p.m., Lucky's dog began to wail and bark anxiously. When Lucky and Billy Ray went to investigate, they noticed a mysterious glow at the rear of the home, followed by a tiny humanoid figure, about 3-4 feet tall, with a large head and long arms that nearly touched the ground. The figure glowed with a silvery hue.

The men quickly armed themselves and fired at the creature, which flipped in the air and vanished into the darkness. Despite this, the beast returned to peer into a window. When Billy Ray stepped outside, a claw-like hand reached down to grab his head from above, but several adults managed to pull him back to safety. Meanwhile, Glennie hurriedly tucked her three younger children—Lonnie, Charlton, and Mary—under the protection of a bed.

Soon, a gunfight erupted, lasting until nearly 11 p.m. Estimates suggested that at least 12 to 15 of these entities were present. Just as quickly as they appeared, the creatures vanished. The family rushed to the police station in Hopkinsville to report their encounter, prompting an investigation. However, upon arriving at the Sutton farmhouse, officers found no evidence of any extraterrestrial activity, aside from some broken windows and holes in the screens that could have been caused by gunfire.

Despite the skeptics who offered various explanations for the sightings—such as misidentified wildlife, specifically great horned owls—residents who witnessed the events consistently stood firm in their accounts, never renouncing what they had seen. Occasionally, others have reported spotting strange objects in the sky. Still, few can claim to have faced aliens as the Suttons and Taylors did.

Kentucky: Herrington Lake Eel-Pig Monster

Notable Characteristics: The cryptid is characterized by its eel-like body, pig-like snout, and curly tail. Reports from sightings indicate that this creature can reach 12 to 15 feet.

Herrington Lake is a large artificial lake in central Kentucky, reaching depths of nearly 249 feet. It was created by Kentucky Utilities damming the Dix River, a tributary of the Kentucky River, for hydroelectric power generation. The lake is home to the Herrington Lake Eel-Pig monster, a mysterious cryptid characterized by its eel-like body, pig-like snout, and curly tail. Sightings suggest that this creature can grow 12 to 15 feet.

The legend of the Eel-Pig monster began in 1972. Professor Lawrence S. Thompson, who taught at the University of Kentucky, owned a second home on Herrington Lake. Occasionally, during the early morning hours, he would spot a creature floating along the water's surface between Chenault Bridge and Wells Landing. He described it as shy and reminiscent of a pig with a curly tail floating 15 feet behind, moving smoothly through the water at the same speed as a boat with a trolling motor.

In an interview with reporter Joe Ward from the Lexington Courier-Journal, Thompson spoke about the mysterious creature with a sense of calm, noting, "It's a monster only in the sense that you'd call an alligator or a crocodile a monster if no one had ever seen one." He added, "What we don't know is colossal; what we do know is minimal." Thompson believed that when encountering something like he did, "the only thing you can do is ask others to look for the same thing and see what you can find."

He was correct; others have had similar experiences. Reports include a sighting in 1976 by Edgar Estes and two companions, who saw a whale-like creature with gray-black skin rise approximately 15 feet above the surface of their 15-foot fiberglass boat. Since then, there have been occasional reports of similar creatures being spotted by visitors to the lake.

Other Notable Kentucky Cryptids

Demon Leaper: In the early 1880s, a winged creature resembling a gargoyle—featuring bat-like leathery skin and wings, sharp claws, and talons—was frequently spotted at Louisville's Walnut Street Baptist Church. The creature perched on the spires, watching the sidewalks below.

Bullitt County Beast: In the Bullitt County area, witnesses have reported seeing a dark-furred entity standing about 7 feet tall. This creature has a German Shepherd's head, a human's muscular torso, and pointed ears. It produces deep, growling sounds.

The Milton Lizard: Also known as the Canip Monster, is a cryptid reportedly resembling a 15-foot-long monitor lizard. It was first sighted in the summer of 1975 near Cable Creek in Milton, Kentucky, by Clarence "Tuffy" Cable at his junkyard, described as having large frog-like eyes and black-and-white striped skin with speckles. His brother, Garrett, also encountered the creature on July 27, 1975, when he spotted it beneath a pile of car hoods in the junkyard. A search party scoured the Blue Grass Body Shop area for any signs of the Milton Lizard, but it had vanished.

Bearilla: In the dense forests of Bath County, Kentucky, there exists a cryptid that stands 7 feet tall, with the body of a bear, a long-pointed muzzle resembling that of a wolf, and hands equipped with dagger-like claws. One of the earliest reports dates to the 1940s when a young boy claimed to have been attacked by the creature near a creek.

Kentucky Mothman: The Mothman legend is mainly associated with Point Pleasant, West Virginia, and originated from sightings reported between November 15, 1966, and December 15, 1967. However, Kentucky experienced its own encounters with the creature much earlier. On November 6, 1868, nearly 30 Mount Sterling, Kentucky residents reported seeing a strange, winged creature circling the Farmer's Bank Building. In 1938, further sightings were reported in Ashland and Elizabethtown of a human-like figure with large, bat-like wings and glowing eyes.

Louisiana: Rougarou

Notable Characteristics: The creature has a muscular, human-like body with the head of a wolf or dog. Its fur is dark or charcoal in color, and it possesses glowing eyes, along with long, sharp teeth and claws.

The Honey Island Swamp is in St. Tammany Parish, Louisiana, within the Pearl River Wildlife Management Area. This swamp is home to wildlife, including alligators, deer, and snakes. One of its most famous inhabitants is the Honey Island Swamp Monster, the Cajun Sasquatch (La Bête Noire), described as an ape-like humanoid creature. However, another creature, the Rougarou, also lurks in the swamps. Rougarou's origins trace back to French settlers exiled to American Colonies sometime between 1765 and 1785.

As Cajuns, they influenced the cattle industry. They introduced unique foods while sharing folklore, including the Loup-garou, linked to werewolf legends from France. It has long been said that something lurks among the mossy cypress trees and murky waters of the swamps in eastern and central Louisiana and the bayous near New Orleans. For centuries, its bone-chilling howl has echoed in the dusky night air. Some describe it as having a man's body but the head of a wolf, with claw-like nails and ferocious teeth hidden behind grinning lips. This wolf-man originated from a human cursed for some wrongdoing. In turn, it seeks out others of equally lousy character to pass on its curse and free itself.

The Rougarou hunts Catholics who ignore Lent for seven years. If someone draws the creature's blood, it breaks the curse and reveals its secret, but the person becomes cursed for 101 days unless they keep it a secret. The Rougarou often targets children, with parents warning them to be home in the dark to avoid the creature. There is a way to protect oneself from these creatures. By placing 13 small objects, such as pennies, marbles, or beans, on a windowsill, you can keep the Rougarou at bay. Because the Rougarou is compulsive, it will obsessively try to count the items. However, since it can only count to 12, it will become so fixated on counting that it will forget about trying to enter the home. As a result, it will have no choice but to retreat back to the swamps when the sun rises.

There have been sightings of the creature—one account describes a black dog chasing two men returning from a visit to their neighbors. In their desperation, the pair jumped a fence to evade the animal. When the dog did not follow, they paused long enough to see a man standing on the other side of the wall, but the dog had vanished.

Louisiana: Honey Island Swamp Monster

Notable Characteristics: A large, bipedal creature resembling Bigfoot, covered in gray hair, has glowing eyes and an overpowering stench. It stands about seven feet tall and weighs around 400 pounds. The creature is known for leaving behind unusual three-toed or five-toed, webbed footprints.

Honey Island Swamp is a vast, remote wetland outside Slidell in St. Tammany Parish, Louisiana. It spans approximately 70,000 acres and is filled with cypress trees, marshes, and bayous. It is home to a diverse array of alligators, birds, and fish. The swamp is also steeped in legends, most notably that of the Honey Island Swamp Monster—a large, ape-like humanoid cryptid said to roam the area. Retired FAA air traffic controller Harlan Ford reported the first sighting in 1963 while exploring the swamp.

Ford was flying over the swamp with Billy Mills when they noted an isolated spot that appeared to be an excellent place for hunting. Then, after setting up a camp, Ford began documenting the different wildlife found there and came upon some strange, unidentifiable signs and sounds of a large creature. One was footprints, unlike those of known animals; they featured four toes with webbing.

Ford's most memorable encounter occurred when he witnessed a large bipedal animal that he initially thought might be a bear. Upon closer examination, he saw that it was at least seven feet tall, had a human face covered with scraggly black hair, and had piercing amber eyes. The creature would become known as the Honey Island Swamp Monster.

Occasionally, the Honey Island Swamp Monster visits the area. About forty miles away in October of 1975, witnesses in Bogalusa, Louisiana, called county sheriffs when they saw "a large hairy black creature standing on its hind legs" and "three-toed hairy monster which made funny noises." Deputies scoured the area but found no monster.

In October 1973, a local swamp tour guide, Greg Faulkner, told reporters he hit some animal while boating along the swampy bayou with his girlfriend near Slidell. He stated, "I rolled over it, the motor kicked up, and I realized I hit something. I stopped and looked but kept going up the bayou a ways." When he looked back momentarily, a creature about five feet tall, black and hairy, was running up the bank on two legs before vanishing. Faulkner, well-versed in the normal creatures who inhabited the area, returned to the site and checked for tracks, finding several along the marshy soil. "There was a size ten foot with five toes, and there were a dozen or so prints where it ran along the bank before it disappeared into the swamp," he said. "And it looked like there was some sort of flesh or webbing between the toes."

Many people who have seen the Honey Island Swamp Monster have been scrutinized by skeptics. However, after Harlan Ford passed away in 1980, his family discovered additional materials related to his encounters. Among these was grainy footage recorded in the Super 8 film, which appears to be an enormous, hairy figure moving through the trees in the swamp. This discovery further solidified the legacy of the swamp monster in Louisiana.

Other Notable Louisiana Cryptids

The Letiche: In the swamps and bayous, there is a creature that is one of three things: an abandoned child raised by alligators, the spirit of an unbaptized infant who died, or a humanoid reptilian born from the swamp environment. This creature is known to attack people in the bayous, occasionally upsetting boats that pass through its territory.

The Grunch: In the eastern part of New Orleans, there is an area called the Little Woods near Grunch Road. It is inhabited by the Grunch, a leathery-skinned creature resembling a goat with horns and sharp spines and standing 3 to 4 feet tall. The Grunch lures unsuspecting victims using injured goats before attacking them.

The Parlangua: This creature inhabits the dark waters of the swamps and is half-man and half-alligator. It walks on two legs and drags its prey into hidden places to eat later. The legend dates to the 1960s when reports emerged of a driver who lost control of his car and crashed into the swamp in Rapides Parish. When they dragged the car out, the creature had feasted on the corpse, leaving human-like bites.

Maine: Cherryfield Goatman

Notable Characteristics: The Goatman is a half-human, half-goat creature that draws inspiration from mythological figures such as satyrs and the Greek god Pan. The Cherryfield Goatman is most often depicted wearing a flannel shirt.

Cherryfield, Maine, is known for its suburban neighborhoods, farms, wild blueberry barrens, forested areas, and wetlands. One local resident was driving his truck along a road lined with woods near Cherryfield when the vehicle began to sputter and eventually stalled. Despite filling the gas tank after leaving home, the truck stopped running, and the gas gauge showed it was empty.

Flustered, the driver got out of his vehicle to investigate. As he walked around the truck, he saw what appeared to be a creature that was half man and half goat standing in the center of the road. The beast had goat-like legs and human features, wearing nothing but a flannel shirt. The strange goat-man remained in place long enough for the driver to gather his wits and race back to the truck, praying it would start. To his surprise, the vehicle started right up, and the gas gauge was back to full. Without hesitation, the man sped away while the Goatman vanished into the woods.

Maine: Tote Road Shagamaw

Notable Characteristics: The Tote Road Shagamaw is a creature frequently described by lumberjacks as having the front paws of a bear and the hindquarters of a moose. This unique combination allows it to walk on its hind legs like a bipedal being, while still having the ability to move on all fours. It was often spotted along the rugged unpaved roads known as tote roads, which were used to transport supplies to remote lumber camps.

The Tote Road Shagamaw is known for its stealth, cunning behavior, and its insatiable appetite for soft secondhand cloth.

It especially covets cotton—which leads it to raid laundry left outside by residents. Its unique ability to move on two different types of limbs may serve as a clever strategy to evade those tracking it. This can lead to confusion among woodsmen, who might mistakenly identify its tracks as belonging to either a moose or a bear.

Gus Demo was from Oldtown, Maine, and he had been a hunter and trapper for over 40 years. One day, he stumbled upon some moose tracks and decided to follow them for about 16 feet. To his curiosity, the tracks then changed to bear tracks. After another 16 feet, they changed back to moose tracks. Perplexed, Demo continued to follow these footprints along an overgrown, marked path of an old tote road.

To his surprise, he eventually came upon a creature that had front feet resembling those of a bear and hind feet like those of a moose. As Demo observed it, the creature paused on its hind hooves, scanned the area suspiciously, and then pivoted to walk on its front bear paw feet. Demo speculated that the Shagamaw had been watching the trappers and timbermen from the shadows and had learned to navigate the old roads itself. To avoid detection in areas where humans were present, it decided to disguise its steps.

Maine: Waldoboro Little Wild Man

Notable Characteristics: This creature stands 18 inches tall and is covered in soft, downy dark hair.

In June 1855, a man was chopping wood in the forest near Waldoboro when he heard an unearthly shriek. His curiosity consumed him, prompting a search. After some time, he gave up, as nothing could be found. He returned to work and struck a blow from axe to wood, and soon after, the scream echoed again.

Upon looking up, he saw a perfectly proportioned miniature human-like being standing between two trees, about 18 inches tall, covered in dark downy hair. The creature fled, and he gave chase, quickly catching up to it. He picked it up, took it home, and fed him some dried beech nuts and water. However, the fate of the little wild man remains a mystery, lost to time and whispers of the past.

Other Notable Maine Cryptids

Specter Moose: For over a 100 years, a moose weighing 2,500 pounds and standing 15 feet tall roamed the state. Known as "Old Moxie," this remarkable animal was first sighted in 1891. The moose had a grayish-white coat and an antler span of 15 feet. Initially spotted in Katahdin, it was later seen ranging from Washington County to Aroostook County and Rangeley. Unfortunately, like many unique creatures of the time, it was shot and killed. The moose was hung up and bled out but reappeared as if alive at the hunting camp afterward.

Billdad: A cross between a kangaroo and a platypus. It jumps into the water and uses its tail to slap fish to catch them. Mostly considered harmless, its flesh may be poisonous if consumed. Bill Murphy ate one, went mad believing he had turned into a Billdad, and jumped into an icy lake, drowning.

The Turner Beast: The mutant canine resembles a husky wolf with bulky shoulders, large eyes, a flat snout, short, mangled ears, a bushy tail, and weighs 120 pounds. Since 1991, residents of Androscoggin County have reported sightings. One was found dead on the road in August 2012, and DNA testing confirmed it was a wolf-dog hybrid.

Maryland: Goatman of Prince George's County

Notable Characteristics: This beast resembles a hairy humanoid figure with a human upper body and goat-like lower limbs. Standing around six feet tall, it is known for its creepy squealing noise before it attacks its prey. The Goatman has been spotted near Tucker Road in Clinton and Fletchertown Road in Bowie, Maryland.

Fletchertown Road is a short stretch, less than two miles long. It's not the secluded place it once was in the 1970s when teens from local high schools made their rite-of-passage trips along the asphalt-buckled street to search for the elusive Goatman haunting the roadway and the surrounding area.

Today, the road is paved, with pockets of woodland and remnants of the past pushed aside for subdivisions and newer homes, accompanied by the constant sound of traffic. The old “GOATMAN WAS HERE” graffiti, once scrawled in black spray paint on discarded refrigerators and worn plywood tacked to fences, has faded away. However, this doesn’t mean the Goatman or those who seek him out are gone. Some believe he remains, just as he has for decades since their parents and grandparents searched for him fifty years ago.

Some believe he might have been the spawn of some crazed scientist from the nearby Beltsville Agricultural Research Center, whose experiments on goats in the 1970s went awry. He mutated into a half-human, half-goat creature. Alternatively, he could be the ornery, hairy old hermit living in a shack in the woods. He is known to walk the Penn Central Railroad tracks wielding an axe, often scaring away pesky kids. Whatever this monster is or was, it depends on who you ask and which generation they belong to.

On November 3, 1971, 16-year-old April Edwards from Old Bowie came face to face with the creature in her yard, which abutted the railroad tracks on Zug Road. “I saw it that night,” April reminisced. “It just looked like a hairy man to me. It was on two legs and stood upright, though it crouched over when it ran, like a hunchback. It had long hair, and I don’t think it was part this or part that; I think it was human.” That night, her beloved ten-month-old German Shepherd mix, Ginger, disappeared. Knowing she was distraught, neighborhood folks went out searching for the pet.

Twenty-year-old Willie Gheen, who was living with April’s family, and a neighbor, twenty-year-old John Hayden, grabbed a couple of baseball bats for protection and went outside. They made a gruesome discovery on the frosted grass—the decapitated head of the beloved pet.

Hayden had also caught sight of the creature. He told reporters, "It was an animal. It was about six feet tall, something like that, and hairy, like an animal. As far as I know, it was an animal on two feet. I remember it made a high-pitched sound, like a squeal." Ginger's body was never found, and other dogs like her suspiciously disappeared in the area.

April Edwards recounted seeing the man-like creature again two weeks later near Hayden's junkyard and towing business. "The second time, it was looking for food or something," she said. "This thing was for real—this was not folklore. I don't know what it was. Whatever it was, I believe it killed my dog and had been living in the woods nearby for some time."

With the rise of expensive homes encroaching on the Goatman's old territory, he may have retreated to more secluded areas in Prince George's County. But he doesn't have to go far. Recently, there have been occasional reports of sightings near Fletchertown. These accounts commonly involve people claiming to have seen a large, hairy, bipedal creature that resembles a goat-human hybrid. Witnesses often describe these encounters as happening late at night or in the early morning hours when there are fewer people around.

Maryland: Snallygaster

Notable Characteristics: Early accounts mention the Snallygaster as having a metallic beak with sharp teeth, octopus-like tentacles, and being part reptile, part bird.

In the 1730s, German immigrants settled in Maryland, Pennsylvania, and Virginia, blending their customs and folklore with the new environment. One such creature that emerged is the Snallygaster, a name derived from the German term "Schnelle Geeschter," which translates to "quick ghosts." These dragon-like ghouls were said to swoop down from the sky to seize their prey.

In earlier times, hunters frequently spotted them on South Mountain, ranging from Frederick to Harpers Ferry. The number "seven" was believed to ward off the Snallygaster, so the best form of protection was to paint a seven-pointed star on the most enormous barn. This symbol had to be precisely laid out, or it would not be effective. Horror stories about the Snallygaster were passed down by word of mouth, often used to explain missing children or livestock and sightings of massive creatures in the sky. As the original name of the beast evolved over the years, so did its appearance. The Snallygaster transformed from an original half-ghoul, half-bird with massive wings, a thick bloodsucking beak, and flesh-piercing talons to a creature described as half-bird and half-reptile. By the turn of the century, its beak had become elongated and metallic, adorned with razor-sharp teeth and a wingspan of twenty feet. Some descriptions even added that the creature had octopus-like tentacles protruding from its mouth.

In January of 1908, the Hagerstown Mail reported that a hiker in the Quirauk Mountain area— the highest point on South Mountain—came across a wild bird he had never seen. It was a feathered, bird-like creature with eyes resembling fireballs. Its beak measured at least six inches and had rows of saw-like teeth on the upper and lower bill. The creature's neck spanned at least two feet, and its feathers shone with a silver and gold sheen, sparkling like diamonds. Weighing approximately seventy-five pounds, it flew past the man, emitting an unearthly shriek. Bullets fired at the bird appeared ineffective, as they did not penetrate its body.

Despite initial skepticism, the Snallygaster's legend resurfaced in the 1930s. In the autumn of 1932, Charles Main, an ice cream dealer from Middletown, claimed to have encountered the creature. "People who say there is no such animal are the ones who need to get it right," he maintained.

He also noted the change in color—it went from white to black. On November 22, Main and another man spotted a winged creature near John Hagan's Tavern, describing it as having streamers from its mouth and a fourteen-foot wingspan. Fortunately, it veered away, and two boys corroborated Main's story, having seen the creature heading toward Middletown from South Mountain.

As these stories spread, public fear grew. Streets were deserted as dusk fell; adults were afraid to venture outside after dark, leading them to lock doors and shut windows. In December 1932, local newspapers sought to quell the reports by declaring the beast's death. They reported that the Snallygaster had been attracted by the scent of alcohol in the Frog Hollow section of Washington County, losing control of its wings and ultimately falling into a vat. By the time it was discovered, only bones remained.

However, the legend of Snallygaster lived on. A couple driving from Frederick to Buckeystown in November 1932 recalled passing Mt. Olivet Cemetery around 5:30 p.m. when they spotted a dark, bulky, winged figure. They quickly identified it as a Snallygaster, narrowly avoiding swerving off the road as the beast whipped a wing into their path.

The Snallygaster may have faded into obscurity over the years. However, the seven-pointed stars, which are said to keep the Snallygaster at bay, can still be seen painted on local barns.

Maryland: Dwayyo

Notable Characteristics: This creature is wolf-like in appearance and as large as a bear, standing 6 feet tall. Its dark-colored fur complements its long, bushy tail, and it possesses a build similar to that of a dog. Notably, it walks upright, which adds to its unique and striking presence.

There were sightings of giant footprints and eerie yowls in Frederick County in 1944 connected to the Dwayyo. The wolf-like beast remained quiet for twenty years. However, in November 1965, John Becker, who lived near Gambrill State Park, reported to the police that he stepped outside as darkness fell to investigate a strange noise. After scouring the area and finding no cause for the sound, he turned back toward his house.

At that moment, Becker noticed in horror a large, dark figure lunging toward him. It stood upright on its hind legs and was as big as a bear, with long black hair and a bushy tail. However, it was not a bear. Becker fought off the creature until it escaped into the woods. He contacted the authorities anonymously afterward, as the idea of being attacked by a wolf-like beast seemed absurd.

On December 7, 1965, a woman in Jefferson, about 10 miles away, complained that a large animal resembling a dog harassed her cows, describing it as big as a calf.

In the summer of 1966, a camper on the outskirts of Gambrill State Park encountered a shaggy, two-legged beast as large as a deer. It had a triangular-shaped head, pointy ears, and dark brown fur. When approached, it screamed and retreated in a remarkable, spider-like walk, with its legs sticking out from its body.

In June 1973, police in Sykesville called in helicopters and a search crew when Anthony Norris reported finding footprints 13½ inches long and 6 inches wide. Other residents described seeing a hairy beast seven to ten feet tall with a bushy tail and dark fur. Some reported that cows and dogs had been killed.

About seven miles away in Ellerton, a woman reported hearing terrifying screams and cries from the mountains for several months. A police search of the area failed to yield clues.

In the autumn of 1976, another sighting occurred when two men were driving off-road near Route 77 between Cunningham Falls State Park and Catoctin Mountain National Park. They were spotlighting deer populations with vehicle headlights in preparation for the hunting season (which is illegal now). Instead of finding deer, they saw a large, wolf-like creature dart in front of their car. The description included a canine-like head and hyena-like banded fur, and the creature walked hunched over on muscled legs in an upright position.

In 1978, two park rangers saw the same type of animal near Cunningham Falls.

The Dwayyo is noted for its connection to the flying reptilian known as the Snallygaster. According to local legends, these two beings are considered mortal enemies, and accounts of their confrontations can be traced back to the early settlements in the Middletown Valley.

Maryland: Sykesville Monster

Notable Characteristics: The cryptid is a large, hairy humanoid creature that typically stands between 7 and 8 feet tall and is covered in dark brown hair. Documented footprints attributed to this creature measure approximately 13 inches in length and 7 inches in width. Witnesses have noted that the monster emits a strong, musky odor reminiscent of fox urine. Additionally, it produces a peculiar ticking sound, which some researchers speculate may be associated with its movement or a form of communication.

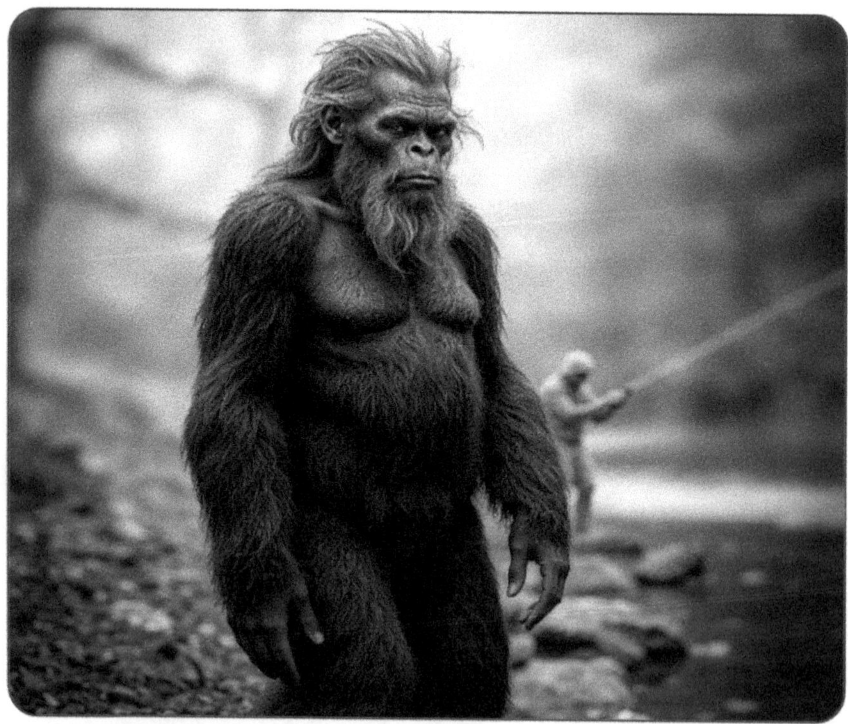

The Sykesville Monster was first sighted in 1972 when an unidentified truck driver witnessed the creature sitting down before it stood up and ran into the woods. He described it as caked in mud from the waist down and appearing like a "man on stilts."

Then, on May 9, 1981, Lon Strickler was fishing along the South Branch of the Patapsco River, not far from River Road in Sykesville. He had set his sights on a particular pool, so with his fishing pole and waders on his feet, he plodded into the water and prepared for a morning of fishing.

Half-heartedly, he noticed a stray dog wandering around the brush along the bank but was too focused on his task to pay it much attention. That was until he heard the growling and then the dog's yapping. Strickler shifted his attention away from fishing and looked up just as the dog's barking suddenly stopped. He was shocked to see a massive seven to eight feet tall creature with dark, matted hair nearly hidden in the bushes on the bank.

He heard a distinct "tick-tick" noise as it ambled out of the bushes and moved toward the forest beyond. The scent that followed was nearly overwhelming—musky and intensely bitter, reminiscent of fox urine.

Strickler immediately left the scene, noting that the dog was fine except for a bit of blood, and reported his sighting to local authorities. He found it strange that the Maryland State Police and federal agents would follow up on his observation. Still, he was not permitted to receive any information about the unusual sighting.

Others also claimed to have seen this Bigfoot-like creature or had encountered its massive footprints. In 1993, an eight-year-old boy in Woodstock reported seeing the beast.

Along Piney Run in Marriottsville, a fisherman discovered bones resembling a human skeletal frame, including a skull. Local authorities were notified and responded quickly, arriving at the scene with helicopters and unmarked vehicles. However, there was no further mention of the incident afterward, which has fueled suspicion among many who believe there was a cover-up regarding this strange encounter.

Recently, there have been reports from individuals who claim to have seen significant figures moving through wooded areas or heard strange sounds at night, which they attribute to the Sykesville Monster. Some witnesses describe experiencing overwhelming fear or unease when they encounter these creatures or hear their sounds.

Other Notable Maryland Cryptids

The Black Dog: The Old South Mountain Inn, located near Boonsboro, served as a tavern for travelers, like waggoneers, stagecoach drivers, and tourists. Local legend describes a huge, ghostly black dog that would waylay travelers there.

The Cecil County Pig Woman: The Pig Woman haunts a lonely bridge on Russell Road, which is also known as Pig Woman Lane. According to legend, a woman trapped in a burning farmhouse jumped from a window, suffering severe burns that left her disfigured. Driven mad by her trauma, she fled into the woods. Nowadays, visitors to the bridge report hearing eerie, pig-like sounds and noticing mysterious scratches on their vehicles. Some have panicked, bolting from their cars into the woods, never to be seen again.

Chessie: Chessie is a serpentine creature measuring 25 to 40 feet in length in the Chesapeake Bay, first reported in the late 1970s. Despite numerous sightings and even video evidence captured in 1982, the true nature of Chessie remains a mystery.

Massachusetts: Dover Demon

Notable Characteristics: The Dover Demon is a cryptid creature sighted in Dover, Massachusetts, on April 21 and 22, 1977. Three separate witnesses (William "Bill" Bartlett, John Baxter, and Abby Brabham) reported seeing a strange being with unusual physical characteristics. They described the creature as four feet tall, with glowing orange eyes, hairless skin, and rough, peachy, or flesh-colored skin that appeared either tan or chalky gray. The creature had a watermelon-shaped head, skinny arms, and legs and lacked a nose or mouth. All the sightings were in a straight line of two and a half miles and near some water.

The initial sighting occurred on the night of April 21, 1977. Seventeen-year-old Bill Bartlett drove with friends along Farm Street near Bridge Street in Dover, a winding road surrounded by woods and fields with fieldstone walls. At around 10 p.m., he spotted a creature perched on a broken rock wall. He saw it from about 10 feet away, driving 30 to 40 miles an hour.

"It looked like a baby's body with long arms and legs. It had a big head about the same size as the body, it was sort of melon shaped," Bartlett stated. It had peach-covered, shark-like skin. He would create a drawing of the creature he saw—a small caricature crawling along a rock wall with an egg-shaped bulbous head, large eyes that glowed, a gaunt torso with a distended belly, and small, thin arms and legs as skinny as a branch. The thin-toed feet adhered to the rock like a gecko's feet cling and mold to a surface. He wrote on the sketch: "I, Bill Bartlett, swear on a stack of Bibles that I saw this creature." In a 2006 interview with the Boston Globe, Bartlett, who was described by the community as a good kid at that time, stated, "It was some kind of creature with long, thin fingers and more human-like in its form than animal," he divulged to the reporter, adding, "Its shape reminded me of kids with distended bellies. I've always tried to guess what it was."

On the same night, around 12:30 a.m., 15-year-old John Baxter was walking home from his girlfriend's house when he got to the intersection of Miller Hill Road and Farm Street about a mile northeast of where Bartlett had seen the creature. Striding toward him, he could see what appeared to be a person with an enormous, bulbous head about 150 feet away. At first, Baxter thought it was a boy from the community called M.G. who had a deformed head due to a childhood disease. He called out to him, but there was no answer.

"As I was getting closer, I could see that it was very small," Baxter said. "The only thought that came into my mind was this—it was this kid walking home from a party, or something, which he usually does at about 12:30, and I called out to him. This was at a distance, still of about fifty yards, and I just kept walking and there was no reply and whatever it was kept walking." As Baxter got nearer to the figure, he noticed right off that it was not M.G. It was much too small for the boy.

He also knew that the other boy would have called out to him. As the two got closer, Baxter began to question what the figure was or who it might be. “Finally,” he went on. “I was about 15 feet away from it when I stopped and it stopped. Well, I stopped when it stopped. We just stood there. I was looking at it and I’m sure it was looking at me. I could barely see the shape of it. And I said one more time, ‘Who is that?’ And so I took another step towards it; the only thought I had was that it might be a very small person like a 4 or 5-year-old, and as I took this step, it just ran so fast into the woods on my left.” Baxter would wonder, at first, if it was a monkey, then got a little worried about how safe it might be and left for home.

On April 22, the following night, 15-year-old Abby Brabham and 18-year-old Will Traintor saw the creature from Traintor’s car on Springdale Avenue. Brabham’s description matched those of Bartlett and Baxter but noted that the creature had illuminated green eyes instead of orange this time. She estimated its height to be about the size of a goat.

The creature disappeared abruptly after its appearance, but its impact remains clear in memory, ensuring it is not forgotten. There are many who wish it would return so they can see it for themselves.

Massachusetts: Bridgewater Triangle

Notable Characteristics: Massachusetts houses the Bridgewater Triangle, a 200-square-mile area in the southeast defined fluidly by Abington, Rehoboth, and Freetown. Communities within include Taunton, Raynham, and Brockton. This region is famous for its alleged paranormal phenomena, featuring various supernatural events and cryptid sightings.

Freetown-Fall River State Forest: This forest is linked to cult activities, including animal sacrifices, ritualistic murders, suicides, and gangland murders.

Profile Rock: A landmark where the ghost of Anawan, a Wampanoag leader, appears on a rock.

Solitude Stone: An inscribed stone near West Bridgewater, found near a missing person's body, reflects themes of loss.

Hockomock Swamp: The largest freshwater swamp in Massachusetts holds historical and cultural significance, having been a strategic location during King Philip's War. It is also a burial ground for Native Americans, and its name in Wampanoag means "place where spirits dwell." Not only does it have a spirited side, but some people have reported seeing Thunderbirds, large birds with a 12-foot wingspan resembling pterodactyls, and Bigfoot-like creatures in the swamp. One hunter even shot at a large animal that cried out in a human-like whine.

Near the swamp is Raynham, where odd bright orange lights appear in the sky, and unidentified flying objects move slowly, unlike an airplane's flight. There are also reports of a shaggy half-man, half-ape creature seen in the woods, known as the Hockomock Swamp Monster. In 1978, resident 24-year-old Joe DeAndrade stood on the shore of Clay Banks, a pond in Bridgewater near the swamp. "I was standing there, and for some reason, I had to turn around," DeAndrade told a Boston Globe reporter. "It was a chill or something inside me. And I turned around, and there, off to the right, maybe 200 yards away, there was this—well, I don't know what it was. It was a creature that was all brown and hairy, like a big apish-and-man thing. It was making its way for the woods, but I didn't stick around to watch where it was going. I ran for the street."

About five years later, a fur trapper, John Baker, was canoeing a river in the swamp. He heard a clamorous crash and rumble of a creature in the nearby woods just before a large, hairy creature lumbered within a few yards from where he was paddling. "I knew it wasn't a human because when it passed by me, I could smell it," Baker expressed in an interview in 1998. "It smelled like a skunk: musty and dirty."

There are differing viewpoints regarding the nature of the area in question. Some suggest it functions as a maelstrom or a powerful vortex, drawing in paranormal phenomena and unusual creatures. Others contend it is merely a secluded habitat that provides an ideal environment for extraordinary life forms to flourish, remaining largely unexplored and unknown.

Massachusetts: Beast of Truro

Notable Characteristics: The cryptid is a sizable feline creature, similar in appearance to a mountain lion or cougar, with an estimated weight ranging from 60 to 80 pounds and a slender physique. It is characterized by a long, curved tail and a furry coat that varies in color from tawny to light brown. Notably, this animal possesses a flat face and moves with remarkable silence through wooded environments.

Truro, Massachusetts, is a small and exclusive town on Cape Cod, known for its beautiful beaches, sand dunes, and the historic Highland Light lighthouse. The town features golf courses, a vibrant arts scene, and a vineyard. In September 1981, the residents began to notice something alarming: a series of gruesome incidents involving local pets. A dozen cats were found dead, and a 175-pound hog had been mutilated, indicating that some sort of predator was on the loose.

More pigs were found clawed within what should have been the safety of their pen. Initially, it was believed that a pack of feral dogs was responsible. However, William and Marcia Medeiros, walking along the bike path near the beach, reported seeing a large, cougar-like animal near Head of the Meadow Beach. The creature was observed ambling for more than five minutes before disappearing into the woods. "My husband put his arm out to stop me," Marcia told reporters at the New York Times. "And he said, 'You see what I see?' Together, we said, 'It's not a fox.' It had a very definite long rope-like tail like the letter J. It hit the ground and went up. We figured it was about as tall as up to our knees and weighed 60 or 80 pounds. We were frightened and froze. He was in the path and didn't see us at first. As we made some noise, he turned, and we saw his face with short ears."

As one stepped aside to grab a branch for defense, the creature wandered into the woods. The couple was convinced it was a mountain lion.

Other residents reported hearing eerie cat-like cries and screams at night that resembled those made by big cats. Police officer David Costa witnessed a large cat-like entity attacking one of his pigs. However, the situation at the beach did not last long; eventually, no more dead pets were found, and sightings slowed. The story has persisted over time, with occasional new sightings reported even decades later.

Other Notable Massachusetts Cryptids

Sea Serpent: Sightings of a mysterious creature have been reported off the coast from Gloucester to Nantucket, with accounts tracing back to 1817. This colossal serpent-like being is approximately 120 feet long and can rise approximately 12 feet above the water's surface. Descriptions of the creature suggest it has a horned head and exhibits features reminiscent of both a snake and a whale, characterized by a long neck, humps along its back, and a head that resembles those of a turtle or a horse. Notably, in 1937, there were several reports, including one from local fishermen Gilbert Manter and Ed Crocker, who discovered unusual web-footed tracks measuring 66 inches by 44 inches while fishing near Nantucket Beach.

Pukwudgies: These creatures are associated with Freetown State Forest in Massachusetts, a notable area within the Bridgewater Triangle. Described as small and troll-like, these beings typically possess gray skin, glowing eyes, and, at times, porcupine quills. Their demeanor can vary; they may appear friendly or threatening based on their interactions with humans. Reports of encounters with Pukwudgies often involve attempts to lure individuals into the woods or engage in various forms of trickery.

Michigan: Dogman

Notable Characteristics: The Michigan Dogman is a cryptid first reported in 1887 in Wexford County, Michigan. This creature is characterized as a seven-foot-tall, bipedal being that resembles a canine, with distinctive blue or amber eyes and a humanoid torso. It produces a notable, shrieking howl that adds to its eerie presence.

According to legends, the Dogman is believed to exhibit a cyclical pattern of appearances, occurring roughly every ten years. Additionally, it is said that the sound of clapping hands may serve as a deterrent against the creature. Sightings of the Michigan Dogman were widespread among lumberjacks throughout the 19th century, who described it as having a human's body and a dog's head.

It's crucial not to take folklore stories about creatures too literally, such as the advice to "clap your hands" if you encounter the creature known as the Dogman. As a predator that may view you as potential prey, the Dogman is a formidable opponent. With an intimidating height of 6 to 7 feet and an estimated weight of around 500 to 600 pounds, it is wise to compare the Dogman to common large animals like wolves or bears, typically weighing between 100 and over 600 pounds. However, you should not clap your hands at them to get their attention, as it may only make them angry; you might end up looking like a five-course meal.

Instead, treat an encounter with the Dogman or other large cryptid similarly to one with a grizzly bear. As the National Park Service advises: "If the bear is stationary, move away slowly and sideways. This allows you to keep an eye on the bear while avoiding tripping. Moving sideways is also non-threatening to bears. Do NOT run; if the bear follows you, stop and hold your ground. Bears can run as fast as a racehorse, both uphill and downhill." So, too, could something larger.

A significant report from 1937 involved a man named Robert Fortney, who claimed to have been attacked by a pack of five wild dogs, one of which was notably seen walking on two legs.

In 2016, in Oceana County, a man was walking through the woods on a snowy day when he noticed how unusually silent the forest had become. Suddenly, he came across a hairy wolf-like creature with broad shoulders and amber-colored eyes. It growled deeply before darting into the trees.

Michigan: Lake Superior Merman

Notable Characteristics: The merman resembles a human child approximately 7 or 8 years of age. Its facial features include strikingly bright eyes, a small nose, and a proportionate mouth. The creature possesses well-defined ears and displays a complexion with a brownish tone. Additionally, its body is covered in short, woolly hair that has a grayish-black coloration. Its body is like a human adult's.

Venant St. Germain was a 31-year-old Canadian fur trader and merchant in the late 1700s. He worked as a voyageur for the Northwest Company, one of the major fur trading companies operating in North America at the time. His job involved transporting goods and furs between trading posts along the Great Lakes.

On May 3, 1782, during a routine fur trading expedition on Lake Superior, he was traveling with companions from Michilimackinac to Grand Portage. Among them was an Ojibwe woman who was on her way to her own destination. They set up camp on Pie Island, which is located between Isle Royale and the Canadian shoreline of Lake Superior.

While preparing for the night and looking out over the waters, the group noticed an unusual creature about 200 feet offshore. St. Germain described it as having the upper body of a human child, around seven or eight years old, covered in gray-brown, woolly hair about an inch long. The creature's features resembled a human's, with brilliant eyes, a small nose, and well-formed ears. Its expression was of curiosity and uncertainty. Its arm and hand were raised above its head, similar to that of an adult male, while its other arm rested below the water.

Initially, St. Germain's instinct was to shoot the creature. Still, he was quickly restrained by the Ojibwe woman, who warned him that harming it would bring bad luck and storms. The Ojibwe people referred to these beings as "Maymaygwashi," which translates to "water spirits" or "merfolk." They believed these creatures were deities of the waters, possessing significant power over natural events such as rain and storms. As she wrestled him to the ground, the sea creature seemed to sense St. Germain's malicious intentions and disappeared into the water.

After he attempted to shoot the creature, St. Germain experienced a violent storm that lasted three days. He believed the tumultuous weather was retribution from the water god for threatening its life. Venant St. Germain testified in court that he had witnessed a merman, providing a compelling account of his experience and the consequences of disrespecting such beings.

Michigan: Nain Rouge

Notable Characteristics: The Nain Rouge is a notable French and American folklore figure mainly linked to Detroit. This creature is often depicted as a small being with red or black fur boots, striking red eyes, and decayed teeth. Its appearance frequently includes a devilish grin, leading it to be described as resembling a baboon with a horned head. The Nain Rouge is steeped in local legend and is considered a symbol of misfortune and impending doom.

The story of the Nain Rouge dates to the early days of Detroit when the city was founded by Antoine de la Mothe Cadillac. The Nain Rouge appeared to Cadillac and warned him of a future encounter with the demon. Regardless, Cadillac did not heed the forewarning. He attacked the creature with his cane and bellowed, "Get out of my way, you red imp!" This led to bad luck and misfortune for the city.

On July 30, 1763, a creature is said to have appeared before the Battle of Bloody Run, during which 58 British soldiers were killed by Native Americans from Chief Pontiac's Ottawa tribe. It is reported that the Nain Rouge "danced among the corpses" along the banks of the Detroit River after the battle, and the river "turned red with blood" for several days afterward.

The Nain Rouge appeared on several occasions throughout the city's history, including before the 1805 fire that destroyed most of Detroit and before the 1967 riots. There have been several sightings of the Nain Rouge throughout the years, including a reported attack on a woman in 1884 and a sighting by two utility workers in 1976. The creature was dancing on the banks of the Detroit River and is often associated with bad luck and misfortune.

Other Notable Michigan Cryptids

The Melon Heads: These angry creatures of Felt Mansion near Saugatuck have bulbous heads. Legend says they are a community of deformed children who fled from an institution and now reside in the surrounding woods.

Panthers: In the 1980s, residents near Wixom began reporting sightings of a large black cat the size of a German Shepherd roaming through yards and woodland.

Pressie, the Lake Superior Serpent: Pressie has a long neck, a horse-like head, and a body exceeding 25 feet in length. Sightings of Pressie have been reported since the 1800s. Some believe it could be a surviving prehistoric creature like a plesiosaur.

Hickory Creek Henhoten: In the 1890s, a giant speckled bird with a massive wingspan created a stir in Benton Harbor. With its hook-shaped head and long neck, locals believed it brought rain. A blacksmith tried to capture it, but the bird's shriek left him deaf. He freed the bird, but a tail feather fell, destroying four rows of grapevine arbors on a farm.

Minnesota: Wendigo

Notable Characteristics: Descriptions of the Wendigo vary among different communities. Still, common characteristics include an emaciated body, ash-gray or yellowish skin tightly stretched over its bones, sunken eyes, elongated claws, and jagged teeth reminiscent of a shark's. Wendigo is often portrayed as much larger than a human—sometimes over 15 feet tall—possessing supernatural abilities such as exceptional stealth and weather manipulation.

The Wendigo is a figure rooted in Algonquian legend representing a man who was once a human—a hunter who succumbed to delirium due to starvation and resorted to cannibalism. This act transformed him into a grotesque creature that embodies perpetual hunger. This evil cannibal spirit can take over an individual and compel them into eating other people.

It has been said the Wendigos are so famished that they eat their own lips and will appear as if they are baring their teeth. It haunts northern forests, particularly during the bleak winter when food is scarce and starvation is prevalent. Once a human becomes sick, is believed to be a Wendigo, *and has tasted human flesh*, nothing can save them. In the late 1890s, a couple of women from Whitefish Lake were brought in for treatment after one of them dreamed that her deceased brother offered her human flesh in a bowl of ice. Both women fell seriously ill and were believed to be Wendigos; however, since they did not consume human flesh, they eventually recovered.

One man was less fortunate. Big Trout Lake is in Canada, north of Minnesota, and is home to a Cree community. In January 1896, a woman and her husband traveled from Wapiska, 80 miles away, to visit the husband's father at Big Trout Lake. The husband, Na-pa-nin, was about 35 years old and well-known in his community; he was well-liked and regarded as a good father. He seemed to be in good health as they started their journey to Trout Lake. However, on the second night of their travels, he began to act strangely, claiming that animals were trying to attack him. His condition continued to deteriorate throughout the journey. Eventually, the wife urged him to go ahead of the family to his father's, fearing for their safety. By the time they reached Big Trout Lake, his mental state had severely declined. His fits and violent episodes worsened over the nearly three weeks they spent at his father's home. His body began to swell, his belly bloated, and his lips were almost chewed off.

During their journey home to Wapiska, the man's hostile behavior escalated significantly. He threatened those close to him, shouting that if they were so distressed about his violent and aggressive behavior, they should kill him.

Fearing for their safety, members of the community bound the man's hands and feet while his wife left with their baby to visit a neighbor. The men discussed the possibility of killing him but had yet to reach a decision. However, when he broke free from his bindings in a state of crazed delirium, they feared he would harm them all. Knowing that an axe must be used instead of a gun to kill a Wendigo, they struck him four times in the head. His body was burned, and trees were felled over the grave. Many days passed before the community began to fear that he might reappear, but he never did.

Minnesota: Hairy Man

Notable Characteristics: The Hairy Man of Vergas Trails is often described as an elusive creature, standing between 7 to 8 feet tall, with long, shaggy hair, a distinct musky odor, and bare feet. This legendary being is reported to inhabit the Vergas Trails, which are located near Vergas, a small city in northern Minnesota.

Vergas is notable for its landmark, the world's largest loon sculpture, a stunning 20-foot replica of Minnesota's state bird. The city is surrounded by picturesque blue lakes and various resorts, making it a popular destination for nature lovers.

Additionally, some locals claim that the Hairy Man, often likened to Bigfoot, roams the area's forests, adding to the region's rich tapestry of folklore and outdoor adventure.

The legend of the Hairy Man of the Vergas Trails is supported by numerous eyewitness accounts, including one from a lifelong resident named Cheryl Hanson. In 1972, while snowmobiling with her cousin, the two girls stopped to explore an old cabin off Lost Highway. As they examined the property, they encountered a barefoot creature with broad shoulders emerging from the cabin, holding a large stick. Following their sighting, the two girls promptly returned to inform the adults about their experience. However, their accounts were met with skepticism.

The Hairy Man is often described as a reclusive and potentially aggressive figure. It has been associated with various animal attacks in the region. One infamous incident involved a local resident who reported that the Hairy Man jumped in front of his vehicle, causing noticeable dents on the hood.

The legend of the Hairy Man began to circulate in the late 1960s. Still, it gained considerable popularity during the 1970s, with numerous reported sightings. Some residents speculate that the legend may have been inspired by an actual hermit living in isolation.

Minnesota: Lake Ada Sarpint

Notable Characteristics: The creature exhibited a light-colored complexion and resembled a sea serpent.

Lake Ada is situated in Cass County, Minnesota, approximately ten miles from Pine River, and is bordered by dense forests. It is famous for its scenic beauty and offers various recreational activities like fishing. The lake is also known for its creature called the "Lake Ada Monster."

In August 1906, Lake Ada gained notoriety due to reports of a mysterious creature observed by local businessmen B.E. Wideman and J.J. Allen. They described the creature as resembling a "serpent" or "sarpint." In their account published in the Duluth (Minnesota) News Tribune Journal, they initially mistook the creature for an overturned boat because of its size and color, which resembled typical boat paint.

While driving home from a trip to Longville, their attention was drawn to what they thought was an overturned boat, given its size and color. The object was about 165 feet from the shore and clearly visible in the bright moonlight. As one of the men approached for a closer look, the creature lunged and disappeared beneath the water, creating significant swells that washed up on the beach. The witnesses believed it was a large animal with a light color whose head was level with its body.

This sighting sparked excitement in the community and led to speculation about organizing efforts to trap or further investigate this enigmatic creature that had captured local interest. Despite their efforts, it was never apprehended.

Other Notable Minnesota Cryptids

Minnesota Iceman: In the late 1960s, the Minnesota Iceman became famous as a spectacle that drew numerous visitors. This exhibit featured a 6-foot-tall creature resembling Bigfoot encased in ice. It was showcased at various fairs and carnivals across the United States.

Pepie, the lake monster from Lake Pepin: Pepie is a serpent-like creature reported to inhabit a local lake, although sightings of this elusive being have been infrequent.

Otter County Dogman: Fergus Falls is an area with farms and lakes. A Dogman story from Fergus Falls in Otter Tail County emerged in early 2009. While driving on Wendel Road, a man encountered a seven-foot-tall bipedal creature with a slender waist, broad shoulders, opposable thumbs, and dark brown fur. He observed the creature crouching behind a tree, seemingly hunting deer. As the man watched, the deer suddenly bolted, and the creature looked directly at him before the man drove away.

Mississippi: Chatawa Monster

Notable Characteristics: The elusive creature is a large, half-man, half-ape entity. It is about 8 feet tall and covered in long, dark hair. It emits a strong, repulsive odor that can be detected from miles away. It is known for its nighttime piercing scream. The beast is also noted for its massive footprints, measuring 20 inches with three prominent toes.

Chatawa is a small town on the border of Mississippi and Louisiana, formerly served by the Illinois Central Railroad. The town is surrounded by forestland and the Tangipahoa Swamps, wetland areas along the Tangipahoa River in Pike County with dense vegetation, including cypress-tupelo stands, water oaks, and sweetgums. This habitat is ideal for diverse wildlife, including alligators, deer, and migratory birds that thrive in slow-moving or stagnant waters.

The town's name is derived from the Choctaw language, believed to mean either "to be swollen" or "hunting ground." This name is fitting, as the secluded, swampy environment has become a hunting area for a creature known as the Chatawa Monster. The origins of this beast remain a mystery, but some believe it may have escaped from a circus train that derailed near the town. While most of the animals on board perished, this creature survived in the surrounding wilderness. There are also accounts of the Kramer Resort that once existed, where exotic birds and animals, including bears and monkeys, were kept in cages on the property.

Witnesses have reported seeing a gigantic, hairy figure moving through the woods and swamps near Chatawa. Strange claw marks, resembling those made by a cat but much more extensive, have been found high in the trees. Livestock, particularly chickens, tend to vanish without a trace.

However, this creature is quite shy and nocturnal and rarely reveals itself in areas where people tend to frequent. Reports of its existence primarily come from the strange cries it emits and its uncanny ability to quickly steal large, dead farm animals. For instance, a farmer in nearby McComb discovered that one of his 150-pound calves had died, prompting him to retrieve some machinery to drag it away. When he returned, it had vanished. Upon scouring the area and wondering what could have possibly carried such a heavy load, he found the calf dragged into the woods and its entire hindquarters devoured in a short period.

Mississippi: Pascagoula 'Elephant Men' Alien Abduction

Notable Characteristics: Humanoid, but feature "carrot-like" protrusions in place of standard human facial features—precisely, one where the nose would usually be located and two additional growths in the positions of human ears. These entities are approximately six feet tall, with pale, wrinkled skin resembling an elephant's flesh and claw-like hands. A significant aspect of their appearance is the absence of discernible eyes; instead, they possess slit-like mouths. Furthermore, their heads attach directly to their shoulders, lacking a visible neck. The movements of these creatures have been likened to mechanical or robotic motion.

On October 11, 1973, Charles Hickson and Calvin Parker were fishing off a pier on the west bank of the Pascagoula River in Mississippi when they noticed flashing blue lights and an oval-shaped object hovering above them. Charles Hickson described the moment: "I was just sitting there fishing when I heard this whirring sound. I looked up and saw this object hovering above us."

They reported being approached by three humanoid beings, later compared to "Elephant Men," who levitated them into their spacecraft for examination. "They had these robotic slit mouths," Hickson recalled, "and they were taking us aboard that craft." The aliens, approximately six feet tall, had gray, elephant-like skin, bullet-shaped heads, and crab-like pincers with slit lips. Hickson and Parker found themselves aboard the craft, paralyzed yet conscious. During the encounter, they underwent what they described as a medical examination conducted by a large robotic eye.

After the experience, Parker and Hickson were returned to the riverbank, reportedly traumatized by the encounter. Parker later revealed how profoundly the experience affected his life, stating, "It changed my life forever; I still think about it every day."

In June 2019, a historical marker was unveiled at Lighthouse Park in Pascagoula to commemorate the abduction event. The marker was funded by local historical societies and approved by city officials. Hickson's family and Parker attended the unveiling ceremony, marking a significant moment for those involved or impacted by the incident. Since then, both men have passed away, marking the end of an era for this particular UFO case but leaving behind a legacy that continues to intrigue both believers and skeptics alike.

Other Notable Mississippi Cryptids

Goat Man: Waynesboro Shubuta Road is called "Devil Worshipper Road" after a farmer known as the Goat Man sold his soul to the devil and now chases cars. The cursed farmer resembles a satyr, standing seven feet tall with glowing eyes, furry legs, and horns while wielding a pitchfork.

Taney-frate Monster: In the Amite River Bottoms, a low-lying area adjacent to the Amite River originating in southwestern Mississippi, there is an 8-foot-tall bipedal creature that resembles a mix between an ape and a human. This creature has shaggy dark fur, glowing eyes, an overpowering stench, loud vocalizations, and massive footprints, which measure over 20 inches long and feature three prominent toes.

Three-legged Lady of Starkville: On Nash Road near the lock and dam in Columbus, a 3-legged woman with a rotting leg saunters along the road. When cars stop, turn off their headlights, and honk three times, she knocks on the roof and races alongside, striking the vehicle as she runs. Some say the leg was removed and attached to her body post-mortem by a lover to create a morbid monster.

Moon Man of Kilgore: The legend of the Moon Man originates from Kilgore Hills, where Gus Goode, the owner of a local saloon, ventured into West Point to renew his newspaper subscription. During this trip, he and his neighbor, Byron Thompson, witnessed strange flying objects in the sky over Clay County, along with a glowing light emanating from a nearby valley. Curious about the phenomenon, they investigated and discovered a large metal cylinder on the ground. They saw tiny beings—"inhuman men"—surrounding the cylinder as they approached. The situation escalated when Thompson shot one of these beings, who was described as about five feet tall, with gray skin and large cat-like eyes. The creature was then returned to the saloon and displayed for public viewing. It became quite a spectacle until it started to decay, and the stench eventually drove away curious onlookers. Goode and Thompson decided to bury the Moon Man in a designated cemetery for extraterrestrial beings.

Pascagoula River Sirens: The Pascagoula River, often referred to as the "Singing River," is rich in legends about sirens and mermaids. One famous story is about a mermaid who lured members of the Pascagoula tribe into the river, ultimately leading them to their deaths. This tale explains the mysterious humming sounds that emerge from its waters. The sounds produced by the river have been compared to flute-like melodies or the gentle rubbing of a crystal glass rim.

Missouri: Momo

Notable Characteristics: Momo, short for Missouri Monster, is a cryptid observed during the 1970s following reports from residents of Louisiana and Missouri describing a large, hairy creature. Momo is 6 to 8 feet tall with a strong, unpleasant odor, a pumpkin-shaped head, glowing orange eyes, elongated arms, clawed hands, and oversized feet.

In July 1971, one of the first reported sightings of Momo occurred when two women, Joan Mills and Mary Ryan, were driving along Highway 79 northwest of Louisiana after leaving St. Louis. They stopped for a picnic lunch off the roadway and were hit by a strong, foul smell. Looking up toward the brush on the hillside, they spotted a black, man-ape creature approximately 7 feet tall, with a head the size of a pumpkin, a furry body, and hair covering its eyes.

Frightened, the women ran back to their car and watched as the creature devoured their picnic lunch before disappearing into the bushes.

Almost a year later, on July 11, 1972, Edgar Harrison's children had a frightening encounter while playing outside. Eight-year-old Terry Harrison and his five-year-old brother, Wally, were in their backyard when they suddenly screamed in terror. Their older sister, 15-year-old Doris Harrison, looked out the window and saw a massive black creature standing near a tree. Observers described the beast as six to seven feet tall, with no visible neck or facial features because of its thick fur. The creature carried a dead dog under its arm and emitted a putrid stench of rotting flesh.

After the creature was reported, newspapers covered the story, and a vigilante mob formed near Marzolf Hill (also known as Star Hill), which was close to the Harrison family home on Allen Street. The police chief at the time, Shelby Ward, was called to investigate the sightings. However, the community was more concerned about an armed gang shooting at anything in sight than about the growls emanating from the woods.

As time passed, numerous reports of encounters with the creature surfaced. One witness claimed to have seen it crossing the highway with either a dog or a sheep in its mouth. On July 21, Ellis Minor checked on his barking dog and spotted the enormous creature moving through his backyard. Although the beast has not been located, it makes annual appearances during the summer, characterized by distinctive snorts and howls, suggesting it may be migrating through the area.

Missouri: Ozark Howler

Notable Characteristics: The creature is a large, shaggy animal that has a bear-like appearance and features glowing eyes. Its howl is particularly notable, as it resembles a combination of a wolf's howl and the call of an elk. In some sightings, observers have reported the presence of sharp horns or antlers on its head, adding to its eerie and mysterious presence in the wild.

The Ozarks extend through Missouri, Arkansas, Oklahoma, Kansas, and Illinois, characterized by remote forested areas, limestone bluffs, rivers, and steep, rugged terrain. This region is home to various wildlife, including white-tailed deer, elk, and mountain lions.

Among its more elusive residents is the Ozark Howler, a large, bear-like creature known for its glowing eyes and eerie howl, which resembles a mix between a wolf and an elk. Sightings of this mysterious creature have been reported throughout the Ozarks for decades.

One witness from Oregon County reported seeing a large, black, panther-like creature early one morning. Initially, the witnesses thought it was a panther, but they realized it was something different upon closer observation. They described the creature as the size of a Great Dane, with long ears or horns, thick black fur, and striking reddish eyes.

Additionally, a seasoned ranger stationed in the remote areas of Arkansas, near the Missouri border, was convinced she encountered the Ozark Howler late at night. She described it as a large black creature that resembled nothing she had seen before but lined up perfectly with other sightings.

Other Notable Missouri Cryptids

Kansas City Winged Demon: In Kansas City, there have been reports of a winged creature that resembles a demonic figure, standing taller than an average person and possessing a wingspan of approximately 12 feet.

Beaman Monster: A hybrid creature resembling a gorilla or wolf is linked to the Sedalia area, with legends dating back to a circus train crash in 1904 that allowed a 12-foot-tall gorilla to escape. Daemon Smith, a Sedalia resident, reported spotting a wolf-shaped being during childhood while riding in his uncle's truck, which paced alongside them as they drove.

Ozark Spook Light: The Spook Light, observed in the Hornet and Joplin areas of Missouri and Quapaw in Oklahoma, appears as a ball of light ranging from the size of a baseball to that of a basketball. It can be seen hovering above treetops or flying down the road. Explanations for its origin include natural gas emissions, reflections from headlights, and even ghosts. Some speculate it may be connected to extraterrestrial activity due to its mysterious and unexplainable nature.

Montana: Shunk Warak'in

Notable Characteristics: The Shunka Warak'in is a wolf-like creature characterized by darker fur and hyena-like features, with elevated shoulders and a sloping back.

It is rooted in Native American legends, particularly among the Ioway people. The name "Shunka Warak'in" translates to "carries off dogs," reflecting its supposed behavior of sneaking into camps to steal dogs. A significant event occurred in 1886 when a Mormon rancher shot and killed what he initially believed to be a wolf that was killing his livestock. Hutchins, the rancher, had the animal stuffed by Joseph Sherwood, who displayed it in his store and museum near Henry's Lake, Idaho, until it mysteriously disappeared in 1980. The animal resurfaced in 2007 when it was donated to the Madison Valley History Museum in Ennis, Montana. Some researchers speculate that Ringdocus could be an unusual wolf or a hybrid species.

Montana: Flathead Lake Flessie

Notable Characteristics: This creature is typically described as eel-like, potentially growing up to 40 feet in length. Its skin displays various colors, from brown to deep blue, accompanied by grayish-black eyes.

Flathead Lake in Montana is the largest natural freshwater lake west of the Mississippi River, featuring over 185 miles of shoreline and covering roughly 200 square miles. Among its vast waters, the lake is home to a legendary creature known as the Flathead Lake Monster, often called "Flessie."

The first recorded sighting of Flessie occurred in 1889. Captain James Kerr, while navigating the lake aboard the U.S. Grant steamboat, along with his passengers, reported seeing a creature resembling a whale in the waters around the boat.

This incident sparked significant interest and intrigue regarding the possibility of Flessie's existence in Flathead Lake. In the 1940s, it was speculated to be a large sturgeon.

Additionally, local folklore recounts a story from the 1940s involving a 3-year-old boy who nearly drowned in the lake. When questioned by his mother about his escape from the water, he attributed his survival to the assistance of the Flathead monster, claiming that it "lifted me up."

In the 1950s, two boaters got too close, and "the spray from the monster was so great that it conked out" their motor, and the monster fled.

A couple reported seeing a large creature while boating on Flathead Lake in 2005. They described it as having humps that rose above the water's surface and moved in a serpentine motion.

Montana: Bigfoot

Notable Characteristics: The creature resembling Bigfoot is portrayed by its reddish-brown hair and more human-like appearance rather than primate features. Notably, it possesses long arms, further contributing to its unusual physique.

Gallatin National Forest is in southwestern Montana, primarily surrounding the northern boundary of Yellowstone National Park. It features diverse landscapes, including mountains, forests, rivers, and valleys. The Bitterroot Mountains, part of the continental divide, extend through western Montana and eastern Idaho, running roughly north to south along the border between the two states. Bowl Creek is a smaller creek near these two prominent geographical features, specifically where Gallatin National Forest meets the Bitterroot Mountains.

In 1991, in Ravalli County, located in a heavily forested area of Bowl Creek with bogs and natural springs, a hunting guide was scouting for an elk hunt as he returned to his base camp. He chose to cut through some dense timber, with the wind blowing in his favor, carrying his scent away from nearby wildlife. Suddenly, his tired horse began to act strangely, which is typical behavior when a bear or moose is nearby. As the guide rode past a fallen tree, he spotted a Bigfoot. The creature, covered in reddish-brown hair, looked more human than an ape and seemed entirely surprised by the guide's presence. Instead of running away, the guide acted as if he hadn't seen the creature and continued his ride. Instinct and experience with wild creatures worked in the guide's favor. The creature remained in place, and they did not cross paths again.

In the autumn of 2005 in Ravalli County, a truck driver and his wife were traveling between Conner and Sula near the Bitterroot National Forest when they saw a creature with long hair flowing behind it. The creature sped down the mountain slope far faster than a human could run, darting past trees and brush. It crossed the road with its arms swinging in just a few steps, quickly crossing US-93. Both the driver and his wife could see it clearly. It made such an impression that they reported it to the BFRO, Bigfoot Research Organization.

Other Notable Montana Cryptids

The Little People of the Pryor Mountains: Known as Nirumbee or Awwakkulé in the Crow language, the Little People are key figures in Crow Tribe folklore, embodying spiritual wisdom. Described as 18-inch, fierce dwarfs with large heads and sharp teeth, they are territorial and have short limbs and little necks. They offer blessings and insights to select individuals, with petroglyphs in the Pryor Mountains linking them to the land. To maintain peace, the Crow Tribe made offerings like tobacco or weapons at sites such as Medicine Rocks. Encounters with the Little People are noted in Crow history, including a story about Chief Red Plume, who received guidance from them during a fast on Big Horn Mountain.

Mountain Man Gorilla: The remote mountainous area between Wyoming and Montana in the late 1800s was primarily traversed by old trapper paths winding through the terrain. In 1892, the Brooklyn (New York) Eagle featured a report about a strange creature resembling Bigfoot found along a particular pass. The article stated, "It Looks Like a Man and Eats Bears and Sheep." Occasionally, trappers would encounter a "varmint"—a creature covered in hair that resembled a human and walked on its hind legs like a gorilla. The creature appeared territorial, as partially eaten large bears and mountain sheep carcasses were often found scattered throughout its domain.

Nebraska: Alkali Lake Monster

Notable Characteristics: The creature is a 40-foot-long, alligator-like entity characterized by its armored plates and sharp teeth. This cryptid has been a fixture of local folklore since at least the 1920s, reflecting a longstanding intrigue and belief in its existence among residents.

In 1921, J.A. Johnson reported seeing a remarkable creature near Hay Springs, Nebraska. He described it as an alligator-like entity measuring approximately 40 feet long and exhibiting dull gray and brown colors. This creature became known as the Alkali Lake Monster or the Walgren Lake Monster.

Various witnesses associated with this phenomenon described a large, horned beast resembling an alligator or an enormous mudpuppy. They claimed it preyed on local livestock and ducks. Observers noted that the creature was so massive that the ground trembled as it moved. It could create a dense fog that could disorient travelers nearby.

Nebraska: Flying Humanoid Monstrosity

Notable Characteristics: The phenomenon of flying humanoids has been reported in various locations around the world, including Nebraska. Witnesses describe entities with human-like characteristics that are seen flying or hovering in the air, with many modern sightings linked to advanced technology associated with UFO phenomena.

In the autumn of 1956, a witness, "Mr. Hanks," reported a bizarre encounter with a flying humanoid while traveling down a rural road near Falls City, Nebraska. Mr. Hanks described the airborne entity as having fifteen-foot-long metallic wings adorned with odd multicolored lights.

The wings were rigid but seemed controlled by a panel strapped to the entity's chest. The face of this flying humanoid was twisted and leathery, and the being stood approximately nine feet tall. This brief encounter startled Mr. Hanks as the being flew overhead and vanished into the dusk.

This sighting is not an isolated incident. In 1948, several witnesses in Longview, Washington, reported seeing three men gliding through the air, each wearing what were described as "flying suits." These suits were believed to be equipped with some form of motorized equipment that allowed for flight. This incident occurred shortly after another notable sighting in Chehalis, Washington, where Bernice Zaikowski and some neighboring children encountered a "birdman" on January 6, 1948. She reported seeing a man with silver wings attached to his back flying over her barn at 200 feet.

There are differing viewpoints regarding the origins of these entities. Some individuals propose that they are merely innovative humans experimenting with new technologies. In contrast, others theorize that they may be extraterrestrial beings or travelers from other dimensions.

Nebraska: Pine Ridge Vampire

Notable Characteristics: The overall appearance of the Pine Ridge Vampire is largely unclear, primarily due to the varied eyewitness accounts from the time. However, it is generally described as having a human-like form, a frothing mouth, and exhibiting unnatural strength. This entity is noted for its capacity to inflict significant harm before vanishing without a trace.

Pine Ridge, Nebraska, had a vampire. In 1895, there was widespread fear about an unearthly entity that was responsible for brutal attacks on cattle and ranchers.

In December of that year, residents of Pine Ridge reported numerous gruesome and violent attacks on livestock with mutilated bodies drained of blood. So grisly were the attacks that they were not merely the work of a large wild animal like a bear or cougar but were attributed to a human-like creature or "vampire." A group of cowboys witnessed a man wrestling a cow to the ground. He ripped its throat out with his bare hands and his teeth. Then, he slurped the blood like a dog lapping water from a bowl. When it attacked the caretakers of animals, it was known to possess colossal strength and could quickly overpower a human.

Jack Lewis was a cowboy who encountered a vampire one chilly night in mid-December while alone on the prairie. The creature knocked him to the ground and clawed ferociously at his neck while he struggled to breathe. Lewis managed to draw his firearm and fired multiple shots at his attacker, who was frothing at the lips. Despite the gunfire, the attacker seemed unharmed and escaped into the darkness before help could arrive. The cowboy had alarming bite marks on his face and neck. Posses were formed to hunt down the vampire-like entity, but it was never captured and mysteriously vanished shortly afterward.

Other Notable Nebraska Cryptids

Blue Springs Bigfoot: The Bigfoot sighting took place in 1974 near the town of Blue Springs, Nebraska. A motorist traveling on rural US-77 encountered a bipedal creature measuring 7 to 8 feet tall, covered in black-brown hair, and having long arms. The beast, weighing about 600 to 700 pounds, stepped out of the ditch and onto the road, so the driver slowed. In just three steps, it had crossed the road. Another motorist traveling in the opposite direction also slowed down, and both drivers stopped momentarily to confirm what they had witnessed.

Oakland Creature: On July 4, 1974, in the small town of Oakland, a couple named Dale and Linda Jones were abruptly awakened from their sleep by unidentified screams from their farm. Dan ventured outside with a flashlight and saw an odd silhouette but could not determine what it was. Linda reported seeing the figure running on two legs across a cornfield. As the townspeople heard their strange story, others began to report sightings of what they believed to be a bear with a monkey's face standing about six feet tall. Law enforcement tried to locate the creature, even using trained tracking animals but found no evidence of its existence. As cooler weather arrived in September, the reports of sightings decreased significantly, and the creature was never conclusively identified.

Nevada: Area 51 Aliens

Notable Characteristics: Descriptions of the extraterrestrial beings associated with Area 51 typically depict them as small, grayish humanoid figures characterized by large, bulbous heads and prominent eyes. The spacecraft reportedly linked to these aliens are commonly described as disc or saucer-shaped, showcasing highly advanced propulsion systems and materials not typically utilized in conventional aircraft. Various conspiracy theories suggest that these crafts may be the subject of study and potential replication at Area 51.

Area 51 is a highly classified U.S. Air Force facility located in Nevada. It has been the focus of numerous stories and conspiracy theories about extraterrestrial life. The site became well-known after a former employee, Robert Lazar, claimed that the government was reverse-engineering alien spacecraft recovered from crashes. Since the late 1950s, there have been reports of Unidentified Flying Objects (UFOs) in the surrounding area, which coincided with secret military tests of high-altitude reconnaissance planes, such as the U-2.

The infamous Roswell incident in 1947 further fueled these theories; it is alleged that debris from a United States Army Air Forces balloon recovered near Roswell, New Mexico, was from a crashed extraterrestrial spacecraft. For years, Area 51 has been portrayed as a secretive hub for government experiments involving aliens and their technology, despite official denials that focus on military operations.

Over the years, many books, documentaries, and movies have shaped the idea that Area 51 is a place connected to aliens and advanced technology. This has created a strong belief that the base is not just a military site but also a hub for studying extraterrestrial life. This combination of accounts and popular culture has inspired intriguing ideas about what occurs in Area 51.

Nevada: Cactus Cat

Notable Characteristics: The Cactus Cat (Cactifelinus inebrius) is a legendary creature often linked to the folklore of the American Southwest, particularly in Nevada. It resembles a bobcat but has thorn-like fur, sharp bones protruding from its front legs, and a branched tail. This unique animal thrives in desert regions and areas abundant in cacti.

The Cactus Cat was primarily observed in the 19th century by cowboys, miners, and pioneers while camping when traversing Nevada's remote and isolated arid landscapes.

The stories often described the Cactus Cat as a nocturnal creature that used its sharp forearm bones to slice open cacti and consume their sap. Since it had a craving for fermented sap, the cat often returned later to drink the juice that had pooled inside. Occasionally, the sap made the cat so drunk that it led to humorous accounts of the creature stumbling through the desert in a drunken stupor and making spooky wailing sounds.

Other Notable Nevada Cryptids

Walker Lake Monster: Known as Cecil, this giant snake-like creature has inhabited Walker Lake in Nevada since the 1800s. Visitors to the lake have reported sightings of it, describing it as thirty feet long, with a crocodile-like head and a long tail.

Jarbidge Monster: In the Shoshone oral tradition, the Tsawhawbitts was a 30-foot-tall cannibalistic giant that terrorized tribes in the remote Jarbidge Canyon of northeastern Nevada. This creature captured humans, stored them in baskets, and consumed them until tribal warriors successfully trapped it in a cave using boulders during an epic confrontation.

Giant Space Clams: In 1925, Don Wood and his companions reported a sighting while flying over the Nevada desert. They observed giant sky clams, with the first measuring about 8 feet long, featuring a wet upper half, a reddish lower half that seemed to breathe, and an injury oozing metallic froth. After 20 minutes, a more enormous clam, estimated at 30 feet in diameter, descended and used its sucker-like appendages to lift the smaller clam. This encounter has led researchers to speculate about the possibility of these creatures being extraterrestrial life.

New Hampshire: Wood Devil

Notable Characteristics: This creature is described as standing between 7 to 9 feet tall, with a slender physique, and weighing approximately 400 pounds. It is covered in shaggy gray or tan hair, with a distinctive horse-like face and large, expressive eyes. The creatures are known to hide behind trees and are extremely fast.

New Hampshire is home to the Woods Devil, a creature compared to Bigfoot but described as having a horse-like face. Reports of the Woods Devil date back to early lumberjacks, who sometimes shared outlandish tales of bizarre creatures to frighten new employees or tourists.

For many years, much of the creature's existence was attributed to campfire stories. However, one notable documented sighting occurred in 1948, when George Lavoie, a hunter in a remote area of Coös County, reported seeing something moving among the trees. Curious, he paused in the dusk and witnessed a tall, thin, hairy creature with the face of a horse.

In 1952, another hunter named Robert Goulet was in Dixville Notch, a short, steep-walled gorge separating Dixville Peak and Cave Mountain in the Great North Woods Region of New Hampshire. An eerie shriek echoed through the valley, and he followed it, eager to discover the source of the strange call he had never heard before. Along his path, an 8-foot-tall, scraggly-haired creature appeared. Goulet took a shot but missed, and the creature quickly vanished.

In 1997, an intriguing incident occurred along Route 26 near Errol, where local farmers had reported unusual sounds emanating from the woods. During this time, Bill Driscoll observed a remarkable figure, a 9-foot-tall creature with long limbs, gray fur, and a face resembling a human. After a brief eye contact with Driscoll, the beast vanished into the surrounding forest.

New Hampshire: Devil Monkey

Notable Characteristics: The Danville Devil Monkey is a reddish-brown creature that stands between 3 to 8 feet tall. It has distinct features, including sharp claws and a face resembling that of a baboon. The creature earned its name due to the panic it caused in Danville and the strange howling sounds it emitted.

In 2001, in the town of Danville, a creature described as monkey-like allegedly leaped through the trees and was heard and seen by multiple residents, including the local fire chief, David Kimball. A local boy claimed that peanut butter cookies left in his treehouse had mysteriously vanished. His mother connected this with the recent monkey sightings.

The sightings began on August 21, 2001, when Kimball witnessed a large monkey-like creature jump into the road in front of his truck. He described it as something not native to the area. He suspected that it could be a Humboldt's wooly monkey, indigenous to the Amazon rainforest. Local authorities and residents tried to catch this elusive creature, even using female monkey urine and fruit as bait to lure it in, but it managed to elude them. Sightings tapered off until ten years later, it was spotted by a family grilling steaks in their backyard after the dogs started barking. They looked, and a monkey was jumping from tree to tree. The mystery of the monkey was never solved. Still, speculation abounded, ranging from a feral or escaped monkey to an extra-dimensional visitor, an evil spirit, or even an alien.

Other Notable New Hampshire Cryptids

Derry Fairy: In Derry, New Hampshire, near Beaver Lake, a legendary creature has garnered attention since its first reported sighting in 1956 by Alfred Horne. Horne described encountering a tiny, green being with a dome-shaped head, wrinkled skin, ears that hung down, and holes for eyes while he was exploring the woods around the lake. This creature stood about 2 feet tall and had short legs and arms featuring stubby hands and feet. This account has since become an integral part of the local folklore associated with Beaver Lake.

Dublin Lake Monster: The Dublin Lake Monster story has been circulating in New Hampshire, specifically around Dublin Lake, since the 1980s. A group of divers wanted to explore the deepest part of the lake. They brought a rope, but one diver reached the end of it and decided to plunge deeper, ultimately disappearing. Two days later, he was found walking through the woods, naked and mumbling incoherently about a hideous monster in the lake.

New Jersey: Jersey Devil

Notable Characteristics: The Jersey Devil is often characterized by its unique physical features, including a body resembling a kangaroo, bat-like wings, a horse-like head, prominent horns, and a long tail.

The Pine Barrens, located in southern New Jersey, is a significant ecological region characterized by its unique landscape and rich history. This area features diverse flora, including twisted trees and resilient shrubs. Encompassing numerous abandoned villages, the region showcases remnants of past human activity, including crumbling brick structures and overgrown paths.

The Pine Barrens are home to various animals, including coyotes, bobcats, beavers, and foxes. However, one creature that people should avoid is particularly significant—a being resembling a combination of a kangaroo and a wyvern.

It had hooves, bat-like wings, a goat-like head, and a forked tail. This creature is associated with Deborah Leeds, known as "Mother Leeds." She had twelve children, and upon discovering she was pregnant with a thirteenth, she cursed the unborn child in anger.

On a stormy night in 1735, surrounded by friends, Mother Leeds gave birth to her thirteenth child, declaring that it would be evil, stating, "Let it be the devil!" Initially, the baby looked like any other newborn, but it soon transformed into a gruesome, monstrous creature. Thus, the Jersey Devil was born. The being growled and screeched before flying up the chimney, escaping into the dark forest of the Pine Barrens, where it continues to prey on the fears of those who venture there. Since then, others have reported seeing the Jersey Devil. Joseph Bonaparte, the older brother of Napoleon, claimed he encountered the Jersey Devil while hunting on his Bordentown estate around 1820.

In January 1909, the legend of the Jersey Devil gained significant attention due to sensationalized newspaper reports, causing a wave of hysteria in New Jersey. This period was characterized by numerous reported sightings, such as one in the Asbury Park Press on January 20, 1909, which documented mysterious tracks found in Gloucester County attributed to the creature. A man later claimed to have faked "some of the prints." The article mentioned that many older residents believed these tracks belonged to the "Leeds Devil."

On October 20, 1909, the Portsmouth Herald reported the Jersey Devil was found dead near Burlington, leaving small hoof prints the previous winter. The creature measured about twenty inches long, with a spine extending six inches beyond its hind leg. It had a kangaroo-like tail, reddish-brown fur, short wings, and a mouth filled with razor-sharp teeth. Its head featured lance-like ears.

They thought it was gone, but it was not. During the 1960s, hoofed tracks and strange sounds were reported in Mays Landing, prompting a reward for the live capture of the creature.

In December 1979, The Asbury Park Press reported on a remarkable incident involving 14-year-old Dale English, ice skating near Chatsworth, a gateway to the Pine Barrens, on January 16, 1979. While enjoying their time, Dale and his friends noticed a strong odor that smelled "like dead fish." Naturally curious, they decided to follow the scent, which led them to encounter "two big red eyes staring at us." Dale described the creature they saw as being seven feet tall before they quickly fled the scene. When they returned the next day, fresh snow had covered the tracks, making it impossible to find evidence of the creature.

In June of 1987, a creature began stalking the Pine Barrens, causing residents to keep their children indoors. Roars and growls echoed through the night, leading police and New Hampshire State Wildlife officers to attempt to locate the creature, admitting that the situation was unsafe. Since January, there had been three reports of household animals being torn apart in Vineland by an unknown entity. Investigators discovered tracks but couldn't determine whether they belonged to dogs, foxes, large cats, raccoons, or bears. Some, however, speculated that it could be another creature known in the Pine Barrens: the infamous New Jersey Devil. One woman had a brief glimpse of the beast in the darkness. "We walked into the woods, and I saw something fall from a tree," she recalled. "Right after it hit the ground, we heard the growls again."

The Jersey Devil is still out there. It is sometimes heard making unusual noises from deep within the woods, and distinctive hoof-like prints have been found in the area.

There are also reports of the creature preying on outdoor pets, such as cats and dogs, especially those left outside by careless pet owners. We may never know if it is the offspring of Mother Leeds' thirteenth child or the same immortal creature born of Hell. If only the whispers of the ancient trees in the Pine Barrens could speak to us and reveal the truth.

New Jersey: Big Red Eye

Notable Characteristics: This Bigfoot-like cryptid is 7 to 8 feet tall, over 400 pounds, walks on two legs, with long hair covering its body. Its eyes appear to glow red when reflecting light. Big Red Eye is reported to inhabit the wooded areas of northwest New Jersey, particularly Sussex County. Its cry is described as blood-curdling.

One of the initial sightings was in 1975. About 12 miles from Newton, two men, Irving Raser and Charles Ames, were walking in a swamp when they noticed two dogs fighting with something partially submerged in the water. The creature was sizable, and the men shouted for the dogs to back off, waiting for whatever they were attacking to come onto dry land.

When it did, the men were stunned. "It was about six feet tall," Mr. Raser recalled. "It weighed between 250 and 300 pounds and was covered with long, brown hair. It had a flat face with deep-set eyes, and the palms of its hands were hairless. If I didn't know better, I would have thought it was a man dressed up in a monkey suit." The animal screamed at the dogs and banged its hand against a tree, frightening them enough to make them back off. After that, it took off into the woods.

About 14 miles away and a couple of years later, reports began emerging in 1977 when residents of Wantage claimed to hear bizarre noises at night that resembled moaning or wailing, sounding much like the calls of primates. The Sites family, who owned a farm on Wolfpit Road, experienced a particularly unsettling incident on May 12. The mother woke up early to prepare the children for school and followed her regular routine of letting the cows out to pasture. However, the cows refused to leave their stalls. While trying to figure out the issue, she heard a strange sound resembling a woman screaming from the swampy woods on the property. Concerned, she went to check on their rabbits, only to discover that the door to the enclosure had been torn from its frame and the rabbits had been killed.

That night, around 9:00 p.m., Mrs. Sites noticed the wire on her shed had been unfastened. "I told my husband that someone was around," she said. He untied their dog, and they went inside the house. Debbie, their 16-year-old daughter, sat in the bay window. She began screaming and yelling that something was in the yard. When they looked outside, they saw a large, hairy creature standing at the corner of the shed. It was big and had no neck; it appeared as if its head was simply sitting on its shoulders. The creature had *big red eyes*.

Their 70-pound dog, Golden Boy, took off after it, but the creature swung an arm and tossed the dog aside quite easily.

Fortunately, Golden Boy escaped and did not return until the next day. Over the following days, the family noticed the strange, human-like creature returning to their farm. During one encounter, they armed themselves and spotted the creature's red eyes staring at them from a distance. After they fired shots at it, the creature fled into the woods.

In July 1977, while returning from Dover Station to Camp Kiamesha, camp counselors spotted a Bigfoot creature in their headlights as it leaped across the road. It jumped "three feet higher than the car in front of us" in just three strides.

In November 2024, another sighting was reported in Ocean County. A hiker was out with his dog and experienced a dark shadow moving through the thick brush. Although he couldn't see the creature clearly, he noted that its size and movement were unlike any known animal.

Over the years, a significant number of eyewitness accounts have documented encounters with this mysterious entity, and new reports continue to emerge even today.

Other Notable New Jersey Cryptids

New Jersey Mothman: The legendary humanoid, known for its glowing red eyes and large wings, is linked to the tragic collapse of the Silver Bridge in West Virginia. Reports of this creature first emerged around Point Pleasant, West Virginia, between November 1966 and December 1967. In 1967, the Silver Bridge collapsed, further connecting the creature to this event. However, in 2017, residents of Burlington County, New Jersey, reported sightings of a tall figure with large wings and glowing red eyes, which was seen perched on a fence post along a rural road. The figure took flight as witnesses approached, soaring into the night sky. Additionally, while investigating unusual sounds in Wharton State Forest, hikers observed a sizable, winged figure gliding silently through the trees.

The White Stag: This elusive animal roams the forests of New Jersey and is known to assist travelers who are lost or in danger in the Pine Barrens. Many years ago, a stagecoach driver halted one night when a white stag blocked his path on a bridge over the Batsto River in the Pine Barrens. When he stepped out of the coach to investigate, he realized the bridge was washed out.

New Mexico: La Llorona

Notable Characteristics: A woman walking along waterways whose siren-like cries lure adults and children to their untimely deaths.

La Llorona, known as "the Weeping Woman," was a woman who married a wealthy man and had two children with him. However, he became distant over time and eventually left her for another woman. Upon discovering her husband's infidelity, she was heartbroken and consumed with rage. She drowned her little children in the river. Realizing the gravity of her actions and overwhelmed by guilt and sorrow, she chose to drown herself in the same river. As a result, she was denied entry into heaven and condemned to wander the earth for eternity. Now, she roams rivers and lakes at night, mourning her lost children and searching for them, often luring others who hear her siren-like wails into the water.

New Mexico: La Mala Hora

Notable Characteristics: La Mala Hora, which translates to "the evil hour," is a figure found in various regions of Mexico and parts of the southern United States, particularly New Mexico. This entity embodies different forms and meanings across cultures, but she is generally associated with danger, seduction, and death. La Mala Hora is depicted as floating, with her feet described as backward.

The legend from southern Mexico has transitioned to New Mexico, where La Mala Hora is often represented as a beautiful woman dressed in white. She appears at night along lonely roads, luring men who pass by with her captivating beauty. Enchanted by her charm, they blindly follow her, unaware of the peril she brings. Many men inadvertently follow her off cliffs or become lost, unable to find their way back.

Some people view La Mala Hora as an evil spirit that haunts crossroads at night. In the past, she was said to appear as a lock of wool that changed size before the eyes of her viewer. She is rarely seen in human form, but when she is, it is often an omen of disaster or death. Modern accounts describe encounters with a terrifying woman dressed in black who signals impending doom.

An old story from the Chiapas region tells of a man walking along a road to visit his girlfriend when he encountered a beautiful woman who resembled her. This woman claimed to have come partway to meet him and wanted to run away together. Initially captivated by her charm, the man soon noticed that her shoes were worn backward. Realizing her true identity as La Mala Hora, he confronted her. He managed to blindfold her before striking her, which caused her to flee.

The following evening, he returned with a blessed needle and pretended to believe she was his girlfriend again. When they reached a secluded spot, he secretly pricked her with the needle, immobilizing her. He then rushed to find a priest and returned with him at dawn, but La Mala Hora had vanished by then.

New Mexico: The Coco

Notable Characteristics: The Coco is a well-known figure in folklore, often depicted in various unsettling ways that intrigue and frighten people. This creature embodies numerous forms, ranging from shadowy figures to frightening hairy monsters or even a sinister cloaked man. A notable characteristic of the Coco is its enormous ear, which is believed to be particularly adept at detecting the sounds of mischief made by children.

The Coco is commonly thought to conceal itself in dark locations, such as under beds, closets, or in the corners of rooms. It is often described as having bright, glowing red eyes that can pierce through darkness and sharp, jagged teeth that enhance its fearsome appearance.

One of the more alarming attributes of the Coco is its shapeshifting ability, which allows it to manifest in different forms, contributing to the anxiety associated with potential encounters. Traditionally, the Coco is regarded as a creature that "snatches" children who misbehave or defy their parents' instructions, serving as a cautionary figure in various cultures.

Other Notable New Mexico Cryptids

Roswell New Mexico Incident: The Roswell incident refers to events in 1947 when the United States Army Air Forces reportedly recovered debris from a crashed unidentified flying object near Roswell, New Mexico. Initially, the military described the debris as related to a "flying disc" but later retracted this statement, claiming the wreckage was from a weather balloon. In 1994, the U.S. Air Force clarified that the materials recovered were from a top-secret project involving a spy balloon designed to detect Soviet nuclear tests. Many remain skeptical and believe that the government may be concealing the true nature of the incident. As a result, various conspiracy theories have emerged over the years, including assertions of extraterrestrial bodies, alien autopsies, and technological reverse-engineering. While many of these theories have been debunked, they maintain popularity among UFO enthusiasts.

Chupacabra: In New Mexico, reports of chupacabra sightings often depict these creatures as resembling dog-like reptiles. Witnesses commonly describe them as having large, glowing red eyes, long, sharp fangs, and substantial claws. Additionally, many accounts note the presence of spines along their backs, contributing to the eerie appearance of these beings.

New York: Sewer Alligators

Notable Characteristics: The American alligator is a large reptile native to freshwater habitats such as ponds and swamps in the warmer southeastern United States. It typically measures between 10 to 15 feet in length and weighs around 1,000 pounds. Their body is armored, and they have a rounded snout. Alligators have powerful jaws and strong tails.

People often say that there are no alligators in the sewer, but—

In 1907, just outside the New York City limits in Kearny, New Jersey—only twelve miles from Midtown Manhattan—a worker cleaning out a sewer was bitten by a small alligator during his job. This incident sparked widespread panic, as newspapers extensively reported the story.

On February 9, 1935, teens James Mitreno and Salvatore Concolucci were shoveling snow into a sewer in Harlem when they heard a splashing sound from below. Curious, they knelt to look into the sewer and discovered a 125-pound alligator. Salvatore used a clothesline to lower himself down and snag the alligator. Unfortunately, they ended up beating the animal to death. The alligator measured 8 feet long, and the boys got their pictures in the newspaper. Teddy May, the Commissioner of Sewers at the time, initially dismissed reports of alligators as hoaxes. However, the frightened public persisted, prompting him to investigate. During his inspections, he reportedly discovered small alligators approximately two feet long. In 1937, a barge captain lassoed a four-foot-eight-inch alligator from the East River, dragging it out after it had become too exhausted to fight. Shortly afterward, another smaller alligator was found crawling along a subway platform in Brooklyn, having emerged from a trash can where it had presumably been discarded.

There is a common belief that alligators do not live in sewers, but they can. Consider this: American alligators in the wild typically have a lifespan of 30 to 50 years. In captivity, they can live up to 70 years, some even older. If an alligator has been in the sewer for 30 or 40 years—whether dumped there or not—it could be around 40 years old. A male alligator of that age would generally measure about 9.25 feet in length. Therefore, if alligators are in the sewers, staying on the sidewalk above is highly recommended.

(It is essential to note small alligators have occasionally been rescued from sewers nowadays—often former pets discarded by owners.)

New York: Hobgoblin of Fort Niagara

Notable Characteristics: This little, human-like creature has pointed ears and wears tattered dark clothing.

For years, people have reported sightings of a hobgoblin in the cemetery at Fort Niagara. The first recorded sighting was by a young man named John Carroll, who, after getting drunk, was thrown into a pit as a form of solitary confinement. While he was there, he was visited by the hobgoblin. In 1812, a soldier also reported seeing a creature resembling the hobgoblin in the graveyard.

Other Notable New York Cryptids

Giant Rat in New York City: A recent study estimated about 3 million rats in New York City, which is close to a third of the city's human population. Among these rats is the Gambian pouched rat, a species not native to New York but has been reported in the city due to the illegal pet trade and escapes from captivity. It is believed that they might be breeding with the common Norway rat. The Gambian pouched rat can grow up to 3 feet long from nose to tail and weigh up to 3 pounds, making them roughly the size of a small cat. A Housing Authority employee recently spotted a Gambian pouched rat and two others. The head of the tenant association at Marcy Houses noted that residents have been aware of these sightings for at least six years, indicating the possibility of an established population in the area.

High Hat: High Hat is from Western New York folklore, known for its cannibalistic tendencies and sharp teeth. Linked with the Allegany Seneca Reservation, it preys on children and resides in marshy areas. Its name comes from the stovepipe hat resembling President Abraham Lincoln's, adding an eerie touch to its fearsome image. During the Kinzua Reservoir construction in the 1960s, workers often joked about seeing a strange figure on the northern shore, referring to it as "old Abe Lincoln" because of the distinctive hat. They were unaware of the story while it lurked along that shoreline for a few years.

White Bigfoot of Belmont: A large, beige, and lanky Bigfoot inhabits central Allegany County around the villages of Belmont and West Almond, near forestland. Two high school girls reported one notable sighting of the White Bigfoot of Belmont in 1999. They claimed to have seen a large, beige creature keeping pace with cars on Route 244 near West Almond, approximately eight miles east of Belmont village.

Manitou Road Demon: Manitou Road in Greece, a suburb of Rochester, comes from the Algonquin word "manitou," which signifies a life force or spiritual energy. This connection to Native American culture, combined with the wooded, rural setting, adds depth to the legend of the fanged Manitou Road Demon, who haunts the area. Over the years, locals have seen and heard this demon, describing experiences of it harassing vehicles or tapping on windows late at night.

The Leaping Loopy: The Leaping Loopy is a cryptid reported in Western New York during the 1940s and 1970s. It has incredible leaping abilities, a long body, and large eyes. Witnesses compare it to a mix between a rabbit and a kangaroo. In the early 2000s, hikers observed the Leaping Loopy hopping over logs and navigating through the brush before disappearing into the woods.

North Carolina: Spearfinger

Notable Characteristics: Spearfinger is a creature characterized by its stone-like skin and witch-like appearance. This entity can shapeshift into the form of an elderly woman, allowing it to present a less intimidating facade. Notably, Spearfinger is distinguished by its long, sharp spear that replaces its right index finger, which it is said to use in its various pursuits.

Many years ago, in the Smoky Mountains, there was a fearsome ogress the Cherokee called "U'tlun'ta," or Spearfinger. Her stone-like skin was impervious to weapons, and she could shapeshift into anything she desired.

Her right forefinger was long and sharp, and she preyed on young children. When she heard them playing outside, she would take the form of an old woman and follow their sweet scent, hobbling as if struggling to walk. "I am tired," she would say, sitting beside them. "Come sit on grandma's lap, and I will sing you a song." And one of them would come skipping and prancing over and plop their little head happily on her lap in anticipation of the special attention.

U'tlun'ta crooned and cooed over the child and slipped her fingers through its hair until the child fell into a blissful nap. Then, U'tlun'ta whipped her hand from its hidden pocket in her clothing, sinking the speared forefinger through the tender flesh of the back of the child's neck until the tip pierced its liver. She would drag out the liver and eat it as it dripped with blood, smacking her lips and sighing contentedly while the other children screeched and ran away.

North Carolina: Vampire of Bladenboro

Notable Characteristics: The creature resembled a bear or panther, approximately three to five feet long and twenty inches high, with a long tail and a cat-like face. It made eerie screams at night.

In the small town of Bladenboro, North Carolina, during the winter of 1953 to 1954, there were several reports of mysterious deaths of pets and livestock, which caused near hysteria among the community. The local newspapers quickly seized on these reports. They began attributing exaggerated, almost horrific characteristics to the creature, describing it as "ghostlike" with "carved claws" and "drunk the blood."

Reports indicated that it was a vampire occurrence and that one or possibly two "vampires" might be lurking in the swamps. Then, on December 29, 1953, a local woman reported seeing an enormous cat-like animal near her home. This sighting was soon followed by alarming reports from farmers and residents claiming that pets had been killed under strange circumstances, including mutilations and the draining of blood. It appeared that any stray or unsupervised pet outside was fair game.

Fourteen miles away in Lumberton, the witch hunt began in the swamps for the creature with Dog Warden Carroll Freeman and a posse of 500 heavily armed men. They found an 80-pound dog that was part collie and part shepherd, hunted it down, and killed it. Freeman suspected it was the leader of a pack of feral dogs responsible for the mysterious killings of several piglets.

On December 31, two dogs belonging to Woody Storm were found dead. He told the authorities that their bodies appeared to be drained of blood, which heightened fears within the community. D.G. Pait reported witnessing a creature dragging a dog into the woods near his service station. Other locals reported hearing eerie shrieks at night that sounded like a high-pitched scream of a distressed child or woman. Around January 1, 1954, additional dogs were found dead in similar gruesome conditions. In January, a woman heard dogs whimpering in the street and stepped onto her porch. A sizeable cat-like creature was running down the street. She screamed, and the frightened beast fled.

The local police chief, Roy Fores, called in additional hunters to track down the mysterious beast. Over 600 hunters descended upon Bladenboro, eager to kill. During this time, most locals avoided going out at night for fear of encountering the creature or the many inexperienced hunters.

After weeks of unsuccessful attempts to hunt down the mysterious creature, Luther Davis and Mayor Woodrow Fussell (who owned the town theater and admitted early on that he thought it was a hoax) made a desperate attempt to quell the panic and possibly gain some fame. They held up the bobcat Davis had trapped, showcasing it to newspapers and for photographs. The bobcat was slightly larger than a large house cat and, when stretched out, barely reached their waists. Despite its size, they claimed it was the "Beast of Bladenboro" and displayed it for the community. A sign beneath the bobcat proclaimed, "This is the Beast of Bladenboro."

Many were skeptical that such a tiny animal could kill and drag both small and large dogs. Still, life continued in Bladenboro, perhaps because people began to watch their pets and small livestock better. Eventually, the so-called "Vampire Beast" vanished, retreating into the swamps from which it had come. In February 2025, a historical marker was unveiled to honor the "Vampire Beast" and commemorate this dark chapter in local folklore.

North Carolina: Santer and Wampus Cats

Notable Characteristics: The Wampus Cat and the **Bristle-haired Santer Cat** are believed to be two different species. However, during a series of mysterious feline sightings in the early to mid-1900s, the two were often confused, as they share similar qualities as feline-like cryptids associated with fearsome traits.

The Wampus Cat and the Santer are from Appalachian folklore in North Carolina. The Wampus Cat is often depicted as a mystical, cat-like entity, while the Santer is known for its terrifying presence and predatory behavior.

The Wampus Cat The creature is often depicted as a fearsome and elusive entity roaming the wilderness, frequently associated with supernatural occurrences. Its origins are thought to be rooted in Cherokee folklore, where it is described as a hybrid of a mountain lion and a woman. It resembles a large cat, characterized by glowing yellow eyes and the ability to run both upright and on all fours. The creature emits eerie sounds that instill fear in those who encounter it.

The Santer Cat is known to inhabit wooded swamps near small towns and is considered a predator of livestock and pets. Its origins are from stories told by lumberjacks in the 19th and early 20th centuries. This creature has a long body covered in reddish or gray fur, a large bald head with small eyes, long legs, and a distinctive tail with eight hard knots resembling beads.

In September 1890, a police officer shot at what he believed to be a Santer Cat while it chased his dog. The next morning, tracks were found measuring 8 inches long and 4 inches wide. It was reported to have eaten 7 pigs and 15 cows. Although a posse was organized to hunt the creature, it managed to evade capture.

In 1897, the Santer Cat consumed several cats from Roaring River to Wilkesboro, heightening local fears. Despite numerous hunting parties sent to track it down, the creature remained elusive, with only its tracks being discovered.

In February 1899, in Chimney Rock, there were reports of savage growls and a wave of missing pigs, believed to be the work of the Santer Cat. This created such a crisis that children were kept home from school.

Sightings of the Santer have been reported since the late 19th century, indicating that it preys on livestock and pets.

In August 1931, Chief of Police Tom Kerr from Iredell County heard a blood-curdling cry that awakened his household. They went outside to investigate, but it was too dark to see anything.

Reports of the creature persisted into the 1920s and 1930s. Even today, these two beasts are blamed for the disappearance of unattended livestock and pets.

Other Notable North Carolina Cryptids

Carpenter's Knob Bigfoot: There is a 10-foot-tall Bigfoot that has been seen walking on both all fours and two legs, frequently spotted at Carpenter's Knob, affectionately known as Knobby. In the deep winter of 1979, locals around Carpenter's Knob in Cleveland County, North Carolina, reported sightings of a large, apelike creature. One prominent witness, 88-year-old Minnie Cook, described the creature as nearly six feet tall and weighing around 250 pounds. After a creature disturbed her dogs, she reported her encounter.

Moon-Eyed People: The Moon-Eyed People are described in Cherokee folklore, mainly in the Appalachian region, as short, pale-skinned, blue-eyed cave dwellers who could not tolerate daylight and were thus active only at night. One version of their story suggests that they were driven from their homeland by the Creek Nation during a full moon. Their sensitivity to light made them vulnerable, ultimately forcing them to hide underground after losing their territory. Artifacts associated with the Moon-Eyed People include petroglyphs at sites such as Judaculla Rock in North Carolina. Additionally, several stone structures, like the 850-foot stone wall at Fort Mountain State Park in Georgia, are sometimes attributed to these mysterious beings.

North Dakota: Miniwashitu

Notable Characteristics: The Miniwashitu is an unsettling aquatic beast, striking fear into the hearts of all who dare to glimpse it. This creature boasts a wild mane of shaggy red hair that ripples in the water, giving it an almost otherworldly appearance. A single, unblinking eye that seems to pierce through the darkness sits at the center of its forehead. At the same time, a prominent horn juts ominously from above, adding to its sinister allure. It has human-like hands. Its back is lined with a jagged, saw-like spine, each serrated edge reminiscent of a deadly weapon ready to strike.

Folklore suggests that merely laying eyes on the Miniwashitu drives people to the brink of madness. Those who pass this test succumb to some horrible fate soon after.

This fearsome entity lurks in the depths of the Missouri River, where it becomes especially active in the springtime, its massive, thrashing body powerful enough to break the frozen surface of the ice, leaving chaos in its wake.

North Dakota: Taku-He

Notable Characteristics: Taku-He is a large, hairy creature resembling Bigfoot, measuring 7 to 9 feet tall. It inhabits the forests of North Dakota, particularly around the forested areas of the Fort Berthold Indian Reservation. Taku-He has a muscular body covered in dark brown or black fur. Its facial features include a large head with a flat face, small ears, and a prominent brow ridge. At night, its eyes glow red or yellow. Taku-He has relatively short legs compared to its body and large feet, each with five toes. Its long arms extend below its knees, and its large hands are equipped with sharp claws.

The name "Taku-He" translates to "big man" in the Lakota language, highlighting its origins in Native American folklore. Considered omnivorous, Taku-He is a nocturnal hunter that consumes both plant-based foods, like fruits and nuts, as well as meat from deer and livestock.

The Bigfoot Researchers Organization (BFRO) reported an unusually high number of sightings in the Fort Berthold Indian Reservation during the winter of 2004, interviewing several community witnesses. In February 2004, near Highway 22, south of Mandaree, North Dakota, a man discovered a line of large footprints in the snow. These footprints extended for nearly a quarter of a mile and had a 5 to 6-foot stride.

On February 22, 2004, at a trailer park on the edge of New Town, children playing outside saw a large, hairy animal standing on two legs. Screaming in fear, they ran towards the trailer for safety. A neighbor rushed outside to investigate the commotion and witnessed the creature quickly fleeing into the trees.

Later that same evening, another sighting was reported approximately 8 miles south of New Town. On February 24, 2004, two women observed a man-like animal peering at them through a window at night near Highway 22. This location was about 25 miles from the children's initial sighting and 17 miles from the second sighting.

On February 25, two men driving south of Mandaree had to stop when they encountered a large, hairy animal walking on two legs down the middle of the road. The creature quickly entered a ditch and vanished when the car's headlights illuminated the area.

North Dakota: Devil's Lake Sea Serpent

Notable Characteristics: A serpent-like monster, measuring between 20 and 80 feet in length, is said to inhabit Devils Lake in North Dakota. This creature has a serpentine body, a snake-like head, and glowing eyes. It is reportedly large enough to capsize a canoe and has been sighted by several people over the years. The legend of the Devil's Lake Monster is similar to those of other lake monsters found around the world.

Since the 1990s, rising water levels have affected the communities surrounding the lake, contributing to its intriguing reputation. According to local lore, Unktehi is said to cause floods by puffing up its body.

Stories of a monster inhabiting Devils Lake have been passed down for centuries, with accounts from Native American tribes describing a large, serpent-like creature often depicted with alligator-like jaws and glowing red eyes.

Notable reports from the 19th century include descriptions of a creature measuring between 20 and 80 feet long, moving slowly along the lake's surface and creating a visible wake. In 1914, during the time it was Chautauqua at Devils Lake—a summer resort that operated from the 1890s to the 1930s—a man and two women rowing a boat witnessed a sea serpent. The creature raised its head above the water, over two feet long, and sported an alligator-like snout. Its body was estimated to be about 20 feet long. The waves created by the creature nearly capsized the boat, but the man managed to row quickly back to shore, and everyone aboard was unharmed.

In July 1915, several individuals at different locations reported seeing the creature gliding through the lake, seemingly unbothered by the onlookers. E. M. Lewis observed the monster from the Chautauqua train, estimating it to be between 50 and 60 feet long with a body about a foot in diameter. Others, including another couple, also noted its presence near the lake's center. The last reported sighting that day was by Reverend C. L. Wallace, who saw it as he was leaving the area of the lake.

Other Notable North Dakota Cryptids

Mermaid: Lake Sakakawea is a large reservoir in North Dakota, formed by the construction of the Garrison Dam on the Missouri River in 1956. The lake has depths that reach up to 180 feet, providing a habitat for various aquatic life. According to legend, it is also home to the Lake Sakakawea Mermaid, who dwells in its depths while waiting for her lost lover. She is often described as a beautiful figure with magical qualities, characterized by long flowing hair that drapes over her chest and cascades down to her waist. The legend tells of how the mermaid and her lover swam the length of the Missouri River for generations. However, the construction of the Garrison Dam created a barrier that separated them. Residents claim that her sad, longing song can be heard on clear, moonlit nights and that she bestows her light upon the creatures living in her domain.

Thunderbird: The Thunderbird holds a significant place in the cryptids of North Dakota, with its origins deeply embedded in Native American stories. The Thunderbird is a colossal bird known for its impressive wingspan, extending to 70 feet. This creature is commonly associated with the creation of storms and the sound of thunder.

Ohio: Frog Man

Notable Characteristics: The creature possesses unique facial features characterized by the absence of eyebrows and a grayish skin tone. Its mouth is enormous and straight, extending entirely across the width of the face, resembling that of a frog. There are no visible lip muscles present. The head is bald with a ribbed texture, reminiscent of a plastic baby doll, which often gives the appearance of painted hair. Additionally, the upper torso exhibits an asymmetrical design, with elements that do not match.

Loveland, Ohio, a suburb of Cincinnati, offers a charming small-town atmosphere with the conveniences of a larger city.

The area features historic districts, bike trails, bistros, and ice cream shops. The Little Miami River flows through Loveland, with the popular seventy-mile Little Miami State Park bike trail running alongside it, following the old Little Miami Steam Railroad path. In the 1700s, along the Little Miami River, there lived a group of Native Americans known as the Miamis (Mihtohseeniaki, meaning "The People"). They were also referred to as the Twightwee by the nearby Delawares. Here, the legend of the Loveland Frogman is said to begin.

Among these early tribes, a legend was passed down to French settlers about a creature known as the Shawnahooc—a human-like being with wrinkled skin and no nose who lived in the waters. The locals spoke of a group of hunters returning home when encountering this demon-like creature. Despite shooting at it, the creature leaped into the water unharmed.

The creature seemed to stay away for perhaps a couple hundred years. However, it made a return. It was around 4:00 A.M. on May 25, 1955, when a witness named Robert Hunnicutt, a short-order chef at a newly opened restaurant, was driving northeast through Branch Hill (in Symmes Township) on the Loveland-Madeira Pike near Hopewell Road. As he crested a rise and began descending a slight grade, the beam of his headlights illuminated a group of figures who appeared to be kneeling along the right side of the road, with their backs turned to the brush.

His first impression was that the men were praying. Believing it to be strange, Hunnicutt brought his car to a halt and pulled over to the side. As realization washed over him, Hunnicutt was stunned to see that the figures were not human—they stood erect and were only about three and a half feet high.

Hunnicutt got out of the left side of his car, noting that the central figure of the three was holding both hands in the air.

He was brandishing dark chains or rods from which blue-white sparks jumped from hand to hand. All three seemed focused across the road and not at Hunnicutt, as if signaling something in the woods. When Hunnicutt progressed further, the figure's arms lowered, and it appeared to tie whatever it held around its ankles. Suddenly, all three figures turned slightly left and faced him simultaneously. They stared at him with browless eyes; the creatures were grayish in color, with large, straight mouths so elongated that they spanned ultimately across their faces—frog-like, with no apparent lip muscles. Their bald heads were ribbed, almost resembling plastic baby dolls with ridged, painted-on hair. The upper torsos appeared lopsided and mismatched.

Curious, Hunnicutt approached the frog-like creatures near the fender of his car, standing about ten feet away. Then, the figures made an odd but graceful motion that Hunnicutt interpreted as a warning for him to stop. He stood there for a few more minutes before the strangeness of the scene washed over him. Frightened, he jumped back into his car and drove to report the incident to the police.

In a subdivision of Loveland called Loveland Heights, Emily Magnone, and her husband were awakened on a hot summer night by their dog's frantic barking outside. They arose and peered out the windows but saw nothing. However, an overpowering, swampy odor filled their nostrils, forcing them to close the windows despite the heat in the house. The smell seemed to cling to the fabric of the home. The following day, while chatting with a neighbor, Mrs. Magnone learned that the neighbor had also peeked outside the night before and saw the strangest thing—a tiny man covered entirely in leaves and twigs who stood still and stared at her. When Mrs. Magnone turned on the lights, he would disappear, but when they were off, she could make out the faint outline of the little man.

In the summer of 1955, a nineteen-year-old Civil Defense worker, an auxiliary policeman known only as C.F. for anonymity, was driving a civil defense truck across a bridge when, for a mere ten seconds, he caught sight of what he described warily as "four more-or-less human-looking little men about three feet high who were moving oddly under the bridge, and there was a terrible smell about the place."

More recently, in 2020, a group of friends reported seeing a creature near the Little Miami River. It stood about four feet tall with webbed hands and feet along the scenic bike path in Loveland.

Ohio: Bigfoot

Notable Characteristics: Bigfoot sightings have been reported throughout Ohio, primarily due to the abundance of forests and its many populated areas that utilize parks and recreational spaces. In southern Ohio, Bigfoot is often called the "Grassman" due to the greenish hue of its fur, which many believe serves as camouflage among the abundant moss-covered rocks in the region. Bigfoot in Ohio is typically described as a large, hairy creature with dark fur, standing seven to eight feet tall. It has a huge torso, big muscular arms that extend down to its knees, and a head set on its shoulders with no visible neck. Its eyes are reddish.

Salt Fork Region: In eastern Ohio, Guernsey County features rolling farmland and forests, along with one of the state's largest parks, Salt Fork State Park, which spans 17,229 acres. The Salt Fork region, particularly within Salt Fork State Park, is known for its notable history of alleged Bigfoot sightings. Since the mid-1980s, there have been over 36 reported sightings, making the park a prominent location for Bigfoot enthusiasts. It has become a hub for Bigfoot research and events, including conferences and guided night hikes that aim to investigate these claims further.

Some key locations within the Salt Fork Region and State Park where sightings have been reported include:

Morgan's Knob at Salt Fork Park: This trail winds through a dense pine forest and then along a road that was once part of a farming community. While walking this trail, three children spotted a Bigfoot stalking a deer.

Bigfoot Ridge at Salt Fork Park: Two campers, a male and a female, were awakened at Bigfoot Ridge Primitive Campground by the sound of something large moving around their tent, along with what seemed like grass being yanked from the ground. The woman opened the tent and stepped outside with her flashlight. When she shone the light into the tall grass, she spotted two yellow, golf ball-sized eyes that quickly turned and vanished into the woods. The male camper heard the footsteps as well. Both were so frightened by the incident that they packed up their camp, loaded it into the vehicle, and left at 2 a.m.

Shadbush Trail at Salt Fork Park: The Shadbush Trail stretches approximately 2 miles from the lodge to the campground. I have observed footprints and recorded howls along this trail, which winds through the woods and runs parallel to the lake for a significant distance.

I-77: I-77 is a four-lane highway that runs alongside part of Salt Fork State Park. Travelers on this route have reported unusual sights. One night in 2003, under a bright moon, a motorist driving along the highway thought he saw a dead bear lying on the road. As he got closer, he realized it was not a roadkill but a humanoid-shaped creature crouching down with its head low as if trying to hide from view. Confused, he put the car in reverse to get a better look. To his astonishment, the creature stood straight, stepped over a guardrail, and walked into the woods. The creature had long, brownish gray hair, elongated arms, and no ears. The driver estimated its size to be around six and a half feet tall and about 500 pounds. It also emitted a strong odor reminiscent of a skunk and dead fish.

Hocking Hills: In the Hocking Hills Region, a vast forested area is located in both Hocking and Vinton Counties, which are well known for Bigfoot sightings.

Some key locations within the Hocking Hills Region where sightings have been reported include:

Hocking Hills State Park Rose Lake: At night, a father and son were fishing on the shore of Rose Lake when they spotted a giant, dark, hairy creature kneeling to drink from the lake.

Vinton County Parks Road to Moonville Tunnel: Along the Hope-Moonville Road, a couple drove at night toward Moonville Tunnel, an area known for its haunting reputation. The man paused the vehicle to use the restroom and stood behind the car. With the headlights still illuminating the road, he saw a Bigfoot-like creature standing directly in front of the car, bathed in the headlights. He quickly turned and fled to the vehicle, getting inside to ask his girlfriend if she had seen what he had seen. To his surprise, she confirmed that she had.

In the same area, I offer night hikes from the ghost town of Moonville to a very remote section of Zaleski State Forest.

It is along a segment of old railway owned by the Vinton County Park District and managed by the Moonville Rail Trail Association. This trail is also used by horseback riders. The night before each hike, I walk the 1.5 miles of the out-and-back trail we will take the following evening, clearing away any mounds of manure to ensure a clear path. This is important because it can be challenging to see while guiding groups through the trail at night, and hikers tend to get a bit irate when they step in six inches of poop up to their ankles.

While hiking after dark with my dog Harley one night, I stopped to watch some beavers move sticks near a section of the trail with a creek on one side and a pond on the other. As I stood there, I noticed Harley's hackles had risen, and she was nudging my leg with her nose in warning. Harley has been backpacking with me in Bear Country and is usually unfazed when we encounter a bear on the trail or when one visits our tent at night. So, I was concerned when I saw her acting spooked. I took a deep breath and heard a deep, guttural growl like a lion's. I froze and then began carefully moving sideways away from the sound, treating it like a bear. As I did, I noticed two huge eyes reflecting red light from the moon, turning to follow my movement. The growl continued, suggesting that whatever was out there—definitely not a coyote or bobcat, as it had a musky odor resembling a damp rag combined with the scents of mink and skunk—was observing my every move until the sound slowly faded.

The troubling part was that I had moved in the opposite direction of my vehicle! I continued down the trail, knowing I would eventually have to return the same way. I did, albeit with much uneasiness. Fortunately, whatever had been there had vanished. The next day, I returned to the area in daylight and discovered an 8 or 9-foot drop-off where those eyes had stared at me. Whatever it was had to be at least that tall!

Ohio: Peninsula Python

Notable Characteristics: The Peninsula Python slithered into northern Ohio's Cuyahoga Valley National Park during the summer of 1944. Witnesses described it as 15 to 19 feet long, with dark coloration and brownish blotches.

The sightings began on June 8, 1944, when Clarence Mitchell noticed an enormous snake slithering through his cornfield near Everett Swamp, just a few miles from the town of Peninsula. For several days, his dogs had been unsettled. They refused to venture into the nearby swampy area, which raised his suspicion about what was disturbing them.

The sound of the dogs barking ultimately alerted him to the snake's presence. He later told a reporter from the Cleveland Press, "I don't know what made me look up, but there, about fifteen paces away, was the biggest snake I had ever seen, sliding along slowly and easily in plain sight on the bare ground. I just stood quietly, not wanting to attract attention. It felt like I watched it for ten minutes. The snake slid into the river, swam across, and climbed out on the other side. It was as thick as my thigh and every bit of fifteen feet long—more like eighteen—sort of brownish with spots. I went over and examined the track it left behind. It looked like someone had rolled a spare tire across my field."

Just a day later, a woman named Missus Vaughn witnessed the large serpent devouring one of her chickens whole. The snake was so full after the meal that it had to climb over the fence instead of crawling underneath it. These accounts prompted a series of reports from other residents in the area, all claiming to have seen this enormous snake. In response, a posse was formed to hunt it down, and local newspapers began to cover the story. Other witnesses, such as Pauline Hopko, recounted experiences in which the snake frightened livestock, resulting in chaotic farm scenes.

Despite many reported sightings and attempts to capture or locate the creature, no definitive evidence has ever been found. The last known sighting occurred around August 1, 1944, after which the snake seemingly vanished. Speculation emerged about how this tropical python ended up in Ohio; one theory suggested that it escaped from a circus truck that had crashed in a local cemetery.

Other Notable Ohio Cryptids

Minerva Monster: Minerva, Ohio, is a small town known for Bigfoot sightings in the 1970s, primarily reported by the Cayton family. In August 1978, the family encountered a large, hairy creature around 7 feet tall with dark fur. The creature was reported multiple times on the Cayton property, drawing media attention and local law enforcement investigations. While some residents claim to still see the creature, it no longer frightens them, and the community seems to coexist with it.

Defiance Dogman: In the summer of 1972, a strange, werewolf-like creature was spotted near the train depot in Defiance. It was 7 to 8 feet tall, very hairy, with fangs and tattered clothes. Initially, the police suspected it was a robber. Chief Breckler remarked, "Very hairy is the first description given by each person who encountered the creature. We don't think it is a prank. He's approaching people with a club in his hand." Two brakemen, Tom Jones and Ted Davis, saw the creature moving side to side like a caveman. Davis recalled, "I looked up and saw these huge, hairy feet. He was standing there with a large stick, then took off for the woods." Reports increased, including one from a woman whose doorknob rattled as something tried to enter her home, and a grocery employee who saw the creature in headlights at 4 a.m. It vanished as quickly as it appeared.

Melonheads: In the 1950s, Dr. Crowe lived in a secluded area near Kirtland, caring for orphans with hydrocephalus. Instead of healing them, he performed cruel experiments that left the children deformed and mentally unstable. Many died, but some survived. One night, the remaining children turned on him and killed him before fleeing into the woods, where they still live today.

Charles Mill Lake Monster: Charles Mill Lake is a reservoir in central Ohio, less than eight miles from Mansfield. It is infamous for the legend of the Green-Eyed Monster, a tale that began on March 26, 1959. On that day, three teenagers—Denny Patterson (16), Wayne Armstrong (16), and Michael Lane (14)—decided to explore the misty lake. After parking behind the boathouse, they noticed a log that suddenly stood upright. Lane later described the creature, saying, "The thing was about seven feet tall, had no arms, two webbed feet, and two green eyes." As the strange thing approached them, the driver panicked and struggled to turn the car around while the creature was only fifteen feet away. Fortunately, they managed to escape the scene.

Oklahoma: Giant Octopus

Notable Characteristics: This creature is described as resembling a traditional octopus but is significantly larger, roughly the size of a horse. It is characterized by its eight-foot-long tentacles, bulbous eyes, leathery red-brown skin, and dome-shaped head.

The Oklahoma Octopus is a notable cryptid linked to three specific lakes in the state: Lake Thunderbird, Lake Oologah, and Lake Tenkiller. Like many misunderstood creatures that appear frightful and ugly, the Oklahoma Octopus has been blamed for several drowning incidents reported in these lakes to explain accidents. However, octopuses are generally not aggressive towards humans; instead, they are curious and intelligent animals. While scientists assert that there are no freshwater octopuses, multiple octopuses have been discovered in the Blackwater River in West Virginia, which is far from the ocean.

Oklahoma: Abominable Chicken Man

Notable Characteristics: The cryptid is described as a large, approximately 6-foot-tall upright primate that resembles a gorilla. It has a muscular build and is covered in dark fur. This creature is known for walking on two legs, similar to a human, which contributes to its distinct appearance in reported sightings.

El Reno is a city situated in central Oklahoma, around 25 miles west of Oklahoma City, making it a suburban area of that city. It has a rural atmosphere and is located along Historic Route 66, surrounded by agricultural land, including wheat and cotton fields. In the 1960s and 1970s, a Bigfoot-like creature appeared to those living in the region.

The slow-moving North Canadian River sometimes floods through El Reno, often flanked by red mud flats and quicksand. On November 13, 1970, along this waterway, two raccoon hunters had a remarkable encounter with Sasquatch on a full moon night. The hunters were parked on the south riverbank, east of the Foreman Road bridge, when one noticed a large shadow behind a fallen tree on the snow-covered ground. Upon closer inspection, he realized that what he initially thought were two reflectors nailed to the tree trunk were actually two blinking red eyes, followed by a shadowy movement.

Suddenly, a tall figure resembling a gorilla dashed along the riverbank, startling both men. The man recounted his encounter with the North American Wood Ape Conservancy (NAWAC), a federally recognized nonprofit organization focused on investigating and promoting the scientific recognition and conservation of the Wood Ape, "About that time, the shadow slid off the bank down towards the riverbed," the witness said. "It sounded like something as big as an ice box had been rolled into the river. We watched as a tall, upright animal ran in a zig zag pattern from sand bar to sand bar towards the west. We just stood there with our jaws hanging open."

In December of 1970, a farmer tending to his chickens discovered that the door to his coop had been ripped off its hinges. The small building's door and walls exhibited huge handprints measuring 7 inches by 5 inches. The farmer contacted the state game ranger, who sent the door to the Oklahoma City Zoo for analysis.

Zoo Director Lawrence Curtis examined the prints and stated that they resembled a primate's; notably, the thumb appeared twisted or deformed, suggesting some sort of injury.

He added, "It resembles a gorilla, but it's more like a man. It looks like whatever made the prints was walking on all fours. Some footprints were also found on the ground outside. Whatever it was, it was barefoot. Barefoot in December!" Around the same time, another man in Stillwater also reported finding strange footprints.

Over the years, occasional reports of similar creatures have occurred in the surrounding areas. In September 2002, wildlife biologists setting up a motion-sensitive camera in El Reno captured footage of a large, black creature running on two legs through the woods.

Oklahoma: Boggy Bottom Monster

Notable Characteristics: Witness accounts of this creature reveal various descriptions, but several characteristics are commonly noted. Generally, it is reported to stand between 7 to 9 feet tall, possessing a large, muscular build and broad shoulders. The creature is typically described as covered in dark, shaggy hair, with some reports indicating a reddish-brown fur color. Additionally, it is characterized by a flat face, large eyes, and the absence of a prominent brow ridge.

The towns of Battiest, Honobia, Octavia, and Smithville are located near each other in the southeastern part of Oklahoma. The Kiamichi Mountains, a subrange of the Ouachita Mountains, provide a scenic backdrop for these communities.

They share a diverse landscape characterized by hills, valleys, rivers, and dense forests. This region includes various state parks that support a rich ecosystem. Additionally, the hardwood and pine forests in the area provide habitats for numerous wildlife species, leading us to another common element among these towns—the Boggy Bottom Monster.

In the early 2000s, Charles Benton went on a turkey hunting trip near Broken Bow, Oklahoma. As dusk approached, he heard strange noises coming from behind him. The sounds resembled powerful moaning and grunting, resonating through his chest. Intrigued yet apprehensive, he decided to investigate the source of the commotion. He spotted a large creature bent over in a creek bottom when he looked around. The beast then stood up and turned its torso toward him, making eye contact. Benton described the being as dark reddish-brown in color, nearly eight feet tall, with a broad forehead and a muscular build. The sight disturbed him so greatly that he exited the scene, leaving behind all his hunting equipment and gear.

A lifelong resident of Honobia had several encounters with what he believed to be multiple Bigfoot creatures in the late 1990s and early 2000s. One incident involved a creature peering through his home window, which terrified his three-year-old daughter. The family also heard loud vocalizations.

Linda Martin, who ran Clancy's Country Store in Honobia, found large footprints measuring 15 inches long and 7 inches wide and heard unusual sounds resembling elk calls.

In June 2009, a family vacationing near Battiest discovered a large human-like footprint while walking along a dirt road next to their cabin by the Glover River. The footprint had five distinct toe impressions and was estimated to be around sixteen inches long. Later that evening, the family reported hearing howls resembling those attributed to Sasquatch.

On January 4, 2012, a witness driving near Octavia spotted a large silhouette next to a power line pole while traveling on Highway 259. The witness described the figure as having clearly defined shoulders and noted that it was too large to be a person or a bear. When the creature was seen, it ducked into the woods. This sighting occurred during dusk in a pine forest environment known for its dense vegetation, which is conducive to concealing such creatures.

The Kiamichi Mountains region has a long history of Bigfoot sightings. Since 1971, the North American Wood Ape Conservancy and the Bigfoot Field Researchers Organization have documented numerous testimonials from this area. The stories about Bigfoot continue to thrive within the community as residents share accounts of personal encounters with the Boggy Bottom Monster that have been passed down through generations.

Other Notable Oklahoma Cryptids

Green Hill Monster: In the early 1970s, two high school football players, identified only by their initials E.S. and E.N., claimed to have encountered the "Green Hill Monster" on a back road called Green Hill Road in Talihina, Oklahoma. E.S. was over 6 feet 3 inches tall and weighed approximately 245 pounds. He reported that the creature grabbed him while he was relieving himself in a wooded area. In shock, he fled to the truck and refused to leave. E.N. described the creature as a large, hairy animal. Following the incident, students and a teacher drove to Green Hill Road to investigate. The local police and highway patrol were alerted due to the many vehicles heading out of town. Officers investigated the area but did not confirm or deny the presence of any creature. They advised the students to vacate the area for safety reasons.

Tuttle Bottoms Monster: There is a Bigfoot in Muddy Boggy Creek near Caney and Tushka (about 90 miles from the Boggy Bottoms Monster near Battiest, Honobia, Octavia, and Smithville). On June 13, 1992, three boys saw a form walking along a country road near a watermelon patch at night. They thought it was a large man standing against a tree. A huge, red-brown, hairy beast stepped out and growled, causing the boys to flee in fear. On July 15, 2006, an 8-foot monster scared two children playing in the water close to Caney.

Boar Man: This cryptid is described by witnesses as a middle-aged male with a strong build, standing between 6 to 8 feet tall. He has large eyes and is said to carry boar tusks, which he allegedly uses to attack his victims. Some accounts suggest that he may be able to transform into a boar or wear the skin of one. Some legends portray him as a man with boar tusks, often depicted wearing a cap or the skin of a boar. Additionally, some stories suggest that he can change between human and boar forms. Sightings of Boar Man date back to the 1920s, with reports primarily originating from the Wichita Mountains Wildlife Refuge.

Elk Man: The muscular Elk Man stands upright and resembles a human but has distinct elk-like features, including antlers and a deer-like head. One notable sighting occurred in early spring 2012 when a group encountered this unexpected creature in the Wichita Mountains while photographing the night sky. They observed that wild animals, such as boars, elk, and bison, were behaving erratically and rushing past them, suggesting they were fleeing from something. Witnesses reported hearing a piercing screech likened to a banshee's wail.

Oregon: Wallowa Lake Monster

Notable Characteristics: The creature is reported to be between 8 and 20 feet long and possesses a distinctive hump-shaped body. Various sightings have characterized it as having a large head resembling a hippopotamus and a long neck.

Wallowa Lake is a glacial lake in Northeast Oregon. It is famous for its crystal-clear, deep blue waters surrounded by the stunning Wallowa Mountains. It is a gateway to the Eagle Cap Wilderness Area and Wallowa Lake State Park. The Wallowa band of the Nez Perce tribe originally inhabited the area around Wallowa Lake. However, conflicts with miners and other trespassers forced them to leave their ancestral land.

In Nez Perce folklore, the legend of the Wallowa Lake Monster has deep roots, featuring tales of a massive serpent-like creature intertwined with the story of young lovers from rival tribes. According to the legend, during a battle between the Nez Perce and the Blackfeet tribes, Tlesca, the son of the Blackfeet chief, fell in love with Wahluna, the daughter of the Nez Perce chief. One night, while they were secretly meeting in a canoe on the lake, they were attacked and killed by a monster from the depths, escalating tensions between their tribes. This tragic event not only led to their deaths but also intensified hostilities between the two groups.

In November of 1885, a prospector rowing a small skiff across the lake reported seeing a creature raise its head and neck out of the water, reaching heights of 10 to 12 feet. Upon noticing the boat, the creature bellowed like a cow before diving back beneath the surface. It later reemerged in the darkness, much closer, with a head that resembled a hippopotamus.

In 1932, two residents fishing on the lake observed a creature longer than their boat. Irene Wiggins, who lived near Wallowa Lake from 1945 to 1983, reported multiple sightings of the monster, describing it as having a large black body and a head like that of a hog.

In 1950, three individuals reported seeing two creatures feeding on fish—one measuring about 16 feet long and the other about 8 feet long. Then, in 1978, witnesses observed hump-like protrusions on the surface, followed by an elongated, snake-like figure measuring 20 feet long swimming in circles.

Oregon: Colossal Claude

Notable Characteristics: A sizeable serpentine creature resembling a horse or camel with a long neck and thick body inhabits the waters around the Columbia River in Oregon and Washington. This beast gained notoriety in the 1930s after a series of sightings that captivated locals and visitors.

The first sighting of the creature occurred on or just after March 15, 1934, when the crew of the lightship Rose reported observing a 40-foot-long creature with an 8-foot neck swimming near their vessel.

In June 1937, Captain Charles Graham of the fishing trawler Viv reported another sighting, describing the creature as a "long, hairy, tan-colored" entity that was 40 feet long and had a waist diameter of four feet.

A notable account came from a couple named White, who were visiting Devil's Churn, a chasm in the basalt cliffs of Cape Perpetua, Oregon. They described the creature as vast and hairy, resembling an aquatic giraffe, with its neck and maned head protruding about 15 feet above the water. Their estimation placed its overall length at around 55 feet.

On April 13, 1939, another sighting occurred when Captain Chris Anderson and his crew aboard the fishing boat Argo encountered what they believed to be Colossal Claude just off the Columbia River. Anderson reported that the creature passed within ten feet of their boat. He described it as having the head of a camel, coarse gray fur, and glassy eyes. One crew member attempted to poke it with a boat hook, but Anderson stopped him out of fear for their safety.

Other Notable Oregon Cryptids

Gumberoo: This fearsome creature is described as a giant bear with sharp teeth, leathery skin, and immune to bullets. It is said to live in hollowed-out trees.

Bigfoot: Oregon has a significant number of reported Bigfoot sightings over the years. According to the Bigfoot Field Researchers Organization (BFRO), there are over 258 credible accounts of sightings and encounters across the state. Heather Winkler described one such case in MarionTalk, a community social network in Marion County, Oregon. In 1970, a woman named Chloe was visiting her father at a logging camp east of Detroit Lake. One night, she was awakened by strange noises outside her cabin. When she opened the door, she saw a Sasquatch standing near an open cooler, holding a large piece of meat under its arm. The two stared at each other until Chloe screamed, which caused the creature to retreat. Later, men at the camp found footprints measuring 14 inches long. It appeared that the Sasquatch had carefully chosen a specific piece of meat, as the contents of the freezer were left relatively undisturbed, unlike the ransacked mess typically left by bears.

Pennsylvania: Squonk

Notable Characteristics: The Squonk is a cryptid from the lumbermen, specifically from William T. Cox's book, "Fearsome Creatures of the Lumberwoods: With a Few Desert and Mountain Beasts." Scientifically known as "Lacrimacorpus Dissolvent," which translates to "body dissolves into tears," the pig-like Squonk's flesh is covered with warts and moles, giving it a perpetually sad appearance.

It is occasionally spotted wandering the hemlock forests of Pennsylvania, primarily during twilight and dusk, as it prefers to avoid seeing its reflection in puddles and ponds, which makes it unhappy.

A squonk can be distinguished from wild pigs by its constant weeping and the tear-stained trail it leaves behind, which can be followed even by the most amateur hunter. However, if frightened, the Squonk will dissolve into a puddle of tears, making it nearly impossible to capture. Hikers have often heard its crying from the woods, but they find nothing when searching for the source.

Pennsylvania: Presque Isle Storm Hag

Notable Characteristics: She exhibits green skin and sharp nails, and her haunting song indisputably lures unsuspecting sailors.

Presque Isle State Park is a sandy peninsula that extends into Lake Erie, located near Erie, Pennsylvania. Lake Erie is known for its unpredictable waves, shifting sandbars, and storms, which have led to an estimated 500 to 3,000 shipwrecks along its coast. Early explorers used the eastern bay of Presque Isle as a refuge from storms, although many did not escape unharmed. The Lake Erie Quadrangle, where Presque Isle is situated, is believed to contain more shipwrecks than the Bermuda Triangle.

According to legend, a fearsome creature known as the Storm Hag resides at the bottom of Lake Erie. She has green skin, sharp nails, and a haunting song that lures unsuspecting sailors before summoning storms to sink their boats. One story recounts an incident in 1782 when a ship was caught in a storm. The captain sought shelter near Presque Isle but hesitated to navigate the dangerous shallows. Just as the storm seemed to relent, they heard the Storm Hag's enchanting song and dark clouds returned. In a violent storm, she struck, dragging the ship and its crew to the depths of the lake.

If you walk along the beach, you might find tiny white crystals, said to be the tears of those left behind. It is believed that holding one of these crystals during a storm may protect you from the Storm Hag's wrath.

Pennsylvania: Albatwitch

Notable Characteristics: The Albatwitch is a cryptid described as a 3 to 4-foot-tall hairy ape-man that resides in the Chickies Rock area near the Susquehanna River in Lancaster County, Pennsylvania. This creature resembles a smaller version of Bigfoot, characterized by its fur-covered body and distinctive yellow eyes. Notably, the Albatwitch has a longer neck and slimmer proportions, giving it a more human-like appearance than Bigfoot.

The name "Albatwitch" translates to "Apple Snitch" in Pennsylvania Dutch, reflecting its reputed habit of stealing apples from picnickers. Sightings of the Albatwitch date back to the Susquehannock, who depicted images resembling the Albatwitch on their war shields.

The Algonquin also spoke of a small hairy hominid known as Megumoowesoos. Many witnesses claim to have seen the creature lurking in trees or darting through the woods near Chickies Rock, a popular lookout point.

Witness accounts often describe the creature as shy yet mischievous. Legend has it that this small furry being terrorized picnickers at Chickies Rock in the 1800s by snatching their apples and pelting the cores back at them. The most recent notable sighting occurred on April 13, 2024, at the Lancaster Conservancy's Fishing Creek Nature Preserve. A witness recounted encountering a stick-thin creature, resembling a monkey, in his car headlights when he stopped to relieve himself by the road. The beast had a distinct wet dog odor, peeked behind a tree, and made strange noises.

When Rick Fisher, an author and researcher, investigated the sighting at Fishing Creek Nature Preserve, he discovered only small depressions that resembled footprints. However, Fisher had previously encountered what he later identified as an Albatwitch in 2002 while driving on Route 23 outside Marietta. He observed a stick-thin figure, the size of a child and covered in hair, walking in the road before it vanished upon closer inspection.

Other Notable Pennsylvania Cryptids

Giwoggle: The Giwoggle is described as a six-foot-tall, wolf-like creature that walks on its hind legs, which have hooves, and has bird claws for hands. Its origins trace back to local witchcraft lore from 1870. Sightings of the Giwoggle are rare, suggesting that it may be a reclusive creature. Since August 2023, reports have emerged from Clearfield County, where witnesses claim to have seen bipedal wolves roaming the forests. It is believed that the Giwoggle was conjured by witches in the 1800s to harass farmers who offended them. Encounters with the Giwoggle typically involve disturbances such as damaged crops and spooked livestock and horses.

Potter Nondescript: In April 1897, a strange creature was spotted in Potter County. A fisherman on Nelson Run witnessed the creature walking upright on two legs, covered in hair and having a hairy head with tusks. The fisherman reported that it was screaming and beating its chest. He quickly fled on his horse, and the creature chased him briefly before stopping. Another witness, William Butler of Denton Hill, described the creature as six feet tall, with an excessively hairy head and tusks measuring six to seven inches long. Butler claimed to have seen the beast eating a groundhog before it noticed him and let out a roar. This surprised him, and he quickly ran away with the creature chasing him for a short distance.

Rhode Island: Glocester Ghoul

Notable Characteristics: The cryptid's behavior resembles that of a hellhound, characterized by its fiery eyes and dark wings, similar to that of a bat. It features spiral ram horns and has a body covered in scales that produce a rattling sound.

The Glocester Ghoul inhabits the woods and swamps of Glocester, Rhode Island. This small town in the northwestern part of the state has become associated with various tales of supernatural encounters, particularly those involving this mysterious beast. One of the first sightings was in 1839 when Albert Hicks, an infamous pirate, and three companions were digging for buried treasure on the Paige Farm believed to belong to Captain Kidd.

While shoveling away, they encountered a creature with fiery eyes, dark wings resembling those of a bat, spiral ram horns, and scales that rattled. It frightened them so badly they did not return to find the treasure.

In 1896, Neil Hopkins saw a creature much like the one Hicks saw while walking home from work. It was the size of an elephant, rattled like metal chain armor, and had hot breath. Some think the Glocester Ghoul was a hellhound guarding Captain Kidd's treasure.

Rhode Island: Mercy Brown, Vampire

Notable Characteristics: When Mercy Brown was alive and as her illness progressed, she suffered severe weight loss and became pale, appearing ghostlike, as if drained by a vampire. Despite this, her cheeks remained flushed and her lips full and rosy. It was believed she contracted the disease from a vampire that had fed on her. After death, Mercy Brown was exhumed on March 17, 1892. Her remarkably well-preserved body contradicted expectations of decomposition, fueling folklore beliefs that vampires do not decay like ordinary corpses. Her skin was flush and lifelike, which made her appear undead. At the autopsy, it was noted blood was still present in Mercy's heart, which, to those in the town, meant that she was feeding on the living, as vampires were depicted as consuming human blood and draining the life force.

The Mercy Brown vampire incident is a historical event that occurred in Exeter, Rhode Island, in 1892. It is one of the most well-documented cases of exhumation and ritualistic practices aimed at combating what was believed to be vampirism. This incident arose during a widespread panic regarding vampires in New England.

George and Mary Brown's family had been living a quiet life in the rural New England town of Exeter until they faced a tragic series of deaths attributed to consumption, a disease caused by bacteria that attack the lungs. The victims experienced labored breathing and a persistent cough. They appeared pale and gaunt, with rosy cheeks and a feverish glow. For most, this illness ultimately resulted in death.

Mary died first in 1883, followed by her daughter Mary Olive in 1884, who lived as a 20-year-old dressmaker. By 1892, 19-year-old Mercy (Lena) and her 24-year-old brother Edwin had contracted the disease. Edwin was sent to Colorado's mineral springs, and while he was away, Mercy died on January 17, 1892. Upon returning from his trip with his wife, Hortense, he suffered a relapse.

As Edwin's health worsened, local superstition led neighbors to believe that one of the dead family members was a vampire responsible for his illness. It did not help that passersby declared seeing already-dead Mercy roaming about the cemetery and through fields. In delirium, Edwin announced that his sister was sitting on his chest, suffocating him. On March 17, 1892, George Brown, under pressure from the community, consented to exhume the corpses of his dead family members. The town marched to the graveyard, eager to find the truth. The exhumation was conducted by local villagers, a doctor, and a newspaper reporter. Both Mary and Mary Olive revealed typical signs of decomposition.

Yet, when they examined Mercy's body—buried for two months—her corpse was well-preserved, and her hair and nails appeared to have grown. They were also shocked to find blood still present in her heart. This extraordinary state of decomposition, or lack of it, led the townspeople to conclude that Mercy was indeed a vampire. Her undead corpse was responsible for Edwin's illness.

The town fell into a vampire hysteria and performed a ritual in line with contemporary folklore. Mercy's heart and liver were removed, charred on a rock, and mixed the ashes with water to create a tonic for Edwin to ingest. Unfortunately, despite these efforts, Edwin succumbed to consumption just two months later. What remained of Mercy's body was buried again in Exeter's Baptist Church cemetery.

Apparently, digging up a grave and tearing the heart and liver from the corpse for a family member to dine upon is quite disturbing to the soul of the dead. After reburial, a glowing blue orb of light occasionally hovers above the headstone of Mercy Brown.

Other Notable Rhode Island Cryptids

Big Rhodey: A creature similar to Bigfoot, characterized by its large size, hairy exterior, and ape-like features, which include a sloped forehead and brownish fur. It walks upright but has a slightly hunched posture. Carl Johnson, the founder of Big Rhodey Research Project, has gathered evidence of this creature, including oversized human-like footprints and clumps of unidentified animal hair found in remote areas of Rhode Island. The most compelling evidence Johnson's team presents is a video that captures a figure moving behind a tree, filmed during an expedition in Exeter. There have been reports of Big Rhodey across Rhode Island in the rural areas of Cumberland, West Greenwich, and Exeter. Most sightings involve a fleeting glimpse of a figure in dark, wooded settings.

Giant Octopus: A mariner named Old Stormalong once sailed the Atlantic Ocean. One day, a large wave caused his ship's anchor to become lodged at the bottom of the sea. Stormalong jumped off the side of the boat. He plunged into the dark depths, where he encountered a giant octopus playfully grasping the anchor with its eight arms and pulling it to the ocean floor. This encounter escalated into an arm-wrestling match between Stormalong and the octopus. Ultimately, Stormalong emerged victorious, claiming he had tied up the octopus's arms in knots before bringing the anchor back aboard his ship.

South Carolina: Lizard Man of Scape Ore Swamp

Notable Characteristics: The Lizard Man of Scape Ore Swamp is a large, humanoid lizard standing roughly 7 feet tall. It has green, scaly skin and long claws on its three fingers. The creature is often depicted as having searing red eyes, which adds to its menacing appearance.

Scape Ore Swamp is a misty and dense wetland in South Carolina's Congaree Sand Hills region. It is known for humid temperatures, low-lying areas filled with cypress trees and bamboo, towering Black Pines overhead, and dark, slow-moving waters below.

Running through this landscape is a lonely stretch of cracked pavement known as Browntown Road, which is often cloaked in the eerie shadows of countless trees when illuminated by dim headlights at night. It is not a place where anyone wants to change a flat tire during the early morning hours, shrouded in mist and darkness. However, one teen did so with nightmarish results.

In June 1988, a notable sighting of a lizard-like creature occurred when 17-year-old Christopher Davis experienced a terrifying encounter. After finishing a night shift at a local fast-food restaurant, he drove home along Browntown Road around 2 a.m. when he got a flat tire. After fixing the tire, he glanced up and saw a frightening creature approaching him. He described it as "green, wet-like, about 7 feet tall, with three fingers, red eyes, and lizard-like skin with snakelike scales."

Davis quickly got back in his car and tried to speed away, but the creature soon climbed on top of the vehicle. He hit the brakes, causing the beast to roll off the car, which gave him enough time to escape. "I wasn't drinking, and I know what I saw," Davis told reporter with The Item Newspaper. "I had just put the tire in the trunk when I saw this thing coming from the trees about 50 yards away, kicking up dust as it ran."

He recounted how the creature clutched the car door as he sped off. When he reached 40 miles per hour, he noticed it had caught up with him. "I looked in the rear-view mirror and saw something. Then I heard a crash on the roof." Thankfully, the soft-spoken teen escaped unharmed, with only a scratch on his fender.

Tom and Mary Waye owned a Ford that was damaged one night while they slept. Its molding was torn, the sidewalls were indented, and the hood ornament was broken. Newspapers picked up the story, and cars lined up along Browntown Road, curiously searching for the creature.

However, it escaped back into the unknown.

The curious eventually left, but over the years following these initial reports, there have been sporadic sightings of the Lizard Man along this lonesome stretch of road. Investigations in the area uncovered footprints surrounding local homes, lending further credibility to these claims. The Lizard Man is noted for its aggressive behavior towards vehicles, with reports indicating instances of mirror removal and damage to car roofs. The combination of eyewitness accounts and physical evidence continues to captivate public interest in this mysterious creature.

South Carolina: Boo Hag

Notable Characteristics: The Boo Hag is a vampiric spirit preying on the essence of the victims to sustain themselves, typically described as having a grotesque appearance, which may include features such as glowing eyes and unkempt hair.

The Boo Hag is a creature commonly represented as a winged witch with distinctive supernatural capabilities. One of its most notable traits is the ability to shed its skin and fly at night. The Boo Hag is often associated with malevolent practices, particularly the act of sitting on the chests of unsuspecting, sleeping individuals. This behavior is believed to enable the creature to drain the life force or breath of its victims, often leading to feelings of fatigue or illness upon waking.

In its true form, the Boo Hag lacks skin. This characteristic highlights its monstrous nature and sets it apart from other supernatural entities, such as vampires. Unlike vampires that primarily consume blood, Boo Hags are thought to sustain themselves by drawing breath from those they target. Many people report experiences with a creature known as the Boo Hag. These accounts often describe feelings of paralysis during sleep or sudden awakenings accompanied by a sensation of being weighed down by an unseen force. These symptoms resemble those of sleep paralysis but are culturally attributed to the presence of a Boo Hag.

To ward off Boo Hags, it is recommended to use indigo blue, commonly painted on doors. Hoodoo practitioners note that a Boo Hag can be easily distracted. Victims of this creature can surround their beds, doors, and windows with salt. Additionally, placing a broom with many bristles at the foot of the bed can help; the Boo Hag will become preoccupied with counting each bristle. Since this task cannot be completed by dawn, the sunlight will expose the witch in the morning, causing her to perish.

The legend of the Boo Hag is closely linked to the history and experiences of enslaved Africans who were brought to America. This belief system merges elements from African spiritual traditions with local stories and folklore, resulting in a unique cultural perspective. The Gullah people, descendants of these enslaved individuals, have preserved many tales about Boo Hags and other supernatural beings. Jacob Stroyer, an enslaved person who documented his experiences in South Carolina during the 19th century, offers insight into how these beliefs were circulated among enslaved populations. Stroyer noted that hags were considered ordinary people who transformed into witches at night, capable of riding humans like horses while they slept.

South Carolina: Third Eye Man

Notable Characteristics: An odd man-like entity dressed in a silver outfit with a third eye in the middle of his forehead.

Beneath the University of South Carolina campus are tunnels constructed from arched brick and stone dating back to the 1800s. Many of the areas have murky, ankle-deep drainage water covering the floor. The identity of the builders remains a mystery. Local theories regarding their original purpose include serving as passages for canal shipments, functioning as secret routes for the Underground Railroad, or acting as escape routes during the Civil War. Today, these tunnels serve as a network of service pathways. Some believe it is the lair of a strange creature.

The first recorded sighting of the creature took place on November 12, 1949. A university student named Christopher Nichols and another student reported seeing a strange man dressed in bright silver entering a sewer portal near Longstreet Theatre. At approximately 10:43 p.m., the figure opened a manhole cover and entered the tunnel. After he went inside, he reportedly replaced the cover. Following this unsettling experience, Nichols wrote an article for the university's newspaper, referring to the man as the "Sewer Man."

On April 7, 1950, a university police officer patrolling near Longstreet Theatre discovered mutilated chickens scattered behind the theatre. Initially, it was suspected to be a strange hoax, but the officer called for backup regardless. When he returned to investigate, he encountered a figure hunched over the remains. When illuminated by the officer's flashlight, the figure revealed a grotesque appearance, complete with a distinct third eye in the center of its forehead. The officer quickly left the scene. When his backup returned, the creature and the chicken parts had vanished.

In the 1960s, students began to explore the underground tunnels more frequently. At one point, it became a requirement for fraternity pledges to enter the tunnels as part of their hazing activities. One night in early October, during their exploration, they encountered what they described as a "crippled-looking man dressed entirely in silver." The figure charged at them, wielding a lead pipe. One pledge was knocked down and sustained minor injuries before they managed to escape and report the incident to campus police.

A search party entered the tunnels to look for what became known as "The Third Eye Man," but no trace was ever found.

Today, the university has declared these tunnels off-limits due to safety concerns and potential legal issues related to trespassing. Maintenance workers have indicated that they only enter the tunnels when necessary due to their hazardous nature and, although they don't say it aloud, the possibility of encountering The Third Eye Man.

Other Notable South Carolina Cryptids

Bush Man: The Bush Man is believed to inhabit remote areas of South Carolina, emerging from a unique lineage that combines Neanderthals and Homo Erectus, along with modern humans.

This being is typically described as shorter and denser than average humans, with strong jaws, an elongated head, a broad nose, and white skin. They have long hair like that of African Americans and a robust physique. They are adept at creating camouflaged clothing from deerskins and plants. Their distinct vocalizations consist of a language made up mostly of vowels. Reports of the Bush Man date back decades, supported by Native American legends of isolated human-like creatures. Encounters include an explorer who felt threatened by a figure with piercing eyes. Residents of South Carolina have reported unusual sounds during nighttime hikes.

In March 1913, rising waters of the Santee River forced a human-like creature resembling the Bush Man to high ground. Residents reported eerie screams and missing chickens over a few weeks. A family discovered a six-foot, hairy figure hiding in a barn, which was subsequently captured and either taken to a hospital asylum for evaluation or released by the local authorities.

South Dakota: Little People of Pryor Mountain

Notable Characteristics: This race of ferocious dwarfs is approximately eighteen inches in height and characterized by their huge heads.

The Lewis and Clark Expedition began in 1804 to explore the newly acquired Louisiana Territory. During their journey, they visited Spirit Mound, located near present-day Vermillion. They had been informed that this mound was referred to as a "mountain of evil spirits," a "hill of little people," and a "place of devils." The Sioux, Omaha, and Otoe tribes shared stories about 18-inch-tall beings with "remarkably large heads" that inhabited the site. Legends describe fierce spirits who, armed with sharp arrows, would launch attacks on anyone daring to approach the hill. Their wrath was swift and unyielding, guarding the secrets of that sacred ground with an eerie intensity.

South Dakota: Walking Sam

Notable Characteristics: Walking Sam is described as standing seven feet tall, characterized by a slender physique, long thin arms, and eyes, but notably lacking a mouth and nose. He is often portrayed as carrying the souls of Lakota men and women suspended from his arms. Additionally, some stories indicate that he may don a stovepipe hat, which enhances his ghostly appearance.

The unsettling legend of "Walking Sam" comes from the Pine Ridge Indian Reservation, where there has been a troubling increase in youth suicides. Walking Sam is a 7-foot-tall figure resembling a bogeyman who has no mouth and preys on vulnerable teens, telling them they are worthless.

When he raises his arms, he shows them the bodies of previous victims hanging beneath so they do not feel alone. He convinces them that life is not worth living and collects their souls. Some believe he is the manifestation of the Lakota people slaughtered near Wounded Knee Creek during a massacre on December 29, 1890.

South Dakota: Taku-He

Notable Characteristics: The Taku-He resembles Bigfoot and is said to inhabit Sica Hollow State Park and the Pine Ridge Reservation. Descriptions of the Taku-He suggest that it typically stands between 7 and 9 feet tall and has a robust body covered in dark brown or black fur. Its head is notably large, featuring a flat face, small ears, and a pronounced brow ridge. At night, its eyes are reported to glow red or yellow, which adds to its eerie reputation. The Taku-He has long arms that reach down to its knees, relatively short legs, and extremely large feet. It is known for its territorial aggression, often demonstrated by mutilating animals and leaving their remains as a warning. "Taku-He" translates to "big man" in the Lakota language.

Sica Hollow State Park is a minimally developed park characterized by its northern climate. The park is notable for its intriguing history and folklore, particularly Sioux legends about mysterious happenings. One significant feature is the Trail of the Spirits, which includes reddish bogs believed by Native Americans to represent the blood and flesh of their ancestors.

In the 1970s, there was an increase in sightings, and a film crew discovered a large 18-inch footprint while scouting locations. This led local authorities and tribal police to organize a large-scale hunt for the creature. It eluded would-be captors. In the summer of 1977, in the Little Eagle and McLaughlin areas near Sica Hollow, more than 28 separate encounters were documented within just two and a half months, including police officers seeing large, ape-like creatures moving through wooded areas.

One particularly notable account comes from LeMar Bear Ribs, who encountered Taku-He while walking home one night. He described it as a “big hairy man” with glowing red eyes, which left him so shaken that he required medical attention.

Recent Sica Hollow State Park reports indicate that interest in Taku-He remains strong among locals and visitors. In December 2023, an experienced trapper reported an encounter after following massive footprints measuring 18 inches long over a distance of seven miles. This was prompted by a frightened local woman who described seeing a “huge, hairy monster” in her yard.

Other Notable South Dakota Cryptids

Roy Lake Eel Creature: Reports have emerged from fishermen and jet skiers at Roy Lake regarding the sighting of large, eel-like creatures in the water. These sightings have generated curiosity and speculation about the possibility of undiscovered aquatic species inhabiting the lake.

Pickerel Lake Serpent: Similar to other lake monsters in South Dakota, Pickerel Lake has had reports of large serpentine creatures that resemble eels or snakes, adding to the tradition surrounding aquatic cryptids in the region.

Badlands Banshee: In old Gaelic folklore, a Banshee is a spirit whose wailing or keening warns a family that a member is soon to die. The Badlands, with their stunning buttes, gullies, and other geological formations, are said to be home to a Banshee that roams the rugged wilderness of South Dakota. Known for her haunting wails that instill fear in those who venture too close, she lures hikers with shadowy gestures. When approached, she remains silent until addressed, at which point she lets out a terrifying scream.

Tennessee: White Bluff Screamer

Notable Characteristics: This mysterious entity is described in two distinct ways: as a spectral white mist associated with omens of death and as a large, cat-like cryptid resembling a mountain lion. Some reports even suggest that it could be an unknown cryptid standing approximately seven feet tall, covered in long fur. One common feature in all descriptions is its horrifying, high-pitched scream, which combines elements of human wails and animalistic howls.

White Bluff is a small town in Dickson County, Tennessee, located in rolling hills and named for the white bluffs along nearby Turnbull Creek. Long ago, in the 1920s, when it was the old town of White Bluff near Trace Creek, a family consisting of a man, his wife, and their seven children lived in a rural cabin in the woods.

For many years, all was well, but then they began to hear unsettling, blood-curdling screams resembling those of a young girl outside their cabin at night and in the surrounding woods. Fearful of whatever creature was lurking out there, none of them dared venture outside after dark without a rifle.

Initially, they dismissed the sounds as the cries of an injured animal. However, as the noises grew louder and more intense, the father could no longer tolerate the terror inflicted on his family. One night, he grabbed his rifle and ventured into the woods to hunt down the creature.

He searched throughout the night, following the eerie calls. But each time he seemed to get close, the sounds vanished. Deeper into the forest he went, until suddenly, the calls ceased altogether. Frustrated and exhausted, he decided to stomp his way home angrily, planning to continue the search the following morning. However, when he opened the door to the cabin, he was met with a gruesome sight. His family had been mutilated in a ghastly way; all of them were dead. He had been lured through the woods by the beast until it sped back to the house and brutally murdered them all while he slowly trudged back.

Local historian Tony England has collected various accounts from longtime residents who claim to have encountered or heard a mysterious screamer. One resident reported hearing its terrifying cries while camping near Trace Creek. Another individual described finding large cat-like paw prints in the area where they believed the screamer had been active. Over the years, many have been haunted by chilling screams in the night, believing they've encountered the infamous White Bluff Screamer. Some brave souls follow the eerie cries into the darkness, driven by curiosity, but few return. Those who do are forever marked by the horror they witnessed, their eyes holding an indescribable terror.

Tennessee: The Tennessee Wildman

Notable Characteristics: Witnesses describe the Tennessee Wildman as a creature with shaggy hair ranging in color from dark gray to dark ginger or light brown. It stands between 7 to 9 feet tall and possesses red eyes, accompanied by an unpleasant odor reminiscent of rotting matter. Unlike other cryptids such as Bigfoot, which are often depicted as ape-like, the Wildman appears more human-like while still exhibiting animalistic features, including claws and an impressive ability to run swiftly and jump to great heights that are not typical of humans.

The first documented sightings of the Tennessee Wildman date back to the early 19th century. One notable account was published in the Hagerstown Mail on March 5, 1871. This article described a "strange and frightful being" observed in the area between Sobby and Crainsville, characterized by its great muscular power and large fiery red eyes. Another mention in the Home Journal of Winchester simply states, "A Wild Man is alarming the people of McNairy County, Tenn."

While many sightings date back several decades, one of the most recent credible encounters occurred around 1995 when Robb Phillips reported seeing the creature during a night hike at Bee Cliffs, a predominantly forested area with scenic views of the popular paddling waters of the Watauga River.

Phillips was accompanied by his cousin, Randy Sparks, on a rainy summer night when they began to notice unusual occurrences in the woods, including the horrible stench of something decaying. According to Phillips, an eerie silence enveloped the forest, with all sounds ceasing abruptly. Following this silence, they heard twigs snapping and an unidentifiable scream resembling no known animal or human sound. This left them dreading, prompting Phillips and Sparks to exit the area as quickly as possible. However, they became separated in the dark woods.

Phillips paused and found shelter against a tree, remaining silent as he listened to the strange stillness around him. Then, he observed something enormous about 20 feet above him in a tree—nine feet tall, with charcoal gray fur that was neither shaggy nor fine. Its long arms had pointy claws, and its red, beady eyes glared down at him. The smell was overwhelming—a potent stench that he likened to that of death, driving him to leave immediately. Only later did he realize what he had desperately tried to avoid was right above him: he had witnessed the Tennessee Wildman.

He was not alone in his encounter. In 2012, Matt Seeber saw the Wildman near his home in McNairy County. It stood 8 feet tall with red hair and eyes and chased his dog after emitting an eerie growl. In 2015, campers near Bee Cliffs heard strange sounds in the woods. When they directed their flashlight toward the noise, they saw a creature with gray fur and red eyes staring back at them, prompting them to quickly pack up their tent and flee.

Other Notable Tennessee Cryptids

Whistling Jack: The creature is described as a large feline, resembling a panther or mountain lion. Eyewitness accounts suggest that it has a sleek black coat, which enhances its stealthy nature. The name "Whistling Jack" comes from a peculiar sound that witnesses claim to have heard in the woods—an eerie whistling noise that some believe the creature itself makes. Reports of Whistling Jack date back a century in Pryor Ridge and Smith's Hollow, with numerous sightings documented by locals who say they have encountered this elusive beast, often accompanied by a horrifying sense of dread. Those who hear the whistling frequently notice that livestock goes missing the next day.

Tennessee Terror: The legend of the Tennessee Terror originated in 1822 when a farmer reported an encounter with a formidable sea serpent in the Tennessee River. In 1827, a man fishing on the river saw a blue-and-yellow creature resembling a snake. Suddenly, he felt his canoe shake so violently that it almost knocked him over. As the story evolved over the years, the creature became associated with a giant catfish called "Catzilla," which is believed to weigh 500 pounds.

Slothfoot: Witnesses have reported seeing a mysterious creature four feet long with four legs. It features a hairless, human-like face, short legs, and a body covered in hair, with heavy paws that have flattened claws. In 2009, a woman reported an encounter with this creature in a Hamblen County, Tennessee cave. Some compare it to a prehistoric sloth.

The Flintville Monster: A massive, hairy creature stands between 7 and 8 feet tall, with glowing red eyes and a foul, skunk-like odor. This beast is known for damaging vehicles. The legend of this creature began in the 1970s when a woman reported that it attacked her car by breaking off the antenna and jumping onto the roof. Throughout the late 1970s and into the 1990s, many sightings were reported. Local farmers have claimed that livestock went missing or were found slaughtered under mysterious circumstances, which they attribute to this creature.

Texas: Chupacabra

Notable Characteristics: Described as a reptilian creature resembling a dog with spines along its back, it is known to drain the blood of livestock, particularly goats.

The Texas Chupacabra is a cryptid that gained fame from attacking livestock, typically goats or cows, and mutilating them, sometimes even sucking the blood entirely out of its prey. It is generally described as being about the size of a small bear with a pronounced backbone, hairless, with a row of spines or quills extending from its neck to its tail.

The Chupacabra is often depicted with long, sharp fangs and large red eyes, accompanied by a distinctive, screeching noise. It has sometimes been seen hopping like a kangaroo. This legend first emerged in Puerto Rico during the 1990s but has since expanded to various regions, including Texas, where numerous sightings have been documented over the past century.

Most of the time, these creatures are misidentified raccoons or coyotes suffering from mange, desperately seeking food due to their compromised health.

However, in May 2022, security cameras at the Amarillo Zoo captured footage of an unidentified creature walking on two legs past a fence late at night. City officials dubbed this peculiar sighting the "Unidentified Amarillo Object" (UAO). The sighting sparked speculation about whether the creature could be a Chupacabra or simply a large coyote standing on its hind legs. Officials encouraged community engagement by asking residents to share their thoughts on what the creature might be, emphasizing that no animals or individuals were harmed during the encounter.

Texas: Houston Batman

Notable Characteristics: The Houston Batman is a large humanoid figure with bat wings, standing approximately 6.5 feet tall and glowing yellow in color while dressed in tight-fitting dark clothing.

On June 18, 1953, three neighbors witnessed a peculiar sighting in Houston, Texas, involving a creature described as a "man with wings like a bat." The witnesses were 23-year-old Hilda Walker, 33-year-old Howard Phillips, and Judy Meyers, the 14-year-old daughter of their landlady. The encounter occurred around 2:30 a.m. while the group sat on Walker's porch during a hot, humid night.

Suddenly, their yard was engulfed in darkness. "All of a sudden, this shadow settled in a tree," Hilda Walker recounted. "We all looked up and saw a 'Batman.' He was balancing himself on a tree limb, and there was a dim gray light surrounding him." She described the creature as six and a half feet tall, wearing a black cape, skin-tight dark pants, and boots, with the appearance of a white man.

As they watched in awe, a mysterious white flame and smoke emanated from behind them, and a burning object that resembled a flying paintbrush swished across the sky before the creature disappeared. Howard Phillips, a tool plant inspector, later told the Houston Chronicle, "I could hardly believe it, but I saw it." Another resident, a 71-year-old man, also claimed to have seen the shadowy figure in the tree but said he simply "went back inside and went to bed."

Texas: Goat Man Bridge

Notable Characteristics: In the shadows lurks a goat-headed figure, its eyes gleaming an eerie red that pierces the darkness with a chilling intensity.

Goatman's Bridge, officially known as the Old Alton Bridge, is in Denton County, Texas. It is an iron truss bridge with a wooden walkway over Hickory Creek opened to traffic—including cattle, horses, pedestrians, and cars in 1884. It was a vital link between Denton and Copper Canyon until it was closed to vehicles in 2001 when a new concrete and steel bridge was built nearby.

The bridge is associated with a successful African American goat farmer named Oscar Washburn, who sold milk, cheese, meat, and goat hides. In the late 1930s, he hung a sign on the Old Alton Bridge that read, "This way to the Goatman," infuriating local Ku Klux Klan members due to his success. One dark night, the Klansmen formed a violent lynch mob, seized Washburn, and dragged him to the bridge, where they brutally hanged him. However, when one of the group went to check if he was dead, they found an empty noose and no trace of Oscar Washburn.

According to local legend, Washburn now haunts the bridge in a cryptid form, perhaps as a shapeshifter. It is said that if someone knocks three times on the bridge at midnight or honks their car horn three times while turning off their lights, they might summon Washburn's angry spirit or encounter other supernatural phenomena related to Goatman. Visitors have claimed to see him—a goat-headed figure with glowing red eyes lurking in the woods. Strange bleating noises can be heard, and something seems to watch from the darkness.

Texas: Black-eyed Children

Notable Characteristics: The Black-Eyed Children look like ordinary kids but have pale skin and completely black eyes. They often persistently ask for rides or knock on doors to seek entry into homes. Witnesses frequently report feelings of dread or anxiety when they encounter these children.

The legend of the Black-Eyed Children (BEKs) originated from an encounter reported by journalist Brian Bethel in 1996 in Abilene, Texas. The earliest reported sighting of these creepy children occurred when Bethel stopped in a parking lot near a movie theater to write a check. He heard a tapping on the driver's side window and rolled it down to see two children outside, aged between 9 and 13 years old.

The older boy asked for a ride to their mother's home so they could get money for a movie that had just started. As he looked into the boy's eyes, Bethel felt an overwhelming dread and "soul-wracking fear." With an unsettling sensation, he noticed that the boy's eyes were completely black, devoid of sclera or iris. The older boy seemed frustrated when Bethel broke eye contact and turned his gaze away. The boy insisted they couldn't enter the car until he gave them permission. Terrified, Bethel rolled up his window, reversed his vehicle, and sped away. The children had mysteriously vanished when he looked back in his rearview mirror.

Afterward, Bethel shared his experience on a ghost-related mailing list and wrote about it for the Abilene Reporter-News. His story gained traction over time and has been recounted in various media formats.

In Houston, residents have reported seeing Black-Eyed Kids (BEKs) lurking in their neighborhoods around Halloween, often appearing at strange and late hours after trick-or-treating has ended. Some people have encountered these children walking alone in rural areas along dark country roads. When they glance into their rearview mirrors, the children have mysteriously vanished, only to reappear further up the road.

The nature of these children remains a mystery. Some speculate that they may be ghosts or extraterrestrial beings. There are theories suggesting that Black-Eyed Kids (BEKs) could be demonic entities that require an invitation to enter homes or vehicles. Exercise caution if you ever encounter children hitchhiking or asking to come inside, as they might be Black-Eyed Kids.

Other Notable Texas Cryptids

Marfa Lights: In the desert of Marfa, Texas, mysterious glowing orbs known as "Ghost Lights" have been reported since 1883, when a cowhand named Robert Reed Ellison mistook them for burning Apache campfires. Eyewitnesses describe them as basketball-size orbs of light, appearing in colors such as white, yellow, blue, or red, dancing and floating across the landscape. The best location to view the Ghost Lights is along Highway 90, overlooking Mitchell Flat, 9 miles east of Marfa. Some speculate that these lights are caused by UFOs, the lost souls of Spanish conquistadors, an optical illusion, or even gases.

Lake Worth Monster A creature associated with Lake Worth is located at the Fort Worth Nature Center and Refuge in Texas. It is often described as a hybrid of man and goat, featuring scales, long clawed fingers, and standing over seven feet tall. The legend became popular in the summer of 1969 when residents reported numerous sightings.

Reports included dramatic accounts such as one where the monster allegedly jumped onto a couple's car from a tree and another where it threw an automobile tire at picnickers. These incidents were widely covered by local newspapers, which fueled public interest and speculation about the creature's existence.

Beast of Bear Creek: It roamed the area of Kimble County, Texas, particularly around Cleo. An old Native American shaman was the last surviving member of his tribe, which had been decimated by white homesteaders who had seized their land. After dark, he could transform from a human into a large, ferocious wolf-like beast, seeking vengeance against the settlers who had destroyed nearly all his people. The settlers were aware of his presence as he patrolled the countryside in his wolf form at night, attacking livestock and targeting those unfortunate to be caught outside after dark. His eerie screams and howls served as a warning, but it was already too late for those who fell victim to his sights.

La Lechuza: La Lechuza is a creature from Mexican folklore, often depicted as a witch who can shapeshift into a large owl with the face of an old woman. This entity seeks revenge on those who wronged her during her life, frequently targeting unruly children and the homeless. Sightings of La Lechuza have been reported throughout South Texas, particularly during the 1970s, when residents claimed to see a giant bird-like figure with human features. One notable sighting occurred in 1975 in Robstown, Texas, where witnesses described a "monster bird" with glowing eyes and human feet swooping down at them. This led to widespread panic and speculation about its connection to the La Lechuza legend.

Utah: Old Briney

Notable Characteristics: The North American Shore Monster, also known as Old Briney, is an aquatic cryptid characterized by its large, serpent-like form. This creature is often described as having a crocodile-like body, a head resembling a horse, two giant eyes, and a tail.

One of the most notable sightings occurred on July 8, 1877, when J.H. McNeil and several workers boiling salt at Barnes and Co. saltworks reported encountering a large creature near the northern shore of the Great Salt Lake at a place called Monument Point, a promontory extending into the water. The company processed salt day and night, burning fires to boil the water in tanks twenty-four hours a day. At 10 p.m., the men heard a "violent commotion in the lake." They looked up to see a large creature approaching them, described by McNeil as having a crocodile-like body and a horse-like head, with an estimated length of around 75 feet.

In his affidavit, McNeil reported, "On the night of July 8, I was working at the salt works at Monument Point when about 10 o'clock I heard a great noise on the lake, and looking in that direction saw a great animal like a crocodile or alligator approaching, but much larger. When we came down in the morning, we saw tracks on the shore but nothing else."

According to his account, the creature approached the shore with a loud bellow, frightening McNeil and his colleagues, prompting them to flee into the nearby mountains for safety until the next morning. Upon returning the next day, they found overturned boulders and disturbed ground along the shoreline, which they attributed to the creature's presence. Many of the men thereafter refused to work.

In 1880, some fishermen from Springville reported seeing a serpentine creature with multiple humps breaking through the water's surface. They described it as 50 to 60 feet long, with a head resembling a horse's head. They noted that it moved rapidly through the water, creating disturbances as it submerged and resurfaced.

In 2023, State Park Ranger Holly Minor recounted an extraordinary story involving two hunters on Stansbury Island who were driven into a cave by a creature described as part crocodile and part horse. "There were a couple of hunters out on Stansbury Island, and they were chased into a small cave by something half crocodile half horse, but this one had the wings of a bat." Minor related. "The wingspan was over 100 feet, and it chased them into this cave and went out over Stansbury Island, and when it came back, it was carrying an entire cow in his mouth. They hid in this cave all night and listened to this chomping on the entire cow." Legends of Old Briney have persisted through the years and will likely endure for many more.

Utah: Wasatch Wildman

Notable Characteristics: The Wasatch Wildman is described as a hairy humanoid figure, typically measuring 7 to 10 feet tall. This creature features long arms, broad shoulders, and a facial structure resembling an ape or primitive human. Its body is generally covered in dark brown or black hair, contributing to its distinct appearance.

The Wasatch Range extends approximately 160 miles, starting at the Utah-Idaho border and continuing down to central Utah. This mountain range is famed for its impressive rugged peaks, picturesque alpine lakes, and scenic canyons, making it a significant natural landmark in the region. Hidden within this range is the elusive Wasatch Wildman.

An unusual sighting occurred in the late 1970s when hikers spotted a large figure moving swiftly through the trees on a trail near Mount Timpanogos. The figure was fast and agile, disappearing into the dense forest before they could get a clear view. Another notable report came from a family camping in the area. They heard strange vocalizations at night, described as deep howls or screams reverberating through the mountains.

The Uinta-Wasatch-Cache National Forest spans 2.2 million acres in northern Utah and southwestern Wyoming. It's a popular recreational destination with diverse terrains and forests featuring wildlife including moose, black bears, mountain lions, elk, and bighorn sheep. In Cache Valley, residents have shared stories of encounters with what they describe as a "big male" Bigfoot. In an interview with Clarissa Casper for the Utah Statesman, Jon Marshall, an author focused on Bigfoot encounters in the area, discussed various accounts from individuals who claim to have seen or heard unusual sounds attributed to the creature. He noted an increase in Bigfoot sightings during the autumn of 2021. Cache Valley is located between the Wellsville Mountains to the west and the Bear River Mountains to the east, both extensions of the Wasatch Range.

"The hotspots for these recent sightings are the White Pine and Tony Grove campsites," Marshall stated. "Most of the individuals who have encountered this creature at these locations have had very similar experiences." The Tony Grove Campground and the White Pine Lake Trail, which leads to White Pine Lake, are located within the Uinta-Wasatch-Cache National Forest, part of Utah's Wasatch Range. "This particular one tends to throw rocks or other objects," Marshall noted. "He never actually hits anyone, but he throws rocks that are softball-sized or larger in their direction."

Other Notable Utah Cryptids

Utah Skinwalkers: Skinwalkers are considered malevolent witches with the ability to transform into animals or control them. They are typically associated with regions in Texas and Arizona, but sightings have also been reported in Utah. These entities are harmful. Those who have encountered Skinwalkers describe experiences involving shapeshifting and other supernatural abilities exhibited by these beings. In Vineyard, Utah, a man recounted an unusual experience outside his home. Initially, he believed he had spotted a cow or horse that had escaped from its pasture. However, as he approached the creature, it began to change into something much more bizarre. He described it as a "white stag with huge antlers and a human face." This description aligns with the traditional characteristics attributed to Skinwalkers, who are often believed to have the ability to transform into various animal forms while retaining some human features.

Provo Werewolves: Witnesses have seen large humanoid figures resembling wolves or dogs in urban settings, specifically University Avenue and south of 600 South. These encounters often describe creatures with glowing eyes and an uncanny ability to disappear quickly. The stories from Provo include accounts from vagrants who claim that werewolves inhabit certain areas near train yards.

Vermont: The Strange Things of the Bennington Triangle

Notable Characteristics: The Bennington Monster is a tall, long-haired creature that lives in an area known for its supernatural presence and missing persons called Bennington Triangle.

"Bennington Triangle" is known for its pattern of regional disappearances between 1945 and 1950, with eerie similarities to the well-known Bermuda Triangle mystery. This region encompasses parts of the towns of Bennington, Woodford, Shaftsbury, and Somerset, with a focus on Glastenbury Mountain. This region has garnered attention for its missing persons cases and various strange phenomena reported over the years, including sightings of unusual creatures.

From early on, strange lights, unusual odors, and untraceable sounds were reported in the region. Glastenbury, now a ghost town, was once a small community with a charcoal-making industry and a logging railroad in the 1800s, peaking at around 241 residents. It later struggled to become a resort but only lasted one season, as flooding destroyed the tracks, leading to the resort's closure. Many peculiar legends have emerged from this area and defy rational explanations.

In 1943, Carl Herrick went hunting in West Townshend. He mysteriously died, found with a punctured lung and injuries described as "squeezed to death by a bear," with bear tracks nearby.

On November 12, 1945, 74-year-old Middie Rivers vanished while hunting in Bickford Hollow, leaving only a handkerchief as a clue.

Eighteen-year-old Paula Jean Weldon, a freshman at Bennington College, disappeared on December 1, 1946, while hiking the Long Trail; despite an FBI search, no trace was found.

Exactly three years later, 68-year-old James Tedford went missing after boarding a bus to Bennington. He was last seen getting off in Brandon, and his absence raised concerns at the Vermont Soldiers' Home.

On Columbus Day, 1950, 8-year-old Paul Jepson disappeared from his family's truck while his mother tended to pigs. Search dogs traced his scent to the same spot where Weldon vanished.

Frieda Langer, aged 53, disappeared on October 28, 1950, while hiking with her cousin, Herbert Elsner, near their family cabin by the Somerset Reservoir. After falling into a stream, Frieda decided to take a shortcut back to the cabin to change her clothes, planning to catch up with Herbert later. Months later, her body was discovered far from the cabin.

Some people believe that strange forces are responsible for the mysterious disappearances in the area, as hikers have reported feelings of confusion and weird experiences. Legends surrounding the "Man-Eating Rock of Glastenbury" warn of a massive rock that ensnares its victims, drawing them in and never letting them go. One of the most intriguing figures associated with this region is the Bennington Monster, reportedly sighted around Bennington County in the late 1940s. Descriptions of the creature vary, but it is often characterized by its height of 6 to 7 feet, long limbs, and an intimidating presence that instills fear in those who claim to have encountered it.

The initial significant sighting involved a stagecoach driving along Glastenbury Mountain near Bennington in pouring rain. The horses were acting skittish on the washed-out path, so the driver pulled the team to the side of the road. When he climbed down to the roadway, accompanied by some curious passengers, they noticed massive tracks in the mud. Moments later, something rushed out of the darkness and knocked over the wagon. As it disappeared, they could see strange eyes glowing in the dark. No one knows if there is a connection between the Bennington Triangle and the Bennington Monster except for their themes of mystery and unexplained occurrences within this geographical area. Both phenomena contribute to the lore encompassing Glastenbury Mountain and its surroundings.

Vermont: Champ

Notable Characteristics: Champ is described as a giant serpentine creature with a long neck and a humped back.

Lake Champlain is a 125-mile-long freshwater lake between the Adirondack Mountains of New York and the Green Mountains of Vermont. It is cherished for its rocky bluffs, sandy and cobble beaches, numerous islands, and various inlets and bays. However, there is a mysterious aspect to this popular recreational area: it is said to be home to a creature known as Champ.

Sightings of Champ date back to the 1600s when French explorer Samuel de Champlain reported seeing a long, serpentine creature in the lake. Historical accounts also include a sighting in 1819, when a captain claimed to have seen a monstrous creature measuring an astonishing 187 feet in length.

Over the years, there have been more than 300 reported sightings of Champ, with descriptions varying widely from a long serpentine figure to something resembling a plesiosaur. In recent years, particularly from 2023 to early 2025, notable developments have occurred regarding Champ sightings. Independent filmmakers Kelly Tabor and Richard Rossi were shooting a fictional film titled "Lucy and the Lake Monster." During their filming in Bulwagga Bay, across from Vermont's Lake Champlain, they used drone technology to capture footage of what they claimed could be Champ swimming beneath the water's surface.

Other Notable Vermont Cryptids

Awful: The large, winged creature, resembling a griffin, has gray skin, massive claws, and a wingspan of about 20 feet. Reports of sightings have emerged from the Berkshire and Richford areas, dating from the 1920s to the mid-2000s. These documented encounters suggest a long-standing presence of this enigmatic creature in the region.

Pigman: One of the most peculiar legends that has become increasingly disturbing over time is that of the Pigman. This creature is half pig and half human. It is believed to inhabit rural areas neighboring Northfield, particularly around Devil's Washbowl, a forested region featuring streams and caves. The Pigman is often described as having human-like features combined with those of a pig, notably a snout and ears. This unsettling appearance has led to numerous reported sightings, and many consider the Pigman an omen of misfortune. These legends contribute to Vermont's rich tapestry of folklore and continue to intrigue those interested in the unusual and mysterious.

Virginia: Bunnyman

Notable Characteristics: A large Man-Bunny brandishing an axe.

There is a chilling legend that originated in Virginia in 1970. It was a time when some people embraced hippie fashion, wearing tie-dye shirts, hot pants, midi-skirts, frayed jeans, and bell-bottoms. Around this time, Project Blue Book, the U.S. government's study on UFOs that had been ongoing since 1952, stopped. Just a year earlier, the Manson family cult and its leader were apprehended and imprisoned.

Amidst these events, a legend emerged—the Bunny Man, who terrorized Fairfax County, Virginia residents. This tale likely left a lasting scar on many children who were taken by their parents to pose on the Easter Bunny's lap for a family photo. Some people recount his story like this:

Once, there was an asylum for the criminally insane located near Clifton. The town's residents were worried about their families' safety if any inmates escaped. They petitioned the government to shut it down, and those who had lived there were relocated far away. Their requests were granted. However, they should have been more careful about what they wished for, as this decision would haunt them for years.

Initially, everything seemed fine. The government arranged for the inmates to be transferred by bus. Unfortunately, during one of the transfers, the bus crashed, allowing some of the inmates to escape into the nearby woods. Eventually, the police captured all but two men—Marcus Wallster and Douglas J. Grifon. As the hunt for the men continued, the police began noticing fresh skins of rabbits hanging from tree limbs. When they returned the next day, the skins would be gone. The chase became more desperate when the rotting corpse of Wallster was discovered near Colchester Underpass in Clifton. His flesh had been peeled from his body, and he was hanging from a limb. His entrails had been gorged.

The local police generally believed that Grifon was hiding in the woods, killing the rabbits for meat and using their skins as clothing. Then, one Halloween night, three local children happened upon the crazed inmate while Trick-or-Treating. Seeing the man dressed in rabbit skins fashioned into a costume that made him appear like a huge white bunny with long ears, they taunted him, "Bunny-Man, Bunny-Man, Bunny-Man."

Their mutilated remains were recovered the next day, lying near the bridge. Above them, their flesh was hanging off tree limbs. So now, those who go to the bridge on Colchester Road in Clifton and call out, "Bunny-Man, Bunny-Man, Bunny-Man," the following day, they will be found with their hides hanging from limbs and their flesh-peeled corpses resting beneath.

Sound like an urban legend? There is some truth to the lore, even more believable and disturbing. Because an ax-wielding bunny was lurking in the brush in Fairfax County and seeking out those who crossed his path—

In the late 1960s and early 1970s, Washington, D.C., was surrounded by a vast expanse of suburbs filled with homes and families. New subdivisions were rapidly transforming small communities and farmland. Even 25 miles away, in the quickly developing areas around Clifton and Fairfax, Virginia, the landscape was no different.

On the night of Sunday, October 18, 1970, in Fairfax, an Air Force Academy cadet named Bob Bennett was visiting his uncle after attending the Air Force/Navy football game. He had parked his car across the street from his uncle's home on Guinea Road and was sitting inside the vehicle with his fiancé, Dusty. Suddenly, a man dressed in a furry costume with long bunny ears emerged from the bushes, brandishing a wooden-handled hatchet. In a deep voice, he cried out, "You're on private property, and I have your tag number!" With a swift motion, the rabbit threw a hatchet at the car's windshield, shattering the glass. The hatchet landed at Bob's feet, and the rabbit then vanished into the darkness of the night. Although the couple was unharmed, the situation was shocking enough to warrant a call to the police, who began their investigation promptly.

Less than two weeks later, this horrible creature returned.

A security guard named Paul Phillips, employed by a private construction company building homes in the area, came across a large, fuzzy rabbit standing on the front porch of a brand-new house just a block away from the previous incident. The guard addressed the strange figure, and the rabbit immediately whipped out a long-handled ax and began striking a roof support on the building. "All you people trespass around here. If you don't get out of here, I'm going to bust you on the head," the rabbit shrieked. Immediately, Phillips rushed to his vehicle to retrieve his handgun. Still, when he returned, the rabbit had disappeared into the nearby woods.

Over the next few weeks, nearly 50 witnesses reported seeing the elusive rabbit in Northeast or Southeast Washington. In Prince George's County, three children were terrified when a man dressed in a bunny costume approached them with an axe on the street as they were returning home from school. Police searched the area but found no trace of the man.

Authorities could not confirm all the reports and never located the Bunny Man. Later, Angie Proffitt, who had visited the nearby tunnel with her boyfriend in her early teens during the 1970s, recounted an eerie experience. She saw two small children at the tunnel entrance, but they completely vanished. Moments later, they appeared at the car's back window, staring at her. Like many others, she is convinced of the reality of these stories. And if you have lived to tell your own account after visiting this frightening site, you believe in them, too.

Virginia: Devil Monkey

Notable Characteristics: The Devil Monkey stands about 3 to 7 feet tall and has powerful hind legs similar to a kangaroo, enabling it to jump as high as 20 feet in a single leap. It features a monkey-like head, small, pointed ears, and a long bushy tail. Its fur is typically dark brown or black, sometimes with white patches on the neck or underbelly. The front paws possess sharp claws, making the Devil Monkey an effective predator.

Virginia has reported numerous sightings of this creature. One notable sighting occurred in Saltville in 1966; two nurses claimed the creature kept pace with their moving vehicle, causing damage to the car before they managed to flee.

In the 1990s, an Ohio woman and her daughter traveled from Nashville to the Outer Banks of North Carolina during the summer. During her trip, she had an extraordinary encounter that lingered in her mind for years. She shared her story of encountering what might be a Devil Monkey with Chad Arment, an author, biologist, and publisher of the North American BioFortean Review, an online Cryptozoology resource and newsletter.

During their journey, they were delayed by orange construction barrels and detours, which sent them four hours off their planned route and driving at night. Unsure of their new path, they became acclimated while passing through Roanoke and nearing Elizabeth City. She recounted, "I saw a road sign that read 'Red Wolf Crossing,' which surprised me. About 20 minutes after seeing that sign, I was navigating some dark, winding roads when a creature leaped across the road in front of my car. I thank God my daughter was sleeping in the back seat. If she had seen it, I swear she'd never have been able to sleep for a month," she stated and went on, "The creature was NOT a wolf. It was completely black, with very short, sleek fur, pointy ears, and a long, thin tail. It appeared catlike, yet unlike any cat I had ever seen. It was very long— or should I say tall— when standing on its hind legs. I would estimate it was easily 6 feet tall while upright. Its torso resembled that of a very thin man, and its head almost looked human, with a pointy beard. However, its hind legs were more like those of a wild cat or dog—very muscular and thin."

The creature had leaped from all fours and crossed two road lanes before disappearing into the night. The strange creature may have vanished but encounters with the unusual force us to see beyond the ordinary, and it lingered in the woman's mind for years.

Virginia: Woodbooger

Notable Characteristics: Witnesses typically describe the Woodbooger as a large, hairy humanoid creature that roams the forests of Virginia, standing between 7 to 8 feet tall and covered in brown or black fur.

The Woodbooger is a regional cryptid similar to the more widely known Bigfoot. It is primarily found in Southwest Virginia, particularly in Norton and surrounding areas. Historically, Norton was a timber and coal boomtown. Still, it is now home to more forested recreational areas, such as the High Knob Recreation Area, which is part of a Bigfoot sanctuary. The name "Woodbooger" likely derives from the Boogeyman or Bogeyman, a figure used in cautionary tales to warn children against wandering into the woods at night.

Other Notable Virginia Cryptids

Chessie: Chessie is a sea serpent believed to inhabit Chesapeake Bay. This snake-like aquatic creature was first reported in sightings dating back to the 1840s near Virginia Beach. Later sightings occurred throughout the 20th century. Various speculations about Chessie's identity include large sharks or oarfish, and some even suggest it could be snakes that escaped from ships. The increase in sightings coincided with local developments, such as the opening of the Calvert Cliffs Nuclear Power Plant.

The Wampus Cat: This notable figure in Appalachian folklore varies in its depiction across different regions. In some areas, it is described as a mystical creature—a cross between a woman and a panther. However, in Virginia, the Wampus Cat is more closely associated with a formidable animal resembling a monstrous cougar, four times larger than a lion. Reports of sightings date back to December 7, 1918, originating from Greeneville, where locals encountered this being. The Greeneville Daily Sun documented these incidents, highlighting that the presence of the Wampus Cat raised concerns among parents about the safety of their children after dark. Eyewitness accounts portrayed the Wampus Cat as a fearsome entity that roamed after dark, making unsettling noises resembling a child in distress and leaving a strong odor comparable to that of cat urine and wet dog mixed with a skunk.

Washington: Sasquatch

Notable Characteristics: Sasquatch is the most famous figure in Washington State, with over 700 documented sightings. This creature is typically described as a massive, upright, ape-like being, estimated to stand between 6 to 10 feet tall and weigh between 500 and 800 pounds. Sasquatch is usually covered in dark brown or reddish-brown fur and is often associated with a strong, unpleasant odor.

Reports of Sasquatch sightings frequently come from remote wilderness areas, particularly the forests and mountains of the Olympic Peninsula and the Cascade Range. In Skamania County, a hotspot for Bigfoot sightings, a law that explicitly prohibits Sasquatch's killing has been enacted.

Violators of this law may face fines of up to $10,000 and potential imprisonment. This legislation was established to protect the creature and prevent hunters from inadvertently harming others.

Here are just a couple of sightings in Washington.

Beacon Rock Area (1970): Beacon Rock State Park is a 4,458-acre year-round camping destination in the Columbia River Gorge National Scenic Area. The park features Beacon Rock, the remnant of an ancient volcano, and consists of a basalt plug formed by cooling lava. The park has forested uplands, including areas with large trees that grow on the mountainside of the rock. One of the most well-known clusters of sightings occurred at the park during the summer of 1970. Witnesses reported seeing a large creature near a cave. They measured its footprints to be approximately 19 inches long and 9 inches wide. One woman, changing her tire at night, had a vivid face-to-face encounter with the creature.

In 1978, a couple and a group of friends stood on Beacon Rock overlooking pastureland when they witnessed a large black creature stepping onto the railroad bed. They saw it take off across a meadow toward the Columbia River. The beast passed by some cows, towering over them and almost doubling their height. Following behind was a smaller creature resembling a chimpanzee that moved on all fours. This smaller creature approached the water, squatted down, and seemed to be searching for salmon before returning across the field.

Stevenson: Stevenson is located approximately 9 miles from Beacon Rock State Park. In September 1969, Skamania County Sheriff Bill Closner photographed two tracks near a logging operation north of Stevenson. This sighting added credibility to local claims regarding the presence of Sasquatch in the area.

Washington: Batsquatch

Notable Characteristics: The legend of Batsquatch began after the significant eruption of Mount St. Helens in 1980. Batsquatch is described as a 9-foot-tall flying creature that appears to be a hybrid of a bat and Sasquatch. It is characterized by its striking yellow eyes, blue fur, tufted ears, a large mouth with sharp teeth, and impressive leathery wings that span approximately 50 feet.

Mount St. Helens is in Skamania County, Washington State, about 50 miles northeast of Portland, Oregon. This active volcano is famous for its cone-shaped appearance, formed by layers of lava, ash, and other volcanic materials. For more than a hundred years, the volcano remained quiet until it began to show signs of activity in early 1980, raising concerns about a potential eruption.

On March 27, 1980, Mount St. Helens began erupting with a series of powerful explosions. These blasts started from the top of the mountain and became more intense over time. The situation culminated in a major eruption on May 18, 1980, at 8:32 a.m. This earthquake caused the north flank of the volcano to collapse, leading to the largest landslide in recorded history and a blast that released hot gases, volcanic material, and an ash cloud that spread across multiple states.

From this eruption emerged a cryptid known as Batsquatch. Shortly after the catastrophic event in May 1980, witnesses reported sighting a creature resembling both a bat and Sasquatch. One notable encounter occurred in April 1994 when 18-year-old Brian Canfield was driving along a remote stretch of highway between Buckley and Camp One in the Mount Rainier foothills above Lake Kapowsin. Around 9:30 p.m., his pickup truck suddenly stalled without him applying the brakes. Although the headlights were still functioning, Canfield witnessed a large creature descending from the sky.

"It was standing there staring at me, like it was resting, like it didn't know what to think," he told reporter C.R. Roberts from the News Tribune of Tacoma. "I was scared. It raised the hair on me. I didn't feel threatened; I just felt out of place." He described the creature as about nine feet tall, with blue fur, yellow eyes shaped like pie slices, and wings that were as wide as the road. "Its eyes were yellow and shaped like a piece of pie with pupils like a half-moon. The mouth was pretty big, with white teeth but no fangs. The face was like a wolf."

After staring at him intensely, the creature began unfolding its wings and suddenly burst upward, flying off toward Mt. Rainier with a wingspan as wide as the road. The turbulence from its flight shook Canfield's truck, causing it to sway. After the encounter, his truck started again, and he drove off, shaken by the experience.

Canfield's story is considered credible, and he was not alone in his encounter. In 2015, a couple hiking near Ape Canyon, a popular trail on the southeast side of Mount St. Helens, reported seeing a large, winged figure soaring above them. This area also has a history of Bigfoot sightings, dating back to 1924, when gold miners described an ape-man in the vicinity.

Spirit Lake, a popular tourist site, was nearly obliterated during the May 1980 eruption of Mount St. Helens. A driver traveling along Highway 504 also reported seeing a large creature with bat-like features perched on a rock outcrop near the lake.

The intrigue surrounding Batsquatch continues among witnesses and cryptozoologists, particularly because of its connection to local folklore related to Mount St. Helens. While descriptions differ, they consistently emphasize the bat-like features combined with those associated with Sasquatch.

Other Notable Washington Cryptids

Lake Chelan Dragon: The creature is a serpentine entity resembling a combination of an alligator and a snake, complete with wings, a long, scaly tail, and sharp teeth. It is believed to inhabit Lake Chelan, Washington's deepest lake, which reaches depths of approximately 1,486 feet. Indigenous cultures refer to this being as N'hah'hahat'q, depicting it as an evil spirit with destructive capabilities.

Tacoma Narrows Octopus: This marine creature can weigh up to 600 pounds. It is associated with the legendary collapse of the Tacoma Narrows Bridge in 1940, which resulted in underwater ruins that have become a habitat for various marine life. Many divers explore these depths, hoping to encounter this elusive octopus. Typically, octopuses are just as curious and well-mannered as the divers who adventure near them.

West Virginia: Flatwoods Monster

Notable Characteristics: The Flatwoods Monster is described as a humanoid figure standing approximately 10 feet tall. It has round red facial features and a distinctive hood-shaped head. Its eyes emit a green light, while its body is dark green. This creature is part of local folklore and has captured the interest of both researchers and enthusiasts of the paranormal.

At 7:15 p.m. on Friday, September 12, 1952, boys played football at Flatwoods Elementary School. Among them were brothers Edison May, age 13, and Freddie May, age 11. As the afternoon shifted from light to dusk, an eerie silence interrupted their game. One of the boys shouted, "Look there!"

Above them, a silver-red ball of fire with flames trailing behind swept across the sky, barely above the trees. They watched in wonder as this object, described as being "bigger than the average aircraft," slowed down, tilted upward, and gradually descended, landing on a flattened hilltop to the southeast—by a cistern on the property of local farmer G. Bailey Fisher.

Believing it might be a meteorite or a flying saucer, the boys raced down the streets in pursuit. As they reached the road where the strange object had landed, they came to the home of Edison and Freddie. Bursting through the doors, they rushed to tell the adults what they had seen. Their mother, Kathleen May, had just finished work at a nearby beauty parlor in Sutton. Not wanting the boys to investigate the site alone, she grabbed a flashlight from the coffee table and followed along with them.

Some boys who saw the flaming object on the football field decided to return home. However, several neighborhood children joined Edison, Freddie, and their mother, including six-year-old Tommy Hyer and fourteen-year-olds Ronald Shaver, Teddie Neal, and Neil Nunley. Eighteen-year-old National Guardsman Eugene Lemon, who heard the commotion, decided to join the group. He had been at home with his mother, enjoying coffee with a friend, when the object passed by, shaking the house and spilling their drinks.

Picking up a flashlight, Lemon accompanied the group with his dog. Freddie May's dog, Ricky, and another neighborhood pup followed closely behind. A little past 7:40 p.m., they walked through a field along an old road path, where they noticed a flashing light. Eugene led the group with Neil by his side. Behind them were Kathleen and Edison, followed by Ronald. Freddie, Teddie, and Tommy lagged behind, stopping at a wooden fence while the others continued onward.

At some point along the trail, the air filled with fog and a mist with a metallic, sulfur-like stench that burned their nostrils, throats, and eyes. About a hundred yards from where the five continued, Kathleen May noticed a massive ball of fire about ten feet in diameter. Next to it was a light pulsing with strange hissing, popping, and crackling sounds, accompanied by a whirring noise like a generator in the air. Eugene Lemon quickly raised his flashlight and saw a tall, green figure standing in the mist. It had a round, reddish face surrounded by a pointed, hood-like shape.

"I saw a pair of eyes near a tree and shone my flashlight on them," Eugene later recounted. "I thought it was an opossum, then there stood this—*thing*." He described it as a ten-foot monster with a blood-red face and a glowing green body. Beams seemed to emerge from what looked like glass on its head.

One dog growled and disappeared into the mist. As Kathleen May raised her flashlight to shine on the object before them, she heard the other dog barking violently. The group stared in disbelief at the towering figure, which illuminated brightly like a Christmas tree and glided within ten feet of Kathleen and Eugene. Suddenly frightened, Eugene Lemon tripped as an oily liquid sprayed toward them. Terrified, the group felt as though their feet were glued to the ground until, in a sudden panic, they bolted, running back down the hillside.

The bizarre incident would later be covered by newspapers. Still, no one could accurately determine what the group had witnessed that evening—a monster, an alien? Many witnesses stepped forward to say they saw several unidentified flying crafts speeding across the West Virginia skies that day. Whatever streaked across the sky shook homes and terrified and mystified people.

West Virginia: Mothman

Notable Characteristics: This creature is characterized by its impressive height, ranging from 6 to 7 feet. It features wings on its back and has a light grey coloration. The eyes are particularly notable, measuring approximately 2 inches in diameter and spaced about 6 to 8 inches apart, with a striking red hue.

On November 12, 1966, Kenneth Duncan was digging a grave in a Clendenin cemetery for his father-in-law when he spotted a flying creature above the trees. Describing it as a "brown human being" with wings, he observed it for about a minute, even though the other men present did not see it.

Duncan was confident it was not a bird. It was the first sighting of the Mothman.

In mid-November, newlyweds Steve and Mary Mallette, both 20, were joyriding with 18-year-old Roger Scarberry and 19-year-old Linda Scarberry in Roger's prized 1957 Chevy. They drove about seven miles from their hometown of Point Pleasant to the abandoned West Virginia Ordnance Works, known as the TNT Area. This vast site, used for ammunition production during World War II, featured about a hundred hidden igloo-like bunkers that stored explosives. By 1966, the area had become a vacant hangout spot, popular for car shows and drag racing.

On that ill-fated evening, that is precisely what the two couples did when they happened upon the creature shortly before midnight. "We were riding through the TNT Area on a side road by the old powerhouse building around midnight on Tuesday, November 15, 1966, when we came over this small rise in the road," Linda Scarberry reported to local police. "All at once, Steve yelled for us to look at that thing in the road. I looked up and saw it go around the corner at the old powerhouse. It did not run but wobbled like it couldn't keep its balance. Its wings were spread just a little. We sat there for a few seconds. Then Roger took off—"

Steve Mallette knew the local wildlife—he had been an avid hunter since he was six. At first, he believed it was nothing more than a raccoon or other woodland critter. "We came over a little rise in the road near the old power plant when we saw the eyes over in the bushes reflecting off the headlights. They glowed red and were six inches apart," he told the press. But the eyes reappeared when Roger Scarberry pulled onto the main road. However, this time, they could see the body attached—a man-like form with a ten-foot wingspan.

"This thing stood about six feet tall with wings on its back."

Roger described the creature. "It was light grey in color, with red eyes about two inches in diameter six to eight inches apart."

Roger Scarberry was driving toward Point Pleasant when a creature appeared at a turn near a billboard. It spread its wings, flew upward, and then followed the car, sending chills of fear. "I was doing 100 to 105 miles per hour, and it was just gliding overtop, sorta moving from side to side," Scarberry revealed. "You could hear a flapping noise. Then it came down at the car, making a squealing noise like a mouse."

Linda Scarberry related that the eyes were large and fiery red. It had a wingspan so vast that the tips were hitting the car's doors as it hovered overhead when they raced down the straight stretch of roadway. Scarberry noted the paint was scratched on the car. They continued into town and did not stop until they realized the creature was no longer in pursuit.

The four witnesses later shared their accounts with Deputy Millard Halstead as they returned to the old building. During this time, the deputy heard a staticky noise but couldn't locate its source. He noted dust rising from a nearby coal pile but could not identify it. Linda Scarberry recalled, "We sat with our lights off for about fifteen or twenty minutes when I heard a strong squeaking sound. A shadow crossed the building on the hill. Mary and I saw the red eyes and told Millard. He shined the light on them. We saw dust rising as he moved the spotlight, and then we finally left."

After the story reached the press, some in the community would laugh at the couples' report, each having their idea of what they thought the creature was including a bird or balloon. Roger Scarberry reacted: "What this thing looked like—it is about six feet tall with large wings on its back. It has the shape of a man. It has two red eyes about two inches in diameter, six to eight inches apart. A wing spread of ten feet.

This thing, whatever it is, is definitely not a crane or goose or balloon or any of the things it has been called. I have seen it and know what it looks like."

In November 1966, Bob Bosworth and Alan Coates rode their motorcycles along Camp Conley Road in the TNT area as they headed to the power plant. As they approached the old power plant building, they noticed something unusual on the roof and stopped to investigate. They tilted their motorcycle to shine the headlight on it, but they decided to enter the building when that didn't work.

They climbed to the third floor and looked across the remaining metal grating catwalks. In stunned silence, they watched as a shadowy figure walked across the catwalk toward them before eventually shooting off into the night. The men estimated the figure's size to be around seven feet and described it as resembling a bird with its wings folded against its back.

West Virginia: White Thing

Notable Characteristics: The creature has a white coat of long, shaggy hair. It has a robust physique resembling a dog's, yet it is as large as a bear. Some eyewitness accounts liken its appearance to that of a lion-dog, distinguished by a long white mane. Notable features are fangs and sharp claws. The White Thing can appear and disappear in a ghost-like manner. This creature exhibits remarkable speed and typically attacks by biting and clawing. It primarily moves on all fours but can also walk on two legs.

The White Thing is infamous for its violent attacks, which reportedly leave no visible scars or wounds on its victims.

In the late 1920s, Frank Kozul could attest to this manner of attack. He was a thirty-six-year-old miner at the Jordan No. 93 mine near Rivesville and Fairmont, and he faced a long walk home each night after work. After exhausting eleven-hour shifts, he sometimes took a shortcut across the ridges instead of opting for the longer route along the road.

One July night in 1929, Frank chose one of those overgrown paths that few people ventured on after dark. As he ascended the steep and wooded incline of Morgan Ridge, he came face to face with a white creature that stood about two feet off the ground. It had an enormous head and a thick, bushy tail, making no noise he could discern. Thinking he could scare it away, Frank kicked at the creature with the toe of his boot, only for his foot to go right through it. The creature started to pounce at him. With his lunch pail in hand, Frank swung it at the White Thing like a sword, but it passed right through the creature. He picked up a stick and began striking at the entity that lunged at his arms and legs while trying to run away.

Frank felt the sting of welts and scratches on his skin during the chase. Ultimately, after a fierce struggle, he passed a cemetery, and it was here that the creature faded away. Once he returned home and checked his arms and legs by lantern light, he found no scratches or marks on his skin. Frank never took a shortcut through the ridge again.

Farmers in the same region near Rivesville have reported that a creature with a spine-tingling scream attacked their sheep and goats. Interestingly, when shot at, the bullets would pass right through it. More recently, in 1994, a man admitted to having witnessed, as a child, a white creature with thick shaggy hair floating next to his family's moving vehicle before it vanished. While the White Thing is sometimes associated with Sheepsquatch, White Thing is generally viewed as possessing a mystical quality and notably lacks horns.

Other Notable West Virginia Cryptids

Sheepsquatch: Described as bear-sized but with sheep features long white wool-like fur and saber-like teeth, Sheepsquatch is said to be carnivorous and dangerous. Its unique appearance combines features from various animals, making it a fascinating addition to West Virginia's creatures. Near Point Pleasant, West Virginia, on snow-covered backroads at the old TNT site, several family members were returning from a reunion. The forest was bare, and the drive was slick. Suddenly, they saw a creature seven to eight feet tall, covered in shaggy fur, with human-like legs and a sheep-like face with ram horns. A hunter also encountered a similar goat-headed beast drinking from a creek before it walked away.

Grafton Monster: A cryptid was first reported by journalist Robert Cockrell on June 16, 1964, near Grafton, West Virginia. Cockrell described the creature as seven to nine feet tall, with seal-like skin and an apparent lack of a head. During his sighting, the creature produced a whistling sound. Following this initial encounter, local teenagers formed search parties to look for the beast, which led to numerous unconfirmed sightings and captured the public's interest.

Wampus Cat of King Shoals: In Appalachian folklore, Wampus Cats in West Virginia are often humans who return from the dead as cats to right past wrongs. One story tells of the Wampus Cat of King Shoals, where a couple settled near the Elk River between two creeks. They had two strong boys and a baby girl until the little girl grew ill. The father delayed getting a doctor, and she tragically died at five months old. He buried her on a hill and was consumed by guilt. He began hearing strange wildcat yowls from her fresh grave on the mountain.

He vowed to hunt the creature responsible. One night, he went out and saw a shadow of the cat, raised his gun, then shot the beast. He was elated and dragged it back to his barn and went into the house, but sometime during the night, the barn burned down. The next day, when sifting through the ashes, there was no sign of the dead wildcat. It hit him then. The man recalled his grandparents' tales of the Cattywampus, spirits of the dead seeking revenge. In his grief, he didn't realize the cat was his daughter in spirit form. He had delayed calling the doctor, which led to her death, but she was too sweet for vengeance. Ultimately, it was he who had killed her twice.

Ogua: The Monongahela River starts at Fairmont, West Virginia, where the Tygart Valley and West Fork Rivers converge. According to Native American legend, the Ogua river monster, a two-headed turtle, lurks in its depths, swiftly dragging its prey underwater at night.

Polk Gap Monster: It walks upright, with broad shoulders and long arms and legs, resembling a cross between man and ape. This creature has been spotted by many near Twin Falls State Park and in Oceana, where Patrolman Bill Pritt encountered a mysterious being while on duty.

One evening in 1978, Pritt was nearing the end of a twelve-hour shift, from 7 p.m. to 7 a.m., when the dispatch received a call about a baby screaming in a neighborhood near the Oceana Town Hall. Pritt got into his cruiser and drove to the location along Monroe Street. There, he saw a figure under a streetlight. "Then it kind of leaped, and I hollered at it," Pritt recalled. "I thought it was somebody who had been involved in something and was trying to get away from me. It jumped down over the bank to the edge of the river."

The creature jumped across the river, and Pritt saw it appear on the opposite side before disappearing into the woods. "It was dark-colored and looked like a man," he said. "It was like a man, only much larger. It must have weighed around three hundred pounds. You can laugh at me and think I'm crazy if you want, but I saw it and don't want to see it again."

Wisconsin: Beast of Bray Road

Notable Characteristics: Eyewitness descriptions suggest the creature stands between 6 and 7 feet tall and possesses a human-like body covered in fur or hair. Its head resembles a wolf, depicted with large, glowing red or orange eyes.

The creature, commonly linked to the rural region near Elkhorn in Walworth County, has often been compared to werewolves or Bigfoot. Sightings of this wolf-like entity date back to 1936. It gained significant attention during the late 1980s and 1990s when numerous witnesses reported encounters along Bray Road.

This elusive being is known for its stealth and the ability to move upright on all fours, much like a human. The first reported sighting occurred in 1936 at the St. Coletta School for Exceptional Children in Jefferson County. Archer Parquette recounts the story in Milwaukee Magazine, featuring Mark Shackleman, who was the night watchman at St. Coletta School, a former convent surrounded by extensive old buildings, fields, and ancient Native American mounds located outside Jefferson.

On one particular night, after arriving at work and beginning his rounds, Shackleman encountered a strange creature. He crossed a field with his flashlight when he saw something crouched down on all fours, digging into the earth at one of the mounds. Initially thinking it was a type of canine, Shackleman watched as the creature stood up to its full height of about six feet. It let out a deep, guttural growl, and a foul odor, reminiscent of decay, wafted toward Shackleman's nostrils. But as quickly as it appeared, it vanished into the darkness. Shackleman would see it one last time the following night, digging in the same mound. This time, prepared for a confrontation if needed, Shackleman stood his ground. The creature bared its white fangs at him, letting out a dog-like snarl as a warning not to come any closer. However, it turned and left without a struggle.

Throughout the 1980s, individuals reported encounters with a mysterious creature, including when it came into contact with vehicles. One notable incident occurred on Halloween in 1991, involving a teenager named Doris Gipson. While driving along Bray Road, she felt a bump against her tire. Assuming she had hit an animal, she stopped and got out to investigate. To her shock, she saw a large creature rushing towards her car. Panicked, she ran back to her vehicle and sped away, hearing the beast leap onto the trunk before it fell off.

In 1989, Lori Endrizzi spotted a hunched, human-like figure resembling a large wolf or dog around 1:30 a.m. while driving home from her job as a bar manager. As she turned on her high-beam headlights, she could see the creature holding a roadkill carcass. Overcome with fear, Endrizzi stalled her vehicle, and the beast lunged toward her car. With trembling hands, she restarted the engine unharmed and sped away into the night.

Wisconsin: Vampire of Mineral Point

Notable Characteristics: This mysterious figure is characterized by his ashen face and pitch-black hair. He often wears a black cape similar to the Victorian figure called 'Spring-heeled Jack.' In 1837, Spring-heeled Jack became infamous for his terrifying appearance and extraordinary leaping abilities, leading to numerous sightings across the United Kingdom.

Once a mining town, Mineral Point is now a travel destination featuring shops and hiking trails in the heart of Wisconsin's Driftless Region. Interestingly, it is also known for reports of a vampire.

On the evening of March 14, 1981, a strange man was seen lurking in Graceland Cemetery in Mineral Point. Officer John Pepper approached a figure described as a 6-foot-5-inch-tall man with a white face and a black cape. When Officer Pepper called out to him, the man bolted, effortlessly clearing a 4-foot-tall barbed-wire fence at the cemetery's edge and running into a field where Angus bulls were grazing.

In 2004, there were reports of a man sitting in a tree outside an apartment complex who leaped from the tree and fled when approached by the police. The most recent sighting occurred in 2008 when a couple fishing on a pier at Ludden Lake spotted a pale-faced man with dark hair and a cape climbing out of the water. They quickly ran to the police station to report the incident.

Wisconsin: Goatman

Notable Characteristics: The Goatman is a cryptid that has become part of the folklore surrounding southeastern Wisconsin. It is half-man, half-goat stalking the woods and back roads of the area.

Hogsback Road is constructed along a narrow, winding glacial esker near the village of Richfield, Wisconsin. The road features numerous sharp curves and steep hills, making it a treacherous drive. It has a reputation for being dangerous, with many lives lost over the years due to the steep drop-offs on either side as it meanders through a gloomy stretch of woods.

To add to this eerie account, there is an old legend. According to a 2006 article in the Times Press newspaper from Hartford, Wisconsin, Janean Van Beckum of the Washington County Historical Society recounted the tale of the Goatman, first sighted along the densely wooded Hogsback Road near Richfield. The story goes that a former Civil War soldier's covered wagon broke an axle, prompting him to seek help. The Goatman appeared and frightened his wife, who hid in the wagon until morning. When she emerged, she found her husband hanging dead and dripping with blood. Since then, the Goatman has haunted the road, luring drivers off and down the steep embankment. When authorities arrive at the scene, the vehicle's occupants have vanished.

On November 9, 2006, in the early morning hours in the nearby Erin neighborhood, Steven Krueger, a contractor who removes dead animals from the road, encountered a seven-foot-tall dark creature on Highway 167 and Station Way.

South Mill Road, located outside of Kewaskum, is mostly unpaved and extends from Highway 28 through the woods to a dirt road and dead end in the Milwaukee River Floodplain Forest State Natural Area. In the autumn of 2006, bow hunter Jason Miller set up a tree stand off South Mill Road. When he returned to hunt, he found that his stand had been moved and had hoof marks on it. After replacing the tree stand, Miller returned another day. Once he climbed up and settled in, a strange beast appeared. It resembled a goat but was the size of a gray and brown deer, with a human head, long beard, and human arms emitting a terrible odor of rotting flesh. As the hunter watched from his perch, the creature cursed under its breath, muttering something about trespassers.

"It was the size of a deer, tan and gray in color," he would report to Washington County Paranormal, a guide chronicling unique urban legends from Texas to Wisconsin to Maryland.

"It looked like a goat but with a human head and arms. I remember it had a beard that was gray and very long. . .I didn't waste any time getting out of there. I left as soon as he was out of sight. I kept an arrow nocked—"

The Goatman has solidified its place in the folklore of the surrounding towns due to its long history in the area. The only question remaining is: who will be its next victim?

Other Notable Wisconsin Cryptids

Man-faced Pigs: A unique legend from Door County's rich Belgian-American heritage tells the story of the Man-faced Pigs from Brussels. This peculiar tale dates back to the late 1800s and early 1900s, originating from a local farmer's curse that inadvertently affected his own livestock instead of the intended targets.

The trouble began when a farmer discovered that a wealthy relative had excluded him from their will. In his rage, he cursed the clergyman who read the will to him and all other clergymen in Brussels. However, due to a mistake in executing the curse—whether it was too weak or misdirected—the curse rebounded onto the farmer himself. Following the curse, strange happenings began on the farm. Furniture would levitate, and his pigs became grisly creatures with "demonic human-like faces." These terrifying pigs relentlessly followed the farmer, maintaining an unbroken stare at him wherever he went.

This torment began to drive the farmer mad, leading to a deterioration of his mental state. Desperate, he sought advice from anyone who could help him escape the curse. Eventually, he received counsel from an elderly neighbor, who suggested he might find solace through prayer and repentance. Frantic for a solution, the farmer built a shrine and fervently begged for forgiveness and divine intervention. Miraculously, the Man-faced Pigs vanished. His livestock returned to normal, and peace was restored on the farm.

Wyoming: DeSmet Lake Monster

Notable Characteristics: The described creature is a large sea organism that measures approximately 40 feet long and features distinctive characteristics, including a horse-like head and a series of bumps along its spine.

The DeSmet Lake Monster, affectionately known as "Smitty," resides in the dark waters of Lake DeSmet, which spans over 258 acres beneath the Bighorn Mountains. When homesteaders began settling in the area around the lake, they shared stories about a massive creature living within its depths. It was described as having a head like a horse, a humped back, and being as thick as a tree and approximately forty feet long. Some even whispered that those who ventured too close to the shore at the wrong time were snatched up by the monster and eaten.

In 1925, a notable reference to Smetty can be found in the book 'Locating the Iron Trail', written by author and railroad surveyor Edward Gillette. In this book, Gillette recounts an incident involving the Barkey family, who reported an encounter with what they described as two sea serpents in Lake DeSmet. "They were all very much excited, stating that they wished I had arrived half an hour earlier as they had seen two sea serpents which had made a great commotion in the water and swam as fast as a horse could trot," Gillette wrote in his book. "Upon asking them to describe these animals as accurately as possible, Mrs. Barkey stated that 'they looked like a long telephone pole with lard buckets attached,' referring no doubt to the fins or flappers along their sides."

According to Gillette's account, the family reported seeing creatures that disturbed the water significantly and swam at remarkable speeds—comparable to a horse trotting. This sighting was not an isolated incident; it contributed to a growing narrative about Smetty as locals began sharing similar stories. Over the years, various individuals have claimed to see large serpentine creatures in the lake, often describing them with characteristics similar to those attributed to other legendary lake monsters, such as Scotland's Loch Ness Monster.

Other Notable Wyoming Cryptids

Jackalope: The jackalope is often described as a jackrabbit with antelope/deer antlers. In the 1930s, Douglas Herrick and his brother from Wyoming created taxidermy mounts by combining the bodies of jackrabbits with deer antlers. This inventive idea quickly spread to other states. The term "jackalope" combines "jackrabbit" and "antelope." While the jackalope is fictional, some real horned rabbits can be infected with the Shope papillomavirus. This virus causes horn-like tumors on a rabbit's head and body, possibly leading to sightings that inspired legends about horned hares across various cultures.

Citations:

• freestateofwinston.org/downeybooger.htm

• youtube.com/watch?v=cyiv8OqOuuU&t=1136s (An amazing story-telling of an early account of the White Thang.)

•Samantha McNamara Staff Writer. (2023, October 11). Legendary 'Alabama white Thang' and Courtland's 'Slough thing': Enigmas of Lawrence. moultonadvertiser.com/news/article_abc5adae-6857-11ee-b5a3-db259d4c6c03.html

• bfro.net/GDB/show_report.asp?id=30680 Wood Booger

• The Anniston Star Anniston, Alabama Sun, Jan 23, 2005 Page 31 White Thang

• Crichton Leprechaun www.youtube.com/watch?v=nda_OSWeyn8

• Huggin Molly Abbeville Herald Abbeville, Alabama Thu, Nov 17, 2005

• pinebarrensinstitute.com/cryptids/2018/8/18/cryptid-profile-the-amikuk

• Anchorage Daily News Anchorage, Alaska Sun, May 12, 1991Page 35

• Tombstone epitaph., April 26, 1890, Image 3

• www.kgun9.com/entertainment/legend-or-lie/legend-or-lie-tombstone-thunderbird-sighting

• Lone Pine Mountain Devil - Weird California.

weirdca.com/location.php?location=292

•Scientific American Gnomes

•Terror of the evil little man Part two. from-the-shadows.blogspot.com/2011/08/terror-of-evil-little-man-part-two.html Gnomes

• USA Today. Gnomes

• The Craig Press Devil Ram

• Steamboat Pilot & Today Devil Ram

• Routt County Historical Society Archives:

• Other regional publications that cover Moffat County and surrounding areas.

• www.texarkanagazette.com/news/2019/jun/14/hairy-monster-hunted-fouke-sector/ Hairy 'monster' hunted in Fouke sector | Texarkana Gazette.

• Pine Bluff daily graphic., July 03, 1902, Image 1Pine Bluff Wild Man

• northamericancryptids.com/ozark-howler/

• Greencastle Herald,Greencastle, Putnam County, 3 March 1914 Wampus Cat

• The Waterbury Democrat. [volume], July 23, 1937, Page TWENTY-THREE,

• Hartford Courant Hartford, Connecticut Wed, Jan 2, 1952 Page 1

• Hartford Courant Hartford, Connecticut · Friday, July 28, 1972

• Meriden, Connecticut Wed, Jan 11, 1939 Page 1

• bfro.net/GDB/show_report.asp?id=7771 Delaware Bigfoot

• www.berfrois.com/2013/04/the-black-dog-w-h-c-pynchon/

• The Syracuse Herald, Saturday, April 03, 1926

• Springfield [MA] Republican 6 April 1926: p. 3

• Daily Advocate [Stamford CT] 6 April 1926: p. 8

• Springfield [MA] Republican 4 April 1926: p. 1

• www.damnedct.com/sea-monsters-serpents-long-island-sound/

• www.news-press.com/story/news/2023/09/13/florida-cryptids-the-skunk-ape-wamp The Miami Herald

• Miami, Florida Sun, Aug 10, 1975 Page 247us-cat-bigfoot-halloween/70830484007/

• Tampa Bay Times St. Petersburg, Florida Sun, Aug 22, 1971 Page 190

• hangar1publishing.com/blogs/cryptids/florida-cryptids?srsltid=AfmBOoopE3IYoUCVHHd0FNfcnQqNDv8NfsIBmtCf6FkVAFem4T6zQ-qc

• The Atlanta Constitution Atlanta, Georgia · February 16, 1981 Altamaha

• The Times-Herald Newnan, Georgia · Sunday, November 29, 2009

• The Times-Herald Newnan, Georgia · Sunday, April 24, 2005

• Werewolf of Georgia: freepages.rootsweb.com/~opus/genealogy/p1800.htm

• www.malamamakua.org/moo-of-mkua-valley

• Honolulu Star-Advertiser Honolulu, Hawaii · Sunday, July 06, 1947

• Honolulu Star-Bulletin Honolulu, Hawaii May 30, 1929 Menehune

• Offutt, J. (2019). Chasing American monsters: 251 creatures, Cryptids, and hairy beasts.

• Bonner County Daily Bee Sandpoint, Idaho Mon, May 7, 1973 Page 4

• Montpelier Examiner Montpelier, Idaho Fri, Jan 31, 1902 Page 4

• Southern Illinoisan Carbondale, Illinois · Wednesday, October 26, 2005

• The Daily Independent Murphysboro, Illinois Mon, Oct 5, 1942Page 1

• The Indianapolis Journal

• cryptomundo.com/bigfoot-report/crosley-monster/

Oct. 31, 2006 Bryce Mayer North Vernon Plain Dealer and North Vernon Sun, Indiana Crosley Monster

• Indianapolis, Indiana · Monday, September 07, 1891 Crawfordsville Specter

• newspapers.library.in.gov/cgi-bin/indiana?a=d&d=CDJ18910905&e=-------en-20--1--txt-txIN-------

• Tipton Daily Tribune Indiana • Wed, Jun 8, 1960 Page 2 Cistern Monster

• The Republic Columbus, Indiana · Sunday, October 31, 1993e Times Hammond, Indiana • Mill Race Monster

• Wed, Aug 17, 1955 Page 13 Green Clawed Beast www.creepyencounters.com/04/dogman-encounter/ Dogman

• cryptidz.fandom.com/wiki/Iowa_Dragons Iowa dragons

• northamericandogmanproject.com/encounters

• www.bfro.net/GDB/show_report.asp?id=1270 Lockridge Monster

• Cryptid Van Meter Visitor - Mythical Encyclopedia. mythicalencyclopedia.com/van-meter-visitor/

• hangar1publishing.com/blogs/cryptids/illinois-cryptids?srsltid=AfmBOoqDN9lF1jGfPtpwdlV5EuSPjN2NqrGNiFZzmpLS2WqC9pVuJ3LQ Chestnut Werewolf

• dogmanencounters.com/jackson-county-ks-encounter/ Dogmen

• northamericandogmanproject.com/encounters Dogman

• The Wichita Eagle. (October 17, 1978). article/the-wichita-eagle/137430215/

Kansas Bigfoot

• The Iola Register. (March 9, 1971).. Newspapers.com. Retrieved February 20, 2025, from www.newspapers.com/article/the-iola-register/72673661/ Chicken Man

• The Wichita Eagle Wichita, Kansas Tue, Oct 17, 1978Page 25 Kansas Bigfoot

• The Wichita Eagle Wichita, Kansas • Sun, Nov 27, 1977 Page 74 Kansas Bigfoot

• Lexington Herald-Leader Lexington, Kentucky Mon, Aug 22, 2005 Page 15 kelly Green Men

• Coffey, L., Coffey, (2018). Kentucky Cryptids: Monsters of the Bluegrass State.

• kentucky.com/news/state/kentucky/article266816586 Mothman

• htmlebarrensinstitute.com/cryptids/2018/8/19/cryptid-profile-the-herrington-lake-eel-pig Eel Pig Creature

• Canip Monster Is Sighted Again. The Trimble County Banner. 31 July 1975.

•The Times-Picayune New Orleans, Louisiana Mon, Aug 22, 1892 Page 4 Giant Frogs

• The Town Talk Alexandria, Louisiana Wed, Oct 24, 1973 Page 7 Honey Island Swamp Monster

• Daily News Bogalusa, Louisiana Thu, Oct 2, 1975 Page 1 Honey Island Swamp Monster

• The St. Albans Weekly Messenger Saint Albans, Vermont Thu, Feb 8, 1855 Page 2 Waldorbor Wildman

• High contrast, fine details, rough textures, dark atmosphere; crisp, sharply detailed creature features.

• The Boston Globe Boston, Massachusetts Oct 29, 2006 Page 115 Dover Demon

• www.cellarwalls.com/ufo/doverdemon.htm Dover Demon

• The Boston Globe Boston, Massachusetts Sun, Oct 30, 2005Page 70 Hocomock Swamp Monster

• Bridgewater Triangle, Massachusetts – Land of Maps - LandofMaps.com. landofmaps.com/bridgewater-triangle-massachusetts/

• Berkshire Eagle Pittsfield, Massachusetts Mon, Jan 18, 1982 Page 13 Truro Beast

• northamericandogmanproject.com/encounters Michigan Dogman

• historyboots.wordpress.com/tag/wendigo/ Wendigo

• The Brandon Mail, April 30, 1896, Page 3 Wendigo

• Perham Focus

• SyFy Channel

• The Duluth News Tribune Duluth, Minnesota Tue, Aug 7, 1906 Page 2 Lake Ada

• pinebarrensinstitute.com/cryptids/2020/11/2/folklore-profile-the-lake-superior-god-of-the-waters-aka-the-great-lakes-merman

• Enterprise-Journal McComb, Mississippi · Sunday, December 21, 1980 Chatawa Monster

• Lyle Blackburn - "The Strange Case of the Missouri Monster"

• cryptidz.fandom.com/wiki/Beaman Beaman Monster

• www.onlyinyourstate.com/experiences/mississippi/ms-legend-of-three-legged-lady Three-legged Lady

• www.bfro.net/GDB/show_report.asp?id=13383 Bigfoot montana

• statecryptids.blogspot.com/2022/11/nebraska-falls-city-metal-winged-demon.html Flying Demon

• blog.nhstateparks.org/tag/new-hampshire-state-parks/feed/ Woods Devil

• www.wmur.com/article/nh-chronicle-the-legend-of-the-dublin-lake-monster/61502845 Dublin Lake Monster

• Valley News West Lebanon, New Hampshire • Fri, Jun 26, 1987Page 16 Jersey Devil

• www.newspapers.com/article/the-portsmouth-herald/1248726/ Jersey Devil

• Asbury Park Press Asbury Park, New Jersey Sun, Dec 2, 1979 Page 35 Jersey Devil

• Brown, Edward. Just Around the Corner, in New Jersey, p. 82, ff. B B& A Publishers, 1984. ISBN 9780912608174. Accessed September 24, 2015. White Stag

Daily Record Morristown, New Jersey Sun, Jun 5, 1977, page 51 Big Red Eye

https://weirdnj.com/stories/big-red-eye/ Big Red Eye

New York Times Stuart Murray Tracking a Mystery Big Red Eye

• multoghost.wordpress.com/2015/08/17/mexican-monstresses-la-mala-hora/

• Daily News New York, New York · Sunday, February 10, 1935 Alligator

• Statesville Record and Landmark Statesville, North Carolina Fri, Dec 17, 1954

• Page 3 Bladenboro Beast

• The Devils Lake World Devils Lake, North Dakota Thu, Jul 16, 1914 Page 1 Sea

• www.bfro.net/GDB/show_county_reports.asp?state=nd&county=Mountrail Bigfoot North Dakota

• bfro.net/GDB/show_county_reports.asp?state=oh&county=Guernsey Bigfoot Salt Fork and Hocking

• The Lawton Constitution And Morning Press Lawton, Oklahoma February 28, 1971 Page 14 Wood Ape

• Tulsa World Tulsa, Oklahoma January 29, 2000 Page 3 Boggy Bigfoot

• reports.woodape.org/data/?action=details&case=02090006#CaseNum

• bfro.net/GDB/show_report.asp?id=31986 Boggy Bigfoot

• reports.woodape.org/data/?action=details&case=02090002# Wood Ape

• cryptidz.fandom.com/wiki/Wallowa_Lake_Monster Wallowa Lake Monster

• mariontalk.com/2024/09/11/oregons-elusive-cryptid-bigfoot-lurks-in-marion-countys-untamed-wilderness/ Oregon Bigfoot

• William T. Cox, "The Squonk", Fearsome Creatures of the Lumberwoods (1910)

• unchartedlancaster.com/2021/10/03/haunted-lancaster-meet-columbias-little-bigfoot-the-albatwitch/ Albatwitch

• pawilds.com/a-cryptid-in-the-woods-of-the-pa-wilds/ Potter Nondescript

• The Item Sumter, South Carolina Wed, Jul 20, 1988 Page 8 Ore Swamp Monster

• The Times and Democrat Orangeburg, South Carolina Bush Man

• northamericancryptids.com/tennessee-wildman/ Tennessee Wildman

• El Paso Times El Paso, Texas Fri, Jun 19, 1953 Page 19 Texas Bat Man

• Corpus Christi Caller-Times Corpus Christi, Texas · Thursday, October 06, 2022 Goat Man

• Mysterious Beings: A Complete Guide. studylib.net/doc/25786603/john-keel---the-complete-guide-to-mysterious-beings

- Eureka daily sentinel. [volume], July 15, 1877, Image 1 Salt Lake Monster
- www.fox13now.com/news/local-news/legends-and-myths-of-great-salt-lake-may-keep-you-up-at-night Salt Lake Monster
- hangar1publishing.com/blogs/cryptids/utah-cryptids?srsltid=AfmBOoo0hPpJwIFG8XrQ1VyJYb8t-LWIxSf-EhrU7o3RzThJhxKkbF5W Wasatch Wild Man
- cbsaustin.com/news/offbeat/a-chupacabra-mysterious-image-caught-on-camera-at-texas-zoo-do-you-know-what-it-is-mystery-zoo-image-ufo-uao-coyote-on-hind-legs-alien-sighting-strange-photo-captured-on-surveillance-cameras-amarillo-zoo Chupacabra
- newenglandfolklore.blogspot.com/2009/10/october-monster-mania-bennington.html Bennington Monster
- www.bfro.net/GDB/show_report.asp?id=28307 Sasquatch Washington
- North American BioFortean Review - Vol 2 No 2 – 2000 Devil Monkey
- Retrieved from www.milwaukeemag.com/the-legend-of-the-beast-of-bray-road Beast of Bray Road
- itsmth.fandom.com/wiki/Beast_of_Bray_Road Beast of Bray
- pinebarrensinstitute.com/cryptids/2018/8/18/cryptid-profile-the-man-faced-pigs-of-brussels Man-faced Pigs
- The News Tribune Tacoma, Washington Sun, Apr 24, 1994 Page 7 Batsquatch
- Times Press Hartford, Wisconsin Thu, Nov 16, 2006 Page 2 Goat Man Wisconsin
- Kewaskum Statesman Kewaskum, Wisconsin Thu, Oct 4, 2012 Page a6 Goat Man Wisconsin
- Casper Star-Tribune Casper, Wyoming Sun, Dec 18, 1955 Page 10
- jackfmcasper.com/wyoming-beasts-where-to-find-them-lake-desmet-monster/ Desmet monster

www.ingramcontent.com/pod-product-compliance
Lightning Source LLC
Chambersburg PA
CBHW070549100426
42744CB00006B/250

9781940087696